I0458679

DEPRAVED OBSESSION

THE GRIPPING TRUE STORY OF LAW ENFORCEMENT'S HUNT FOR A SADISTIC SERIAL KILLER

ROD SADLER

AUTHOR OF 'KILLING WOMEN'

WILDBLUE
PRESS

WildBluePress.com

DEPRAVED
OBSESSION

This book is dedicated to the memory of Kenny Myers, Shawn Moore, and all of those who were victimized by the killer. It is also dedicated to those who worked so fervently in bringing a killer to justice.

"A child's innocence is the one gift, that once stolen, can never be replaced."

— Jaeda DeWalt

NOTE

Some names have been changed and denoted as such by an asterisk (*).

Quoted material was taken from printed sources and interviews with the author. They appear as is. Any mistakes are the original authors'.

TABLE OF CONTENTS

Acknowledgments   13
Preface   17
The Oakland County Child Killings   21
The Beginning   33
Kenny   51
Shawn   67
The Investigation Begins   81
The Jeep   99
A Task Force   104
The Tips   116
Up North   139
On the Run   156
Mr. Personality   170
Tombo   182

Photos   197

How Safe Are the Children?   208
The Exams   224
The Reagan Effect   247
Without Kids, There Is No Tomorrow   256
The Leak   265
The First Trial   289
I Was Killing Me   347
Leavenworth   371
The Existence of Evil   380
Questions Remain   391

ACKNOWLEDGMENTS

I am indebted to those who fought the good fight—to those who spent countless hours in bringing a child killer to justice. I am also indebted to those who made sure the killer received fair and impartial trials. This wasn't an easy story to tell, and a reliance on media reports alone wouldn't have done this story justice.

Dave Ostrem, a former patrolman for the Green Oak Township Police Department, set this book in motion when he asked if I would be interested in documenting the case. I agreed, knowing full well that Dave would be an invaluable initial source for the most accurate information.

Edwin Moore, a former detective for the Livingston County Sheriff's Department and now a cold case investigator, was another resource I reached out to. Both he and Dave Ostrem were the initial officers involved in the abduction of Shawn Moore during that beautiful Labor Day weekend in 1985.

As my research progressed, I recognized names of people who were involved and through those, I met others who put in countless hours during the investigation. I am grateful to Don Brooks and Roger Bittell, both of whom are now retired but worked tirelessly until the killer was caught, along with so many others. They graciously shared their stories with me.

Jess Lopez, now retired from the FBI, provided intrinsic details of how the killer was identified and how the manhunt for him began after he fled to Florida.

I would like to thank the Honorable Frank Del Vero (ret.), who served as Livingston County's prosecuting attorney, and his chief assistant, David Morse, for their willingness to share details about the investigation and the roles they played in the prosecution's efforts to ensure the trial was fair.

Beyond the prosecutors, Raymond Cassar was more than willing to share intimate details about his participation in this case and his defense of the killer. Mr. Cassar wanted to ensure that the readers of this book understood there was a sort of redemption on the part of his client after being convicted in the abduction and murder of Shawn Moore and, by that, he spoke of his client's interview with the FBI to help them understand the mind of a child predator with the hope of preventing something similar in the future.

The Honorable Timothy Kenny (ret.), who, as the chief trial lawyer in the Wayne County Prosecuting Attorney's Office in 1985 prosecuted the killer there for the abduction and murder of Kenny Myers, shared details of the prosecution's case that were invaluable to me as I wrote about the connections between the two murders.

Dr. Harley Stock, a psychologist and the prosecution's star witness in both cases, was very forthcoming in providing information that allowed me to understand the State's position about the killer's sanity and how dangerous he truly is.

I couldn't have written this book without the help of former and current reporters from both the print and digital media. They did an outstanding job in documenting the cases from beginning to end. I would like to thank Jack Kresnak, Dan Grantham, Stephen Cain, and Chris Hansen.

Thank you also to Cory Williams and Denise Powell. Your efforts haven't gone unnoticed. While there are no definitive answers, your dedication and the work done by so many others on the re-opened investigation into the Oakland County Child Killings have provided hope that someday, justice might prevail.

Even the smallest of help in getting an introduction or referral to someone, or simply having the use of an office for an interview, didn't go unnoticed. Thank you to William Worden, Hillary Elrod, Maria Miller, Ken Ouellette, Jeff Weiss, the Michigan State Police, the Livingston County Sheriff's Department, the Livingston County Prosecuting Attorney's Office, the Wayne County Prosecuting Attorney's Office, and the Williamston Police Department,

Finally, thank you to the people at WildBlue Press— Steven Jackson, Michael Cordova, Robert Davis, Jazzminn Morecraft, and Donna Marie West.

To all of those who helped in some way, you have my deepest gratitude.

PREFACE

In the early seventies, my family moved from the mid-Michigan area to a place we referred to as "up north." Cadillac was a tourist destination in northern lower Michigan with two beautiful lakes sitting side by side and connected by a small channel. Mitchell State Park sat between the lakes and today, it looks much like it did back then. Cadillac was a great place to be a kid. With Lake Cadillac and Lake Mitchell, there were endless activities year round that included camping, fishing, boating, hiking, snow skiing, snowmobiling, hunting, and a host of other things to keep someone busy. While we only lived in Cadillac for three years, it was a time filled with great memories.

As kids, my brother and I would mow our neighbor's lawn during the summer to earn some money, and in the winter, we would trudge up and down Chapin Street shoveling snow from driveways to keep the cash flow coming in. Our goal was to save enough money to buy our first bikes.

At the local hardware, the awkward-orange Schwinn Stingray with the matching banana seat was my reward for the laborious hot summers cutting grass and snowy winters shoveling drives. My brother chose a lime green ten-speed, and Dad paid for half of each.

We were mobile. No longer having to walk to our friends' homes, we were able to traverse the distances around the neighborhood in half the time on our bikes. During summer vacation, a select few of us in the neighborhood would leave home at any given time with the goal of riding around Lake Cadillac. It seemed, at least as a kid, an all-day journey. There were no cell phones and not a dime in our pockets to call home if we needed to. To this day, I am not sure our parents even knew where we were for most of the day. That's just how things were.

Our home was a two-story house with four bedrooms. My brother and I shared a room on the second floor that faced the street. The houses were so close that it seemed you could almost reach out a side window and touch the neighbor's home. With an optometrist on one side and a Presbyterian minister on the other, we settled comfortably in our new surroundings.

I think our time in Cadillac was also the time when I first discovered some of the evils in the world. It was a fall day, and I had stayed home from Franklin Elementary because of some perceived illness, though I don't recall exactly what my symptoms were. Bored, I picked up a *Reader's Digest* magazine and began looking for something interesting to read. I normally thumbed through the pages quickly, looking for the section titled "Laughter, the Best Medicine," but on that particular day, I read a story that affected me for the next few years. I don't recall the particulars but remember it involved the abduction of a teenager. Afterward, I couldn't stop thinking about it. As a pre-teen, the story lingered in the back of my mind and, for our remaining time in Cadillac, I was fearful the same thing could happen to me.

Today, I recall how frightened I was after reading that story, and later, as a young police officer in the mid-eighties, hearing about the abduction and murder of a young teen named Shawn Moore from Green Oak Township in Livingston County. It all came back to me, and I could only imagine how frightened Shawn must have been. At the time, I had no idea where Green Oak Township was until I was driving down US-23 and saw the Green Oak Township Police Department along a service road next to the highway shortly after Shawn's kidnapping.

As the investigation unfolded and Shawn's body was found "up north," I couldn't help but wonder how investigators had found him over 100 miles from his home. Shawn's case captivated me as it developed, and I followed it to the end. At least I thought I did.

When I began writing this book, I interviewed investigators, prosecutors, judges, attorneys, and members of the media. I searched through old police reports, newspapers, photos, and trial transcripts. As I researched the case of Ronald Bailey and his victims, I was fascinated by the courage and determination of the victims' families and how they turned tragedy into something positive in their attempt to prevent the same thing from ever happening to other children.

The abduction and murder of Shawn Moore became a defining moment for Brighton, Michigan and for Livingston County as a whole. Anyone who remembers that time forty years ago will tell you it was a time when an entire community lost its innocence.

It was also a defining moment for anyone directly involved in the investigation. Each time I did an interview with a former law enforcement official, attorney, or someone from the media, I would mention the name of another person I had already interviewed, and the response was always, "Oh, I remember him. If you see him again, tell him I said 'hi.'" It was a common phrase I heard again and again because it was a case they could never forget.

This book goes beyond just reporting the facts. Those whom I interviewed went beyond that by sharing some of their personal stories, struggles, and thoughts about the investigation.

They are, no doubt, despicable crimes, but this book moves beyond them by highlighting the camaraderie and determination of multiple law enforcement officers from several jurisdictions who set their egos aside while connecting the dots in their desperate search for a killer. It also highlights the true genuineness, courage, and determination of the victims' families.

1

The Oakland County Child Killings

On the west side of south-central lower Michigan, I-96 begins near Norton Shores, just south of Muskegon. The freeway, which is mostly two lanes in each direction, continues around the east side of Grand Rapids, the state's second largest city. Continuing to the east, the landscape is mostly agrarian countryside with gentle curves in the highway, an abundance of trees, and an occasional small city along the way. Nearing Michigan's median, the freeway swings to the south around the west side of the Mitten State's capital, Lansing, then changes direction one more time to the east and continues toward Detroit.

Along the way, small towns and cities dot the landscape, and while each has its own uniqueness, they somehow seem all the same. They boast small industry and businesses, agriculture, high school sports, and hometown pride. Like thousands of other small towns across the country, they are pastoral communities with names like Williamston, Webberville, Fowlerville, and Howell, each seemingly an uninteresting equal distance apart from one another, and each with their own history and charm—Small Town, USA.

Driving to the east from the small village of Webberville, drivers cross from Ingham County into Livingston County, one of a group of ten Michigan counties referred to as Cabinet Counties, each of those honoring one of President

Andrew Jackson's Cabinet. In this case, it was US Secretary of State Edward Livingston.

The geographic location of Livingston County offers commuters easy access to Lansing, Detroit, Ann Arbor, and Flint, with three highways passing through the county: I-96, US-23, and M-59. Just east of Brighton, I-96 intersects with US-23, the north/south highway running from Jacksonville, Florida to Mackinaw City, Michigan. US-23 also serves as a bypass to the Detroit metropolitan area.

Between 1984 and 1986, the populace in Livingston County increased from just over 100,000 people to almost 104,000. In comparison to that 3.6 percent gain for the same period, the US population increased by only 1.8 percent, while the entire state's population grew by only .9 percent.

The fastest growing age group for those same years was the thirty-five to forty-nine-year-old age group, amounting to a 9.8 percent increase.

Within Livingston County, Howell and Brighton are the two major cities, if they could be called that, while there are two villages, Fowlerville and Pinckney, and three incorporated townships that include Brighton, Genoa, and Green Oak.

Green Oak Township, at the southeast corner of Livingston County, borders the city of Brighton to the north.

With only four traffic signals in Brighton, driving from one end of town to the other, a person could easily find themselves waving to a friend within the six-block business district. The small-town feeling held an attraction for many in the tight-knit community at a time when houses were left unlocked, keys left in the ignitions of cars, and everyone seemingly knew everyone else. The Mill Pond, the Kiwanis Gazebo, and the Farmers' Market all added to the sense of hometown and community that made Brighton such a special place to live and raise a family.

To many, the quintessential city marked the beginning of the Detroit suburbs. Commuters in and around the small town who worked in Detroit or Flint navigated the day-to-day traffic jams to and from the industrial hubs. Made up of both young professionals and retirees, the picturesque downtown area was considered an ideal place to live with very little crime. As an innocent commuter community, Brighton's most serious offense was an occasional quick-change artist passing through the small town, and violent crimes were few and far between. The most recent had been the murder of Kimberly Louiselle, a sixteen-year-old girl who was reported missing in Green Oak Township in 1982. She was found murdered three weeks later near the Island Lake Recreation Area in the township, and her killer still hadn't been found. Her case remained cold for the next thirty-eight years.

With the largest number of Detroit's northern suburbs, bordering Livingston County to the east is Oakland County. Northville, a smaller historic Detroit suburb, lies both at the southern border of Oakland County and partially on the northern border of Wayne County.

Northville Township was home to both the Hawthorn Center, a children's psychiatric hospital that provided intensive inpatient psychiatric services to children and adolescents, and the Northville Regional Psychiatric Hospital, providing those same services to adults.

Wayne County is the largest in population for the entire state of Michigan, with over two million people in 1985. The county is largely urban with cities like Detroit, Wayne, Dearborn, Livonia, Westland, and a host of others. To the average driver, it can be difficult to identify jurisdictional boundaries when traveling from city to city in Wayne County because it seems they all run together.

Ferndale, in Oakland County, lies ten miles northwest of Detroit. Along the Woodward Avenue Corridor, it is considered an inner suburb of the Motor City.

In February 1976, across southeastern Michigan and beyond, people were gripped in fear with the seemingly random murders of children in and around Oakland County that spanned the next fourteen months. The murders began in January when Cynthia Cadieux, a sixteen-year-old student at Roseville High School in Macomb County, began a ten-minute walk home from a friend's house. It was the last time she was seen alive. Less than six hours later, her body was found lying in the middle of Franklin Road in Oakland County. Her body was fifteen miles from her home. She had been beaten and sodomized before her skull was crushed with some sort of blunt object.

It had been four days since Cynthia's body was found. In Birmingham, another Detroit suburb, fourteen-year-old Sheila Srock was babysitting in a quiet neighborhood. The high school freshman, whose parents had both died from cancer, lived with her older brother. When the home where she was babysitting was broken into, the man raped and sodomized her. Afterward, he shot her five times. When neighbors heard the gunshots, they gathered in front of the home, and Sheila's killer snuck out of the house in silence, mixed in with the small crowd, and then drove off in a 1967 Cadillac two-door.

One month after the murder of the two high school girls, it seemed like an early spring day. On February 15, temperatures were already in the fifties by 1:00 p.m., though the sustained winds were in the mid-twenties and wind gusts reached the mid-thirties. Still, even with cloudy skies, the spring-like temperatures were welcomed in Ferndale and across southwest Michigan.

Twelve-year-old Mark Stebbins sat with his older brother as the two of them watched a pool tournament at the American Legion Hall. Their mother, Ruth Stebbins, worked there as a bartender. Mark had other things on his mind. He would have rather been watching *Destination Tokyo*, a World War II movie on TV, and at around 1:15, he decided to walk home. He said goodbye to his mom and brother, and the seventh-grader put on his hooded blue parka over his maroon sweatshirt and left for the three-quarter-mile walk home. By 11:00 p.m., Mark still hadn't shown up at home, and his mother, divorced from Mark's father, reported him missing.

No one in the area ever saw Mark walking home, and Ferndale Police Chief Donald Geary said, "This is not a routine missing person case, and we are quite concerned."[1]

Four days after Mark Stebbins disappeared, the weather had returned to more seasonal temperatures and at 11:30 a.m., Mark Boetigheimer left his office in Southfield, approximately four miles from the site of Stebbins's disappearance, to stop at the nearby pharmacy in the New Orleans strip mall. In the parking lot, Boetigheimer thought he was looking at a mannequin. He walked closer to the four-foot-high brick wall separating the pharmacy parking lot from the office complex next door. He quickly realized it was the body of a boy wearing a hooded blue parka and maroon sweatshirt. The boy was lying on his back with his hands folded across his chest, the hood of his parka up around his head.

The twelve-year-old boy with strawberry blond hair and blue eyes had been suffocated. There was evidence that he had been bound and sexually assaulted.

The Southfield Police began to interview witnesses and, after talking to a man who had walked his dog in the area at 9:30 that morning, their belief was that Mark's body had been dropped off sometime between 9:30 and 11:30. The

---

1. Kennan, Marney Rich, *The Snow Killings*, Exposit, Jefferson, NC, 2020

witness was certain that the body wasn't there when he was walking his dog.

On August 7, six months after Mark's murder, fourteen-year-old Jane Allan was hitchhiking to her boyfriend's home in Auburn Heights. She had left around lunch time, and after she had gotten there, she ended up leaving after they had some sort of disagreement. She was last seen hitchhiking in Pontiac, and police believed she was likely trying to get back home. Her body was found four days later in Miamisburg, Ohio. She had been dumped in the river with her hands tied behind her back. Because of decomposition, the coroner wasn't able to determine if she had been raped but believed she was dead before being thrown in the river.

On December 22, Karol Robinson, a court reporting teacher, was making dinner at home in Royal Oak, another Detroit suburb in Oakland County. She knew her twelve-year-old daughter, Jill, was upset but also knew her daughter didn't want to talk about whatever was bothering her. She had been quiet and moody lately, perhaps from the stress of her parents' divorce, moving to a new home and school, and making new friends. Jill had also had a premonition that she was going to be murdered. Only a few months earlier, she had confided to her mother that she was fearful that someone was going to shoot her.

Four and a half months after Jane Allan's body was found floating in the Great Miami River in Ohio, the divorced mother of three girls asked Jill, the oldest of the three, to make some biscuits for dinner. One of Jill's favorite things to do was to bake with her mom but on this night, she was visibly upset, and she refused to tell her mom why. Karol couldn't break through her daughter's emotions and finally told her to go outside and think about it.

Jill grabbed her Levi's backpack, a green-and-blue plaid blanket, a brush, and two books. Karol told her she didn't have to leave; she only wanted to know what was bothering her. Her daughter was determined and simply walked out the front door.

Mrs. Robinson was certain her daughter would just sit on the front porch and eventually come back inside. When Karol asked one of her other daughters to call Jill in for dinner, Jill was gone.

After driving through the neighborhood looking for her daughter, Karol Robinson called other family members to see if anyone had seen Jill. No one had, and at 11:30 p.m., she reported Jill missing. The girl was last seen wearing a denim jumpsuit, snow boots, a bright orange winter parka, and a blue knit cap with a yellow zigzag stripe.

Four days after Jill was reported missing, her body was found in Troy, north of Royal Oak. The sixth-grader was found on the shoulder of northbound I-75, just north of Big Beaver Road and within sight of the Troy Police Department. It was 8:45 a.m. when a car passing by spotted her small body. She was wearing her backpack, which still contained the plaid blanket. Jill had been shot in the face.

Based on the initial investigation, police believed that Jill was carried from a car and placed on the ground before being shot once with a shotgun from a range of six to ten inches. They also believed she had been left there between 2:00 and 4:00 a.m.

During her autopsy, Oakland County Chief Medical Examiner Dr. Robert Sillery didn't find any evidence of Jill being sexually assaulted.

On January 2, 1977, ten-year-old Kristine Mihelich wanted to read all about her new favorite teen idols, Donny and Marie Osmond, and begged her mom to let her walk to the 7-Eleven store four and a half blocks away so she could buy a copy of *Teen* magazine. She promised her mom she would be careful crossing the streets.

Kristine's mother, Deborah Ascroft, worked at the Hartfield Bowling Alley on Twelve Mile Road and, at twenty-nine years old, she was the mother of four. Kristine was her bright-eyed fifth-grader, and she couldn't wait to get back to school after the Christmas break and tell her friends about Donny and Marie.

When the Berkley teen was reported missing, police checked every possible route she might have taken to the 7-Eleven in addition to looking into parked cars, trash bins, alleys, and tool sheds within a half-mile radius of her home. When police checked at her intended destination, the clerk remembered selling the *Teen* magazine to the fifth-grader.

As the days passed, both Deborah and her ex-husband appeared in news conferences, pleading for their daughter's safe return. Her father said, "Since it's been four days and she still hasn't been found"—he paused—"well, I'm hoping she's alive… that the person who is holding her will let her go… that he won't hurt her."

It was January 21 when Kristine was found just fifteen minutes from her home.

Franklin Village was a quiet community, and "should have been hanging from a Christmas tree back then, encased in glass."[2]

Jerome Wozny, a local mailman, saw some color in the quiet snow along the side of the road and was drawn to it. It was Kristine's body. There was no blood.

By now, it was clear to the police that at least three of the victims—Mark Stebbins, Jill Robinson, and Kristine Mihelich—bore many of the same characteristics. All three children had been held captive for days, and all three had died within hours of their bodies being found. The clothing worn by the kids was clean, and so were their bodies. Their bodies were placed near well-traveled routes so they would be easily spotted.

Many believed if the killer wasn't found, there would be more.

---

2. Appleman, J. Reuben, *The Kill Jar*, Gallery Books, New York, NY, 2018

Three months had passed since the murder of Kristine, the third victim of a killer—or killers—now called the Oakland County Child Killer.

On Wednesday, March 16, Cathy King gave her brother, Tim, thirty cents so he could buy some candy at the nearby Hunter Maple Pharmacy in Birmingham. It was just four blocks from their home. Cathy knew that her brother would have to cross a very busy road, but he assured her he would be careful. Then seventeen, she hesitated but quickly gave in to her eleven-year-old brother's sweet smile.

Cathy was going out for the evening, and her parents, who also had plans for the evening, had agreed to allow Tim to stay home alone. One of his two older brothers was at play practice while the other was babysitting. Cathy told Tim she would leave the front door slightly ajar for him to get back into the house. Tim left the house at 7:45 p.m. with his skateboard.

At 9:00 p.m., Tim's parents arrived back home after spending the evening with some friends and then going to dinner at the nearby Peabody's restaurant. The restaurant was less than 500 feet from the Hunter Maple Pharmacy.

After Tim's parents, Marion and Barry King, arrived home, they were quickly followed by their two oldest sons. When they couldn't find Tim, Marion and one of her sons got in the car and began to search the neighborhood for him. Barry stayed home with his other son in case Tim called.

Cathy arrived home at 2:00 a.m., and she was the family's last hope. Those hopes were replaced by fear when Cathy explained how she had given Tim thirty cents to buy some candy and how she had left the front door ajar for him so he could get back into the house.

In a press conference the following day, Tim's dad, Barry, said, "You couldn't have a more ideal child. He's active and into all kinds of sports. He knows the dangers of talking with strangers." He continued, "Just three weeks ago, in a talk with his mother, he told her he would run if a man ordered him into a car. We've been realistic about the problem since [the child murders] happened."[3]

In a desperate effort to find Tim, Oakland County Prosecuting Attorney L. Brooks Patterson authorized all local law enforcement to stop and search every vehicle on the streets of Oakland County after midnight. No one doubted that Patterson's order was unconstitutional, but authorities were "driven by the urgency to find Tim King alive."[4]

Tim's body was found on March 22, 1977, six days after the boy was kidnapped. Two men from Detroit were making a U-turn when the headlights of their car swept across a shallow ditch on Gill Road near Eight Mile Road in Livonia. They noticed something red in the snow. It was the hockey coat Tim was wearing. He was lying face down, his skateboard tossed a few feet from his body.

Like Mark Stebbins, Tim had been sexually assaulted. He was the last known victim of the Oakland County Child Killer or Killers.

As the investigations progressed, police believed the murders of Cynthia Cadieux, Sheila Srock, and Jane Allan weren't related to the murders of the other four children. Sheila's killer, a man from North Carolina, was arrested and convicted of her murder fifteen months after her body was found. Three years after Cynthia's murder, a Roseville man was convicted of the crime. Jane Allan's murder remains unsolved but an informant for the police linked her to a young girl seen with the Dayton Outlaws, an Ohio motorcycle gang, though none of those leads were ever confirmed. Police still believe that whoever picked her up hitchhiking was responsible for her death.

---

3. Kennan, Marney Rich, *The Snow Killings*, Exposit, Jefferson, NC, 2020

4. Kennan, Marney Rich, *The Snow Killings*, Exposit, Jefferson, NC, 2020

The Law Enforcement Assistance Administration published an analysis of the remaining four child killings, and the report alluded to the belief that the murders were committed by "a single killer or small group of killers."

- All four victims were alone when abducted; also, they were all taken from business areas, in or near parking lots.
- Two victims were abducted on a Sunday afternoon, two on a Wednesday evening.
- Victims were held captive for periods ranging from three to nineteen days.
- Victims appeared to have been well fed while held and not subjected to weather or other exposure.
- The victims were well cared for during their period of captivity, including caring for their normal biological needs. All the bodies were clean, and Tim King's body was described as clinically clean (his fingers and toenails had been scraped).
- All four victims were dressed in their own clothing (possibly by someone else) just before or after death.
- All four bodies were deposited along roadsides where they would be readily found.
- There was no evidence of sexual molestation of either girl; both boys showed obvious anal dilation.
- Apparently little if any force was used in the abductions; no commotions were reported in this regard.[5]

The Oakland County Task Force, formed in 1977 as the investigative body to solve the murders of the four children, disbanded in December 1978 with no one ever being

---

5. Corrigan, C.H., *Oakland County (MI) Special Task Force-Finding the Child-Killer in the Woodward Corridor-Major Case Investigation-Team Manual-Police Technical Assistance Report*, US Dept of Justice, Washington, DC, 1978

charged with the killings. The murders of Mark Stebbins, Jill Robinson, Kristine Mihelich, and Tim King remain unsolved.

2
The Beginning

The boundaries of Livonia Township were set in 1835, and the once-forested wilderness was replaced by orchards and dairy farms as new settlers from New York and New England moved to the area. Farming was the way of life for 100 years, and in the early forties, the township made a bold move from farming to industry when Ford and General Motors moved into the area. The entire township was incorporated as a city in 1950. By the mid-eighties, the Big Three automakers all had factories in Livonia.

Between 1950 and 1960, the population in Livonia increased by over 250 percent but by 1980, it gradually began to decline.

Much like many of the larger Detroit suburbs, Livonia lacked a defined downtown area. While there were some older neighborhoods, over 100,000 people lived there, and with five major shopping malls, over two million shopped in Livonia during the day. Even though the northwest part of the city was somewhat rural, it was still extremely busy.

—

Large shade trees lined both sides of Scone Street. One- and two-story homes sat across from one another on the quiet street where children roamed free with their bikes on warm summer evenings, oftentimes not returning home until the streetlights came on. Biking, fishing at Hines Park, and Little League baseball were favorite pastimes for many of the kids in the neighborhood, and being gone for hours at a time was commonplace.

Alfred Bailey, in his early fifties, was well liked and respected in the Livonia community where he lived with his wife and kids in their white brick home with the neatly manicured lawn. Mr. Bailey worked for Electronic Data Systems, a subsidiary of General Motors. With the advent of data processing, Alfred Bailey got in on the ground floor and often worked as many as sixteen hours per day. For a few years, his work week consisted of seven days per week with Thanksgiving, Christmas, and New Years his only days off.

The Baileys were friendly, typical neighbors. Alfred coached the Livonia Blue Jays, a Junior Football League team for eight- to fourteen-year-old boys. His team was always well coached, and the league was well known for not emphasizing any sort of competitiveness. As a matter of practice, the coaches didn't keep statistics, and there weren't any championship games. He was career oriented, and he ran a strict home.

Alfred's oldest son, Ron, was born in February 1959. The family lived first on Lahser Road near Eight Mile in Detroit before moving to the Scone Street home, just a few blocks from the Livonia Police Department. For Ron's formative years, Alfred Bailey seemed to be away much of the time. His wife, Charlotte, often complained about the problems she was having with Ron while he was growing up.

Ron was independent, an adventurist, and his dad knew he really enjoyed being outdoors with gardening and science as his hobbies. He liked to go skiing and bike riding, and oftentimes he would jump on his bike and be gone for hours, riding through the various neighborhoods in the area with his friends. His parents had set boundaries for his bike riding adventures, but there were many times when Ron Bailey stepped outside those boundaries. Fishing was a favorite thing to do. He loved catching walleye and bass and would often grab his fishing pole and head for Hines Park in the southwest corner of the city. There were times when he wouldn't show back up at home until long after dinner.

Before the family moved to Livonia, Mr. and Mrs. Bailey ran a strict household. She used to discipline her oldest son with a two-inch-wide Air Force belt when Ron and his brother would get into arguments about cleaning their room. Ron was the neat one and he considered his brother a slob. Ron would be the one to suffer his mom's discipline because he was older and should be the one to do more work. If he did what he was told, he was fine. If he didn't, he knew he would be punished. The whippings with the belt often left red marks, and if he ran to avoid them, it was worse. The beatings stopped after the Baileys moved to Livonia and instead, Ron would often be grounded.

As a youth coach in the neighborhood, Alfred saw some promise in his son as a baseball player, but that promise would soon fade and be replaced by psychiatric hospitals, family counseling sessions, and court battles. Ron never saw his dad very much because he worked seven days a week. If Ron was awake, his father was sleeping. It seemed as if he only saw his father when he was leaving for work or coming home, and if he was able to help him out on the weekends, he felt as if he could never do anything right in the eyes of his dad. Unlike his mom, Ron's dad only hit him once when he stole a Hot Wheels car from a local store. Enraged that his son had stolen something, he paid for the toy and left the store with Ron. When they got home, he used a belt on his son, then picked him up and threw him into the wall. When his son got up, Alfred Bailey picked him up and threw him into the wall again.

There wasn't anything pleasant that Ron Bailey remembered about his childhood. There weren't any good times.

In September 1973, at the age of fourteen, Ron Bailey had an unexplainable urge and, with a knife in hand, he held it to the throat of a fifteen-year-old boy and kidnapped him from a shopping center in Dearborn Heights. He took the boy to a clearing at the south side of a bus yard in Livonia. He tied the teen's hands behind his back and forced him to lie face down on the ground. When he heard someone nearby, he forced his captive onto his bike with the boy's hands still tied and moved to a different spot. He tried to make the boy pass out by pressing on his stomach in rapid succession in an attempt to have him hyperventilate. It didn't last long. He had to move the teen again when he noticed a police car in the distance. Bailey untied his fifteen-year-old captive, then re-tied him to the bike through his belt loops. He moved to Frost Junior High but this time, the teen captive was tied with leather straps that Bailey had with him. He tied the boy's hands, hit him, then molested him before letting him go. He pulled the teen's pants down, along with his underwear, and tried to arouse him by fondling him. The teen told Bailey he'd had enough and wanted to be released. The boy's kidnapper demanded his victim's phone number and scratched it into the fender of the bike. Bailey hit him several times in the face and stomach, and he told the boy to make up some story about an older man picking him up in a car. The teen was then let go.

The police were quickly notified, and there was evidence of rope burns on the boy's wrists along with marks on his face and neck. In the one-story brick building that housed the Livonia Police Department, the teen was shown a school yearbook to see if he could identify his kidnapper. He picked out Ron Bailey but when Bailey came to the Livonia Police Department with his parents, he denied kidnapping and sexually assaulting the boy. He said he had seen the other boy playing on a large pile of dirt at the intersection of Stark and Schoolcraft, and the two of them had a fight after the teen had started to yell obscenities at him.

The next day, Ron Bailey showed up at the Livonia Police Department without his parents and confessed to what he had done. He had talked it over with his parents and decided to come in. The only difference in his story and the police report was that Bailey maintained he didn't have a real knife, and he didn't scratch the boy's phone number on the fender of his bike. Shortly after he got to the police department, his dad, Alfred, showed up. Bailey was read his Miranda warnings for a second time that day, and he admitted that the original statement given by the victim was the truth.

Alfred Bailey knew his son had a problem, and it was getting worse.

Two weeks after confessing to the abduction, Ron Bailey was sent for psychiatric treatment at the Hawthorn Center in Northville Township, just five miles or so from his parents' home. The Bailey family worked with a doctor who was the director of the hospital, and they weren't allowed to see Ron for ninety days. It was all part of their son's treatment. While he was at Hawthorn, he said he never had any intention of harming his victim, and there wasn't any "aggressive" reason why he had kidnapped the teen. He simply wanted to see the boy's genitals. He was resolute in his promise that it would never happen again. "I learned my lesson, and I wouldn't want to hurt my family's feelings."[6]

Ron Bailey was released from Hawthorn almost four months later, just one month from his fifteenth birthday. Now living back at home, he seemed to be doing well. Riding on his twenty-six-inch red Schwinn bike was still his favorite pastime.

---

6. Dr. Harley Stock to Mr. Frank Del Vero and Mr. Charles A. Murphy, June 23, 1986

Five months after his release, a twelve-year-old boy was returning some library books at the Alfred Noble branch of the Livonia Library when Ron Bailey asked him for help in repairing a broken bicycle chain. As the boy tried to help him, Bailey grabbed him by the throat. "I have a knife in my pocket. Just do like I say and you won't get hurt," he growled.[7] Bailey took him across the street from the Westland Mall and ordered him to breathe heavily while he pressed on the boy's chest, trying to get him to pass out. While it didn't work, Bailey was able to pull the boy's pants down and fondled him before eventually walking away. The boy was able to identify Ron Bailey from the *1972-73 Frost Junior High Yearbook*, and when Bailey was interviewed with his dad, he confessed to it. The next day, Bailey was re-admitted to the Hawthorn Center. He admitted to trying to get the boy to hyperventilate but wouldn't admit to any sexual assault. In a second therapy session, he finally admitted to fondling his victim.

Bailey's counseling sessions at Hawthorn seemed to be productive when he said he had become curious at the age of ten or eleven after seeing an athletic supporter at his cousin's house. He was curious if other boys had begun to "sexually mature" like him, and that was the reason he had kidnapped his two victims. He said he had never intended to harm either one of them, and the threats were simply used to intimidate them. After two months, Bailey was released to his parents again. He had been a model patient at Hawthorn.

It was at the Hawthorn Center where Ron Bailey met another patient his same age. Her name was Deb Chesney, and the two became quick friends.

The treatment he received at Hawthorn involved many hours of family therapy with his parents, who were quick to realize that after their son entered his teens, he became

7. City of Livonia Police Department, *Incident Report,* P. Beyer, 7414849, Livonia, MI, 1974

"a mixed-up boy who never really had a chance to grow up like normal kids."[8]

Each week, Mr. and Mrs. Bailey had a family session with Dr. Jose Tombo and Ron on Thursday afternoons at 2:00 p.m. The sessions would last over an hour, and they continued for a little over one year.

—

Opening in 1956, the Hawthorn Center was a part of the Michigan Department of Community Health and considered one of the Midwest's finest psychiatric treatment facilities for children and adolescents. Before Hawthorn, children who were psychiatric patients were confined in hospitals with other adult patients because the state didn't have any programs for children. It was built on fifty-eight acres on the southeastern corner of the Northville Regional Psychiatric Hospital property. The premier facility was named for the numerous hawthorn bushes that seemed to consume the property.

Hawthorn stood out from regular state hospital services for children and was "intended to manage seriously disturbed children within a therapeutic milieu."[9] Considered a comprehensive children's psychiatric hospital, it included day treatment programs, research programs, in-patient and out-patient services. There was also a training program for psychiatric residents, psychologists, social workers, and special education teachers. The Hawthorn Center had associations with the University of Michigan, Wayne

8. Martindale, Mike, "The People vs. Ronald Lloyd Bailey," *Detroit News*, February 16, 1986

9. Cesaro, Robert and Hirshbein, Laura, "The Ambivalent Role of the Institution in the History of Child and Adolescent Psychiatry: A Case Study of the Hawthorn Centre in Michigan, USA," *Henry Ford Health Scholarly Commons*, 2020

State University, Michigan State University, and Eastern Michigan University. There weren't any other facilities in the state quite like Hawthorn.

In order for a child or adolescent to be admitted to Hawthorn, specific criteria had to be met. A "minor requiring treatment" meant that a youth had to have "a substantial disorder of thought or mood that significantly impairs judgment, behavior, capacity to recognize reality, or the ability to cope with the ordinary demands of life." If they didn't qualify under that, then a minor had to qualify under the second set of criteria that included "having a severe or persistent emotional condition characterized by seriously impaired personality development, individual adjustment, social adjustment, or emotional growth, which is demonstrated in behavior symptomatic of that impairment." The in-patient treatment could last anywhere from a few days to a few months.

The goal of the doctors and staff at the Hawthorn Center was to prepare a youth to go back home. For the treatment to be successful, the youth would have to be well enough to participate in skills to learn and make a successful return to home more likely. The programs included work therapy, development of daily living and social skills, and peer support.

Hawthorn also allowed its patients to participate in special events and field trips under the direct supervision of the staff.

—

By 1975, Ronald Bailey was out of the Hawthorn Center and living back home with his family. He had dropped out of high school.

Unable to control his depraved obsession with young boys, Bailey went hunting for his next victim. Now sixteen years old, while riding his bike, he spotted a ten-year-old boy who was walking home from a nearby shopping center. He asked the boy for directions, then pulled out a white-handled knife, held it to the boy's throat, and said, "You're coming with me."[10] He ordered the boy to get on the bike or he would kill him. The two of them rode to an empty field near the intersection of Plymouth Road and Middlebelt in Livonia. They walked 200 feet into a bushy area. The boy was told to "hyperventilate thirty times."[11] Bailey was hoping he would pass out. When it didn't work, he forced eight sleeping pills—likely taken from home—into his victim's mouth and made him swallow them with a can of Coke, then forced his victim to jump up and down to get the pills into his system faster. Bailey pulled the boy's pants down, ran his fingers across the boy's stomach, then fondled him. When Bailey's victim began to pull his pants up, Bailey pushed him to the ground and kneeled next to him as he began strangling him. He choked the boy into unconsciousness and, thinking the ten-year-old was dead, he threw the boy's body into some bushes. The boy was asked by police what happened when his kidnapper began choking him, and he said, "I went to sleep."[12]

The Livonia Police interviewed Ron Bailey again, and when he was asked about the sleeping pills, Bailey said he had used them to calm the boy down.

Bailey was sent to the Hawthorn Center for a third time and, if he was released from there, he would be returned to jail with a $50,000 cash or surety bond. In an interview there, he claimed he had been given some drugs by a friend, and they caused him to sexually assault children. He

10. City of Livonia Police Department, *General Incident Report*, A. Cheney, 7512414, Livonia, MI, 1975

11. Dr. Harley Stock to Mr. Frank Del Vero and Mr. Charles A. Murphy, June 23, 1986

12. Dr. Harley Stock to Mr. Frank Del Vero and Mr. Charles A. Murphy, June 23, 1986

eventually admitted his story wasn't true, and officials felt Bailey needed long-term and intense therapy that couldn't be offered to him at the Hawthorn Center. They recommended a private boarding school. While Ron Bailey's parents were receptive to this idea, the recommendation was changed. Wayne County Juvenile Court Judge Gladys Barsamian described the future killer as a danger not only to himself but to others. Bailey needed extensive long-term treatment he couldn't get in the juvenile court system. He was described as a pedophile with a history of bizarre sexual practices who had impulses to sexually molest and physically harm young males. There was a recommendation that Bailey be prosecuted through the Juvenile Court system. The recommendation included him being under the supervision of the Court until he reached the age of seventeen and a half. Beyond that, it was recommended that Bailey be transferred for additional private treatments.

Dr. Cyril Jones noted in his report that Bailey had said the reason for the abductions he had admitted to was to "show them things I know." He wanted to "tickle their bellies" and teach the boys about hyperventilation. He wanted to show them the "good feeling you get from it."

Dr. Jones recommended long-term treatment in Hawthorn Center, yet Ron Bailey was released to his parents until he was re-admitted for a fourth time in August. Now, instead of being a model patient, he began to test authority figures at Hawthorn, and until he was confronted with a police report by a therapist, he claimed he couldn't remember the kidnapping and assault of the ten-year-old boy.

In therapy, Ron Bailey spoke of the hyperventilation experiences with his victims and described them as "funny and good feeling."[13]

---

13. Dr. Harley Stock to Mr. Frank Del Vero and Mr. Charles A. Murphy, June 23, 1986

He wanted to spread the word to other kids so they could experience it too.

Even at Hawthorn, Bailey was accused of hyper-ventilating another patient, and when the patient woke up, Bailey was fondling him. By mid-September, Bailey escaped the Hawthorn Center but was captured later that night. Instead of being returned to the Center, he was taken to the Wayne County Youth Home for his second stay. The staff at the Youth Home was concerned about Bailey's lack of remorse and the fact that he didn't understand that what he had done was wrong. He talked about it as if it were a science experiment. The staff felt Bailey's illness was psychotic, and it was becoming more severe each time he did something.

In his report, Dr. Jones wrote that Bailey had a "borderline personality with sexual arrestation disturbance... in addition to severe impulse control." He characterized the borderline personality as having anti-social behavior and brief episodes of psychotic behavior, as well as sometimes hurting himself or someone else.

Bailey had confessed to Dr. Day that he had hurt another young male by choking him in a bizarre sexual act and even though he knew it was wrong, he couldn't control his impulse. "He himself admits it could happen again. He couldn't control himself even though he knew he would be caught." She added that the Bailey family couldn't handle him, and Ron had a history of fleeing institutions when those impulses struck. She diagnosed him as having "severe impulse control defect, poor sexual judgment, and immaturity with consequent criminal behavior toward minor male children."[14]

Bailey was moved to the Northville Regional Psychiatric Hospital in November under the care and treatment of Dr.

---

14. Kresnak, Jack and Bowles, Billy, "Reports on Bailey Cite 'Bizarre' Sex, Psychotic Episodes," *Detroit Free Press*, September 17, 1985

Jose Tombo. Three weeks later, he fled from the hospital but was caught shortly thereafter. He was returned for a third time to the Wayne County Youth Home. One month later, he was re-admitted to Northville.

In January 1976, when the case against Bailey was charged, it was waived in Wayne County Juvenile Court, and he was charged as an adult for the 1975 kidnapping, sexual assault, and attempted murder of the ten-year-old. He was sent for a competency evaluation at the Center for Forensic Psychiatry in Ypsilanti, where he was found competent to stand trial. He was placed back at Northville for treatment while awaiting his day in court.

Police took note of two things about Ron Bailey: his victims all had blond hair and blue eyes, much like himself, and the severity of his attacks on young boys had escalated.

By May, Alfred and Charlotte Bailey asked for their son to have off-ground privileges so he could attend classes at Schoolcraft College. In January 1977, according to Dr. Tombo, Ron Bailey was making excellent progress, and Dr. Tombo asked that the Court grant his patient those privileges. In May, Bailey approached another patient at Northville in some sort of sexual manner, and he was also using drugs, but Tombo simply referred to it as a normal growth pattern given his past history.

In August, Ron Bailey was caught with a male patient in bed with him, and Bailey denied it. Tombo said his staff was mistaken.

When Bailey was released for his weekend passes, he would often lie to his parents about where he went. In spite of that, Tombo continued to give Ron the weekend passes. Dr. Tombo still saw Ron as a model patient. In October 1977, Ron Bailey was released from Northville.

Bailey now faced sentencing in the abduction and assault of the ten-year-old boy. The parents of the victim wouldn't allow their child to testify, and Judge Theodore Bohn knew there was only one option to keep a grip on Bailey; a plea deal would have to be made rather than having the charges dismissed. In the deal before Judge Bohn in Wayne County Circuit Court, Bailey pleaded guilty but mentally ill to kidnapping. In exchange for the plea, the sexual assault and attempted murder charges were dropped. Bohn had a dilemma and was faced with a difficult decision: He had the option of sending Ronald Bailey into the state's prison system, where he wouldn't get any treatment, or he could leave him in the state's mental health system, where he would receive psychiatric treatment. Psychiatric treatment or the prison system? Even though Bailey had been involved in three separate sex crimes over the previous three years, Judge Bohn thought he had a better chance of turning his life around at age sixteen through the state's psychiatric system. Ronald Bailey was sentenced to five years of probation, continued out-patient therapy with Dr. Tombo, and $825.00 in court costs.

—

Michigan was in need of a new state mental hospital by the mid-forties. The Northville Regional Psychiatric Hospital opened in 1952. The 453-acre campus was beautifully landscaped and, with twenty separate buildings, it was welcomed as one of the best psychiatric hospitals in the entire country.

Northville was designed for 650 patients and for the first time anywhere, music and art were offered as part of a patient's treatment. Other treatment opportunities included home economics, mechanics, working with the ground crews, or working inside the hospital.

By the seventies, budgets around the state were reduced, and other hospitals were either closing or had already closed. This resulted in overcrowding at Northville, sometimes with over 1,000 inpatients. At times, some of those were sleeping in the gym until rooms could be found for them. It was part of the reason that some of the doctors began relying more on medicine and drugs to treat symptoms.

Because of the overcrowding and other problems in the mental health system within Michigan, deinstitutionalization was one approach that was used. A researcher described deinstitutionalization as, "The reduction of the number of patients in state hospitals, and it may involve measures that reduce admissions to, and/or increase discharges from these hospitals. While in principle, deinstitutionalization, systematic pre-release, and community service planning for patients [works], in practice there has, at times, been little regard for the disposition of released patients."[15]

Such was the case for Ronald Bailey. After being treated by Dr. Jose Tombo, he was released just two years after entering Northville. He had managed to complete his high school education from Bentley High School in Livonia while he was at Northville and even registered at Schoolcraft College but never took any classes. The Bailey family was certain he was cured, and his probation was set to end in October 1982.

Jack Zaccardo* was working at Northville as an attendant nurse when he met Ron Bailey in 1977. Zaccardo was gay, and he was pretty certain that Bailey was too. Their friendship developed because they both had a dislike for Dr. Jose Tombo. Tombo, whom many suspected was gay, was Bailey's treating psychiatrist and had made advances to Zaccardo on occasion in addition to other male patients at Northville, including Ronald Bailey.

During the time that Bailey was at Northville and Zaccardo was working there, Zaccardo prodded his new friend about why he was being treated there. Bailey didn't hesitate to tell him that he enjoyed having anal sex with

15. Smith, Gerald H., *The Rise and Decline of Mental Health Hospitals in the State of Michigan*, ScholarWorks at Western Michigan University, 1992

males, especially young males. When Zaccardo pressed him about how he had gotten admitted to Northville, Bailey simply said that he had just gotten an urge. In Zaccardo's opinion, his friend was the type of person who would definitely go after a child, but he didn't think Bailey was the type of person who would kill. Bailey liked to be in control, but if the pressure was on, he would retreat. His friend couldn't handle pressure.

After Zaccardo left his job in the late seventies and Bailey was released, the two men stayed friends. They would see each other as friends at least once a week, skiing in the winter and canoeing in the summer. Six months after Bailey's release from Northville, the two drifted apart for a few months until they decided to move into a home with Phil Hildebrand* on Trinity Street in Detroit. Zaccardo moved out after only a few months and moved to a place of his own.

While Ron Bailey was living with Hildebrand, he was helping restore the home. He became friends with a neighbor, George Soper, and found out Soper was moving to Florida. Soper was a convicted pedophile and drug dealer, and Ron wanted to tag along to Florida.

Alfred Bailey knew nothing of Soper's background but saw Ron's ambition to move to Florida as his chance for a new start. Ron told his dad that he wanted to work in Florida with his friend, Mike Slavin, and he already had a job lined up there. He said he wanted to live there, go fishing, and be able to do everything he wanted to do. It was his getaway. Since his son was still on probation, Alfred told him to contact the courts to see if it could be arranged. In hindsight, others simply saw it as a predator moving to new hunting ground.

Moving his case to a probation officer in Florida wasn't an unusual request. Bailey's case would simply be transferred to a probation officer in the Sunshine State, and he would have to follow the same probation stipulations that he had in Michigan.

In Florida, Ron Bailey reported to Marion County Probation Officer Susan Sharp. He was required to have a place to stay, a job, and a plan of action. Bailey moved into a trailer park with George Soper, the convicted pedophile from Michigan, who was living with his mother in the Summerfield neighborhood south of Belleview, Florida. He found a job installing burglar alarm systems, but the business quickly folded and Bailey was without a job. It didn't take long to find a second job delivering tires with Mid-Florida Tire Wholesalers in Ocala. Soper was the manager.

Ron Bailey was just getting started.

The owner at Mid-Florida Tire Wholesalers had no idea that one of his drivers was a pedophile from Michigan. Bailey always dressed neat and clean, and he was always friendly with his co-workers and customers. He salary was almost $300 per week with a one-dollar commission on every tire he sold. He also had health care coverage.

In July, the daily temperature in Ocala hovered around ninety degrees, and radiating heat rising from fresh blacktop was a common sight.

Bailey was making tire deliveries when he spotted his next victim, a fifteen-year-old boy. Driving the company truck, he slowly pulled to the side of the road. He asked the boy if he wanted to make some money and the fifteen-year-old said, "Sure." Bailey told him he would give him ten bucks if he would take off his clothes so Bailey cold take pictures of him.

Immediate fear overtook the teen, and he grabbed a nearby rock for self-defense when Bailey started to get out of the truck. It was the only thing he had with which to protect himself, and he threatened his potential abductor with it. Ron Bailey fled. The victim was able to identify the truck Bailey was driving, and when police showed the teen a photo lineup with Ron Bailey's picture included, the teen identified Bailey as the man who had solicited him.

One month after Bailey tried convincing the fifteen-year-old teen to take off his clothes, it happened again when Bailey approached a twelve-year-old boy. In the aftermath of those two cases, Ron Bailey was charged with two counts of contributing to the delinquency of a minor. He pleaded no contest to one count in January 1983, and since his Michigan probation had expired in '82, he was put on one year of probation in Marion County, Florida. The second charge of contributing to the delinquency of a minor involving the fifteen-year-old was dropped.

—

Nine months after Bailey was put on probation in Florida, a thirteen-year-old boy told police that a man who called himself "Gary" had fondled his genitals. He was driving a tire delivery truck when the teen was first picked up. The man drove him around in the delivery truck and got him drunk by giving him beer and whiskey. He picked him up the next day in a brown two-tone station wagon and did the same thing. The man took him to a house trailer south of Ocala, and although the thirteen-year-old boy was intoxicated, he recalled that while they were at the house trailer, the man had fondled his genitals before eventually taking him home.

The Marion County Sheriff's Office began an investigation, and the boy was able to identify the delivery truck from the tire store and the driver. By now, the Marion County Sheriff's Department was very familiar with Ron Bailey. They knew where he worked, the kind of car he drove, and the delivery truck he used. A sheriff's deputy drove to Mid-Florida Tire and waited for Bailey to return from his daily routine.

Ron Bailey knew he was in trouble and he panicked.

At work, Bailey was out on the road making tire deliveries. The deputy waited. When Bailey didn't show back up at the tire store, police began checking the neighborhood. They found the delivery truck abandoned on a nearby street. Bailey was gone, and he had taken several hundred dollars with him that he had collected from his deliveries throughout the day.

3
Kenny

Ron Bailey was facing another arrest in Florida for violating his probation and would likely be charged with molesting the thirteen-year-old. There was a two-count warrant issued for him. The Marion County Sheriff's Office theorized that he had seen a patrol car at the tire store waiting for him to return and made his decision to run. He left a note for Soper at the trailer that said he had been "fooling around with boys again."

By the summer of 1984, Ron had reconnected with his old friend Jack Zaccardo in Michigan and ended up moving in with him and his roommate, a Highland Park police officer, on Hilldale Street in Detroit. He was driving the two-tone Buick station wagon with Florida plates. After a few months, he moved from Hilldale to a ramshackle apartment on Pilgrim Street in Highland Park. It was owned by an attorney he had become acquainted with at a bar in Northville. The apartment was managed by a woman in Livonia, and Bailey enlisted the help of her seventeen-year-old son to clean the place up before he moved in.

Bailey's parents still didn't know he had returned to Michigan from Florida, nor did the Livonia Police Department or the Marion County Sheriff's Office.

That September, when he was asked to leave the apartment, he moved in with another friend he had known for years who lived on Lehigh Street in Dearborn Heights. Bailey was working at LaLinda's Restaurant on Grand River in Detroit when his old friend reached out to another friend who worked at ARA Coffee Services in Livonia, just a mile from his parents' home. He was hired in September 1983 to work as a warehouse attendant and was later assigned to make deliveries and service coffee vending machines. His delivery routes spanned from Detroit to Lansing and at one time, he had a northern delivery route because he knew the area so well.

Bailey had been warned about drinking at work. At lunchtime, he would often have a couple beers, and his boss knew it. He could smell it on his breath, so Bailey switched from beer to vodka and grapefruit juice. He was also doing speed to keep him going. He would be out late at night at the bar and would counteract the speed with Valium. They seemed to be his preferred drugs since his days in Florida. It was a daily occurrence, and he couldn't stop.

At work, he was frustrated. He didn't think he was getting paid enough even though he thought he had a huge responsibility. He was in charge of the warehouse and kept it spotless, but the new employees were getting paid more than he was.

During any given week, Bailey was spending fifty to sixty dollars on alcohol and thirty to forty dollars on drugs. He was worried his boss might find out by running some sort of check on him because he had lied on his application about ever being arrested.

Anxious and scared, he went to a bar at Five Mile and Farmington Road for happy hour. He started with a couple martinis before switching to vodka and grapefruit juice. He still had Valium in his system that he had taken at work because he was angry. He left the bar and headed to the Winner's Circle, another bar. He smoked a joint on the way there. He was comfortable at the Winner's Circle because he felt everyone knew him. He sat in the corner by himself, worrying about what he would do if he lost his job. He was also worried because the girl he was seeing, Deb Chesney, had been talking about marriage, and it made him uncomfortable. He was trying to find a way out of it. His parents had warned him that she would try to get him to marry her.

After Bailey left the Winner's Circle in Northville, he went for a drive before stopping at a party store for some wine coolers. He started for Deb's house but got off the freeway and decided to head toward a bar in his old neighborhood in Detroit. He knew he couldn't go home drunk, so he changed his mind and instead headed for the Livonia Mall.

—

It was 8:00 p.m. on June 7, and a sixteen-year-old teen was sitting on a bench at the Livonia Mall while many of the stores were getting ready to close. To Ron Bailey, he looked alone and bored. His mom was in a nearby women's store.

"Are you here with somebody?" the teen heard someone ask. Mark Chadwick* looked up to see a blond-haired man in his early twenties wearing a beige-colored button-up work shirt, brown pants, and brown leather work shoes. He also noticed a gold, non-digital watch on the man's wrist.

"Yeah, my mom," the boy replied.

The man asked the boy if he knew how long his mom was going to be in the store.

"I don't know," he replied.

The man offered him some cash to do him a favor. Ten bucks sounded pretty good. The sixteen-year-old boy agreed to help the stranger, who said he was having car problems in the parking lot. Besides, he was bored while he waited for his mom to finish shopping, and he would be back before she even realized he had left.

Ron Bailey had eyed the youth and thought he looked good. He admired the way the teen wore his clothes, and he wanted to have sex with him.

Bailey hated his own body and thought he was too fat. When he was a teen, every time he tried to dress like the other kids his mom would make him change into something else. He really admired the teen at the mall and was a bit jealous because he figured the boy could get girls easily enough. He thought about asking him to have sex and paying him but wasn't sure at what point he should bring the subject up. He was both scared and aroused at the same time.

It was only June, and the summer of '84 promised to be a scorcher as temperatures had already reached eighty-eight degrees.

In the parking lot, the Chadwick boy looked at the old white-over-brown-colored 1970 Buick station wagon parked outside the mall theater. The front grill was missing, and there were a couple large dents on it. He stood outside the car while the man sat in the driver's seat and fiddled with some wiring under the dash as he turned the ignition. Nothing happened. He asked the teen to get in and try the ignition as he looked under the hood and tapped the car battery terminals. Still nothing. The teen noticed there were tears in the front seat, and the radio didn't fit into the dash very well. It was no wonder the car wouldn't start; it was fourteen years old.

Ron Bailey stood at the front of the car with the hood open. He was stalling. His anger had built to a point where he figured, *What the hell.* He walked back toward the driver's door and told the boy to slide over so he could try the ignition again. The sixteen-year-old slid across the front seat to the passenger side as the man got in the driver's seat a second time. The teen casually watched as Bailey reached under the dash and immediately came up with a six-inch lock-blade knife.

"Move, motherfucker, and you're dead," he said as he pressed the knife to the boy's throat, then to his groin. He tied the boy's hands behind his back. "Don't mess up or you'll never see your family again."[16] He told Chadwick to sit still and he wouldn't be hurt. Bailey put the main fuse back in so the car would start.

Gripped with fear, for a split second Mark Chadwick wondered if he was dreaming. The kidnapper ordered him to close his eyes and told him to lean against his shoulder as they drove out of the parking lot. It would look as if the boy was sleeping. The teen was smarter than that, and he kept one eye slightly open as they left the mall in the dilapidated station wagon.

Back inside the mall, the boy's mom knew something was wrong when she came out of the store and didn't see him on the bench. She turned her head back and forth, searching the area where her son had been waiting for her, hoping to catch a glimpse of him. It wasn't like him to simply leave, and she had a sinking feeling as she frantically started to look for him. She began to worry.

"I just saw your son with one of his cute friends," her best friend said as she walked up to the worried mother. Now terrified, she thought her friend offered a glimmer of hope that he was nearby. Her fear only intensified when her friend said she saw the pair walking to the parking lot. She knew Mark would never leave the mall without her.

—

Bailey and his victim drove out of the parking lot and turned onto Seven Mile Road. The kidnapper's mood had changed from apprehension and anger to being happy that he was going to have sex.

---

16. Martindale, Mike, "The People vs. Ronald Lloyd Bailey," *Detroit News,* February 16, 1986

With his one eye still slightly open, Mark Chadwick was trying to see where he was being taken. They were heading west before turning south on Northville Road. The boy was petrified yet still remained calm. After driving for five miles, Bailey turned the car into Hines Park in Westland and stopped in a secluded area near some swings and slides. He told the boy he had to "finish a contract" and take some photos of him in bikini briefs.

The teen was confused and asked, "Why don't you just pay somebody to do it?"

Bailey took a blanket from his car, untied one of the boy's hands, and led him up to an even more secluded area at the top of a small hill. He had warned the teen not to run and told him he had a .357 Magnum.

At the top of the hill, Bailey looked at his prize. He studied the boy's body from different angles. He forced the boy to remove his shirt and put it over his victim's head as a blindfold. "Do you get buzzed easy?" he asked.[17] He forced the teen to guzzle two cans of Old Milwaukee beer. "Drink it straight down. Don't stop," he ordered.[18]

Chadwick was terrified. Fearful for his life, he talked with his kidnapper in a friendly tone, trying to stay calm. Bailey performed fellatio on the teen, then got on top of him and ejaculated. As the two walked back to the car, Bailey suggested they go to another area of the park instead, but the teen refused. When they got back to the station wagon, Ron Bailey said, "I want you to do me a favor. I want you to give me a blowjob."[19] The boy refused. He told his kidnapper he just wanted to go home. Knowing the boy was at an

---

17. Martindale, Mike, "The People vs. Ronald Lloyd Bailey," *Detroit News,* February 16, 1986

18. Written statement of [redacted], *Supplemental Report*, 84-16525, Livonia Police Department, June 12, 1984

19. Written statement of [redacted], *Supplemental Report*, 84-16525, Livonia Police Department, June 12, 1984

age where a simple threat would likely keep him quiet, he agreed to Chadwick's request.

As Ron Bailey was driving the boy back toward his home, he told the teen his name was Greg, and he sold drugs for a living. He also said he had a wife and a young daughter. It was all a lie.

Chadwick was certain his kidnapper was going to kill him.

After driving by the boy's home to make sure the police weren't there, he told Mark that if they had been, he wasn't going to let him out. Now a block away from the home, Bailey made the ominous threat as he released the boy: if he told the police, he and his family would be killed.[20]

As the Livonia Police began their investigation, a composite rendering of the kidnapper was done based on the boy's description. The imaged was created with an Identi-Kit, a series of pre-printed plastic overlays of facial features and hair styles. If the kit didn't contain a facial feature similar to the person being described, the victim had to choose the facial feature that was the closest. There was no way to change those features if they weren't correct. In terms of Mark Chadwick rating how close the rendering resembled the kidnapper on a scale of one to ten, the teen rated it at six to seven. Afterward, because of Mark's response to the drawing when it was done, the police weren't certain there was a close enough resemblance to the kidnapper so it was never shown to the media.

The next step was a photographic lineup. The lineup included a photo of a known pedophile by the name of Ronald Bailey, but the photo was from Bailey's teen years, and Chadwick couldn't identify him. Bailey's file at the Livonia Police was as thick as a phone book. It didn't really matter that the teen couldn't pick him out. He would have

20. Kresnak, Jack, "Teen Victim Believes Bailey Twisted His Life," *Detroit Free Press*, November 24, 1986, p 1

been their first suspect, but they just assumed that Ron Bailey was still living in Florida.

Chadwick's mother brought the clothing he had been wearing to the police, and it was sent to the crime lab. There were semen stains on the clothes.

—

Like his older brothers, the fourteen-year-old boy with the wide grin was anxious to get a job. The former Warren paperboy had already saved 3,000 dollars. He couldn't wait to find another job, and he knew there were a lot of opportunities for part-time help at some of the party stores south of Nine Mile Road along John R., a thoroughfare named after John R. Williams, a businessman, army general, and politician from Detroit's early days.

Marie Edenstrom spent most of the day painting, and she had made a picture frame for their new home. Marie, her husband, and Kenny had moved from Warren just two weeks earlier. Her son had his evening plans set, but dinner first. It was almost 6:00 p.m., and the small, modest home smelled of barbequed pork chops, potatoes, and string beans, a favorite of the young teen. They were done eating by 6:30.

Kenny Myers changed from the black cutoff t-shirt he was wearing to his favorite blue jersey with the number "66" emblazoned on it. "Mom, I'm going to the other side of the Holiday Inn, and I'm going to come back with a job," proclaimed Kenny.[21] Even though his mom had warned him that he was too young to be hired at a lot of stores, he was still determined.

It had been five weeks since the kidnapping in Livonia. Kenny Myers checked his digital Byron wristwatch, a gift from his mom, at around 7:30 to see how much time he had

21. Ingersol Gave, Brenda, "Bailey's Second Kidnap-Murder Trial Begins," *Detroit News*, November 13, 1986

before his 10:00 p.m. curfew, then set off from his home in the 2000 block of Almont Street in Ferndale as the Michigan lottery numbers were being announced on TV. It was the last time Marie Edenstrom would ever see her son alive.

—

In the month since Ron Bailey had kidnapped Mark Chadwick, he was still angry and depressed about everything ranging from his work to Deb Chesney. He knew his parents had caught on to his mood swings, and they attributed it to booze, but Ron knew it was from the drugs he was doing every day. He would normally come home, change his clothes, and head right back out.

Ronald Bailey left work at ARA and headed toward the bar. He was upset and restless, angry, and depressed as he drove around drinking beer in his car. He stopped at several bars including the Wagon Wheel, the Majestic, and the Winner's Circle. He was drunk. He didn't feel like he fit in anywhere. He decided to head to another of his regular watering holes, a gay bar called the Gas Station where he and his buddy, John Zaccardo, used to hang out. He knew he could sit there and no one would bother him. The more he drank, the more paranoid he became, and he thought everyone was looking at him. He decided to leave and head to John's house.

Zaccardo wasn't home. Bailey decided to just drive around for a while and made a loop through Highland Park looking for some friends, but he couldn't find them either. As he came back down John R., he stopped at a party store at 10 Mile. He bought whiskey and ginger ale before heading back toward Zaccardo's house, hoping to find him. Bailey was desperate to find him. Zaccardo always made him feel better. Still wearing his work shirt and pants, he realized he was out of cigarettes after he had left the last party store.

He would just stop at another one. By now, Bailey's sexual appetite had become insatiable.

Inside the store, he noticed a blond-haired boy. Bailey was at one end of the counter, and the young teen had walked toward the back. *Gee, that kid looks good,* he thought to himself.[22]

The boy came walking back toward the front, and he stopped to talk with a man near the candy rack. Bailey noticed the boy was staring at the candy, and he thought he looked depressed. Maybe the boy needed some money because he had been staring at the candy but hadn't bought any. Bailey became even more aroused as he admired the boy. He fantasized about showing him some sexual things that he had learned and, like a wild animal stalking its prey, Ron Bailey began to follow Kenny Myers.

Bailey followed the teen out of the store. Kenny sat down in the parking lot, and Bailey sat down next to him. He asked the boy what was wrong. Kenny told him he couldn't find a job, and he had already checked several places along John R. They talked for just a minute or so, and Bailey went back to his car. He began formulating some way to grab the boy and thought about asking if he wanted to make some money. It had worked before.

Bailey was apprehensive. What if the boy said no? He wasn't paying attention, and while he was trying to come up with some sort of plan to grab the teen, he realized Kenny had ridden off on his bike.

Bailey decided to follow him. A half mile down the street, Kenny stopped at a combination gas station-donut shop and went in. Ron Bailey thought about circling the block but Kenny came right back out. He must have simply walked in and asked if they were hiring.

---

22. Dr. Joel Dreyer to Raymond Cassar and Charles Murphy, August 26, 1986

Ron Bailey started to feel sorry for the boy but as he looped around Eight Mile, his sympathy disappeared and his sexual appetite took over. He simply wanted to have sex with the boy. As he was coming back up John R., he saw Kenny riding southbound, and he stopped in the street to ask if the boy had found a job.

—

Marie Edenstrom trusted Kenny. He was always on time. If he was going to be late, he always called but by 9:00 p.m., with no word from her son, she paced the living room floor in the single-family home at the corner of Almont and East Breckenridge. He was never past his curfew. Since it was mid-July and the summer days were longer, maybe Kenny had lost track of the time. It didn't get dark until almost 10:00. In the back of her mind, she feared that her trusting son might have gone with someone for the money if they offered him a job. She waited, nervous, for any sound of Kenny coming home on his bike.

—

Dolly Mae Banks lived alone on John R., south of Eight Mile. Her home was just north of Remington Street, and the elderly woman loved to sit behind her living room window and watch traffic go by her house.

On that warm summer evening in July 1984, she watched traffic from her front window and noticed a teenage boy on a blue ten-speed bicycle riding south. He was across the street, and as she watched him, she saw a two-tone station wagon driving northbound. The car slowed, and so did the boy on the bike. Mrs. Banks could see the driver was talking to the boy. As she casually watched, the car suddenly backed into a parking lot, blocking the boy's path. She could see the station wagon was an older model, and she thought it might have a lighter top. There was damage to the right rear quarter panel. The driver got out, walked over to the boy, yanked him from his bike, and hurried him to the car.

Concerned, Mrs. Banks quickly thought, *Oh, my God, maybe he's going to snatch him.*[23]

The man pushed the boy into the car and drove off as the bike was left lying on the ground. Dolly Banks wasn't sure what she had just seen, and for a brief moment she thought she might have witnessed a kidnapping. In disbelief, she convinced herself it was nothing more than a father reprimanding his son, and it was quickly forgotten.

—

Twenty miles to the southwest of Ferndale was Edward Hines Park, and it was a favorite of Ron Bailey's.

The Holliday Park Cooperative Townhouses sat between Hines Park and Wayne Road. It was 10:00 p.m., and three teens sat behind the townhouses in the park as dusk took hold and the last glimmers of daylight surrendered to darkness. The teens casually noticed a man in his early twenties with straight blond hair walk from the woods. He asked for directions to Ann Arbor Trail. He was lost.

—

At 10:00 p.m., Marie Edenstrom and her husband got into their car and began looking for their son. An hour later, they pulled into the Ferndale Police Department. Kenny's stepfather tried to reassure Marie that Kenny would be

---

23. Kresnak, Jack, "Two Say Bailey Was Near Site of Boy's Body," *Detroit Free Press*, December 3, 1985

found, but she already knew she was never going to see her son again.

The next two days were agonizing. There were two possibilities to Kenny's disappearance: He had either run away, or he was the victim of foul play. Kenny's mom knew he hadn't run away and she, along with the rest of her family, were going through hell. Every minute that passed seemed like an eternity, and the Ferndale police had no leads in Kenny's disappearance.

—

Hines Park was once a flood plain from the Middle Rouge River in Wayne County. Running for over seventeen miles, the park connects several communities in southeastern Michigan and has miles of recreational paths, playgrounds, and fishing areas to enjoy.

It was Tuesday, July 17, not long after Kenny Myers had been reported missing. A clinical psychologist who lived in the Holliday Park Townhouses was walking in the wooded area behind the apartments when she found a royal blue, teen-size football jersey with the number "66" on it. It was folded neatly on the ground near a fence that separated the apartment complex from the park, and she later said it looked as if it had been "compulsively laid there." She picked it up and hung it on the fence. Later that night, as she heard the news of Kenny Myers's abduction and his description, she realized she had found the jersey that the teen had been wearing. She called the Ferndale Police, and they were at her door by 2:30 a.m. on July 18. It was their first break in the Myers abduction.

After calling Kenny Myers's mother, the detective raced back to Kenny's home in Ferndale. He knew there was nothing more they could do that night but showed the shirt to Marie Edenstrom. She was certain it belonged to her son.

Later that morning, police began a door-to-door query of the residents in the apartment complex; a couple of them had seen Kenny's shirt the previous day near the collapsed fence.

As the police started to search along the river, they heard over their radios that a body had been found in the park.

It was almost lunch time, and a fourteen-year-old boy and his four-year-old brother were spending their summer doing what they loved to do. They were fishing near a waterfall in the Nankin Mills area of Hines Park at around 11:30 a.m. when they made a grisly discovery along a footpath near Ann Arbor Trail and Edward Hines Drive; it was the body of a young teenage boy with blond hair. He was lying on his left side 150 yards from where the football jersey was found. He was wearing cutoff shorts, tennis shoes, socks, and sneakers. He had no shirt on. The boys flagged down a retired Wayne County sheriff's deputy.

Word spread quickly in the media, and two days after the discovery in Hines Park, Dolly Mae Banks saw the news reports on television. She remembered the boy she had seen being pushed into the car across from her home. Mrs. Banks called the police and described what she had seen on Monday evening. Ferndale Police began to piece the case together with a timeline but had nothing more than that.

The Ferndale Police began to release information about Kenny's kidnapping and murder to the media, and one of the first questions to law enforcement was whether there was any connection to the Oakland County Child Killings in the seventies.

"We're examining all possibilities but have made no correlation at this time," said Nancy Mouradian, the Wayne County sheriff's press secretary. "We only have theories at this point," she said, then added, "The preliminary medical examination does not show signs of sexual molestation but additional tests are being conducted to determine this more conclusively."[24] It was a question on everyone's mind.

—

As the media covered the disappearance of a young Ferndale teen and the discovery of his body in Hines Park, Ron Bailey returned to work at ARA. He drove his 1970 Buick station wagon with Florida license plates around to the back of the business and backed it into some weeds. He left it there for a month, which his co-workers thought was very unusual. Instead of driving back and forth to work like he normally would, Bailey would either walk to work or have other co-workers pick him up and drop him off. Management got tired of the station wagon sitting in the weeds, and they finally told Bailey to move it. Bailey had been telling his friends that his car had broken down, and that's why he had been walking to work or hitching rides.

Bailey's co-workers thought he was strange. He seemed obsessed with his appearance, and he would comb his hair repeatedly throughout the day. Some suspected that Bailey was gay while others assumed he was asexual.

By September 1984, the media coverage of the Kenny Myers abduction and murder had faded, and Ron Bailey had been promoted to warehouse manager. No one had made the connection between Bailey, his two-tone Buick station wagon, and the kidnapping and murder of a Ferndale teen.

Even with his job at ARA, Bailey was having trouble making ends meet. In the few months that he hopped from apartment to apartment, he was already in debt to the utility company for $300.

Ron Bailey knew that sooner or later, someone would identify his Buick station wagon, so in December, he drove

---

24. George, Maryanne, "Ferndale Youth Was Strangled," *Detroit Free Press*, July 20, 1984, p 28

to the Bob Saks Oldsmobile dealership on Grand River in Farmington Hills. Bailey felt comfortable there because he had worked there as a detailer in 1977 before he was fired, along with another detailer, for trying to defraud the Michigan Employment Security Commission.

The station wagon had been purchased in Ocala Florida at the McNeal Motor Company for $725.00. At trade in, the wagon had over 86,000 miles on it. He bought a 1985 Toyota pickup with only seventeen miles on it and took delivery on December 10, 1984.

Alfred Bailey and his wife were surprised when their son showed up at their house out of the blue on Christmas Day. Like the Livonia Police, they had assumed he was still in Florida and didn't realize he had moved back to Michigan a few months earlier. Alfred sat down with his son and, after discussing the financial problems that Ron was having, he suggested that his son move back home. He couldn't survive on the $172 per week he was making at ARA. He could sleep in the family room in the basement of the Bailey home until he could get back on his feet.

By May, with summer quickly approaching, Ron Bailey stopped at Wonderland Marine in Livonia. He decided to purchase a pleasure boat, and he financed the water craft through the Michigan National Bank after his application for financing was denied through the National Bank of Detroit. He financed a total of $6,000 for the Aerocraft Malibu inboard/outboard motor boat. During the summer, he would take his girlfriend, Deb Chesney, or some of his other friends out on the boat. Two months after he bought the boat, he traded in the Toyota pickup at Bob Saks for a 1985 Jeep Renegade with a hardtop. He had owned the pickup for just eight months. Alfred Bailey co-signed for the Jeep, and Ron Bailey told his friends that he had bought it so he could tow his new boat around.

4
Shawn

At 6:38 a.m. on August 31, the sun began to peek above the horizon. It promised to be a gorgeous day.

The silver Jeep with the black hardtop and blue pinstriping slowed as the driver made a turn into the driveway on Kearn Road south of Fowlerville. Tom Bailey was just getting ready for a shower when he peered out the window. He had never seen the Jeep before, but he recognized his cousin, Ron, when he got out of it. The two hadn't seen each other in six months, and it was an unexpected visit.

Tom Bailey walked from the house in his bathrobe. "What are you doing here?" he said to Ron as he reached out for a handshake.

"Just heading up north."

Tom lived with his parents and his two brothers but he was home alone, and Ron said he had just stopped by to see how everyone was doing. He had brought a six pack of beer, and the two cousins drank as they talked and watched TV for a while.

Ron had brought some guns along for target shooting and said he was heading up north to a cabin near Midland for the weekend. He said his girlfriend's dad owned it, and he was going to get it ready for hunting season. His girlfriend and her young son were going to come up later that night.

Tom asked to see the guns his cousin had brought along. Ron took a single-shot .22 rifle and a single-shot 12-gauge shotgun from their soft cases. Tom took each one and looked them over. He glanced inside the Jeep as Ron put them back in behind the driver's seat, and he noticed a couple gym bags and a wooden box.

"What's in the box?" he asked.[25]

Ron said it was ammo for the guns.

As the two cousins were talking, Ron asked Tom if his dad would allow Tom's younger brother to go up north with him. Tom didn't think he would.

Tom's parents and two brothers pulled into the drive just after 1:00 p.m. They had been shopping for a refrigerator at the Meridian Mall in Okemos for one of their other son's dorm at Central Michigan University where he was a freshman. They were as surprised as Tom when they saw Ron Bailey in their drive.

The relatives all stood around chatting, and Tom's dad looked over his nephew's new Jeep while asking Ron how his family was doing. Ron mentioned he was going to his girlfriend's cabin up north to get it ready for hunting season. Some boys were going to meet him up there to help him get it ready. After a few minutes, the adults headed into the house. Tom had a wedding he had to be at by 3:00, and the afternoon was moving along. He still had to shower in order to make it to the wedding on time, and he left Ron with his little brothers, Fred and Jerry, Jr.

Jerry, Jr. wandered inside the house and started watching television. After Tom left Ron standing with his other brother, the two walked into the house and asked his uncle if Jerry, Jr., just twelve years old, could go up north with him. Jerry had just gotten back from a ten-day vacation trip with his mom, so Ron's uncle told him no.

---

25. Deering, Ivan, Supplemental Report, Livingston County Sheriff's Department, 12-4872-85, September 17, 1985

When Tom got out of the shower, he noticed his cousin was still chatting with his younger brothers. By the time Tom left at 2:30 p.m., his cousin was already gone.

—

"Look. These clothes don't match," the four-foot-ten-inch middle-schooler said to his mom.[26] He was subtly trying to tell her that he needed to have some of his clothes washed. He pointed to the beige short-sleeve collared shirt he was wearing and his gray shorts with maroon stripes down the sides. She ignored the remark but noticed the high-top tennis shoes he had on and told him to change into his old tennis shoes. The new shoes were for school, which would begin in a little over a week. She knew he would be working in the yard with his dad all day, and she didn't want them ruined before he even had a chance to wear them to school.

At eighty-five pounds, Shawn Moore turned and went back into his bedroom. He was conscientious about how he looked, and he liked the new tennis shoes but changed to his old ones for the yard work. There was an ominous warning on his small, second-floor bedroom door. It read, "Warning: This room is protected by an attack moose." Like most seventh-graders' bedrooms, it was a disorganized assortment of things one might expect to find: seashells, encyclopedias, tennis shoes, paintings, Legos, baseball cards, and a *Crossbows and Catapults* game set. He had a cat named Mr. Peabody, and he kept his hamster, appropriately named Mouse, inside a small cage. The sun was bright, and with his blond hair parted down the middle, he put on a painter's hat with the word "Scranton" emblazoned across the front, advertising the name of his school. He wore it, seemingly, everywhere.

---

26. Smith, Amy and Cain, Stephen, "The Death of Shawn Moore," *Ann Arbor News*, August 31, 1986

Shawn had spent Saturday morning watching cartoons, and he was joined by his dad. Everyone agreed that he wasn't an ordinary child. Some of his teachers thought he was very mature for being a sixth-grader and had joked that he might someday start a law firm with his brother Scott, who was attending the University of Detroit. Shawn was very creative, and during the previous school year he had built both a bookcase and a small radio that he could talk on. He was really looking forward to starting seventh grade at Scranton, and his teachers described him as intelligent and personable with a sparkling personality beyond his years. Basketball, baseball, and football were Shawn's favorite sports, and he loved music too. He played clarinet in the school band, and he could even identify some of the classical music composers by listening to their music.

He lived with his parents, Bruce "Bud" and Sharon, and his older brother, Scott. Shawn's older sister had married and moved to the northwest coast. He really admired Scott, and even though there was thirteen years between them, they still found time to do things together. Scott would often bring home *The New York Times*, and he found it humorous when he discovered his little brother reading the paper. The Moores were a very loving family, and when they would travel to the family cabin in Copper Harbor, Shawn loved to do the things that most other thirteen-year-olds do: he loved to fish, swim, hike, and go canoeing.

Shawn's friends might have considered the Moore home a strict one. He loved to ride his bike but was often not allowed to ride it outside the subdivision they lived in. He had a 10:00 p.m. curfew during summer break, and if his parents were gone for the evening, he wasn't allowed to go out and do things. They would oftentimes call and check on him. Like most parents, as their son grew older, they taught him not to go with strangers and to resist if anyone ever tried to abduct him.

Saturday evening was set. An early dinner was planned, and they were all going to see the 7:00 showing of *Back to the Future* at the local theater. But the lawn work was waiting, and it would be Shawn and his dad mowing and trimming what seemed to a thirteen-year-old like a vast expanse of grass. Shawn didn't mind mowing because he liked to drive the eight-horsepower lawn tractor, and at around 11:00 a.m., Bruce and Shawn set out to get the lawn work done. Bruce cut the lawn on one side of the yard because of a steep embankment, and he didn't want his son to roll the tractor. Within the first hour, the choke cable on the tractor broke along with two other things. Bruce began trying to fix them so they could finish the lawn, and Shawn wanted him to hurry. He had to push the grass sweeper by hand, and he was hot, tired, and thirsty as his dad worked to fix the tractor.

It was 2:00 when Shawn had some lunch, and by 3:00 p.m., he and his mom came out of the house. Since the tractor still wasn't working, he asked his parents if he could ride his bike to the Pump and Pantry gas station and convenience store for a can of pop.

Shawn Moore was proud of his new ten-speed bike, and he loved to ride it. He hopped on the silver-gray Huffy and, as Bruce and Sherry Moore watched him ride away, they had no way of knowing it was the last time they would ever see their thirteen-year-old son.

Shawn pedaled out of the Horizon Hills subdivision and headed north on Whitmore Lake Road, riding with traffic. At around 3:00, Robert Redford and his wife, neighbors of the Moores, left their house and were driving to Marv's Meat Market. As they turned out of the subdivision, they passed Shawn and Mrs. Redford waved at him. He was on the east shoulder of the road, and the Redfords thought that was dangerous. They commented to each other how it might be safer if he rode on the west side of the road so he could see approaching traffic.

Redford needed gas, and he stopped at the Pump and Pantry. As he was filling the tank, Shawn rode into the parking lot on his bike and walked inside. The station was being remodeled and the counter had been moved. When Mr. Redford walked inside, he wasn't paying attention. His head was down and he was concentrating on getting money out of his wallet as he walked behind the new counter. Shawn was standing in line to pay for his root beer, and when Redford realized that he was behind the counter instead of in line, he looked up and noticed Shawn laughing. Redford starting laughing with his young neighbor at the awkward situation too. He quickly positioned himself on the right side, three or four people behind his neighbor. When Shawn left the store, it was the last time Robert Redford ever saw him.

—

The blond fourteen-year-old boy, a ninth-grader at Hartland High School who was shopping with his mother, loved motorcycles, and the advertisement intrigued him. They had been to the bike shop, but it was closed. They had stopped at Kroger and grabbed a few groceries. Now they had to make a quick stop at Kmart in the Brighton Mall. As the two walked in the mall entrance, her son said he would wait for her as he stopped by a couple bulletin boards outside the entrance doors to the Kmart. There were video games inside the mall doors they had just come through, and she assumed that was where he would be.

Inside the store, she headed for the school supplies, looking for a specific folder her younger son wanted for school. It wasn't in stock and she kept on walking. She walked to another section to pick up a doorbell button, then headed for the cashiers. She paid for the doorbell button, and her receipt was stamped at 2:50 p.m.

In the mall entrance, the overhead lights were flickering on and off sporadically as the boy stared intently at the cork bulletin board. His mom would be done shopping soon, so he was wasting some time until she was finished. He never noticed the man walk up from his left side. "What are you looking at?" he asked the boy.

"Motorcycles," he said as he pointed toward a picture on the bulletin board.

"Your mother is doing some shopping, huh?"

"Yeah."

The man glanced suspiciously to his left and right to see if anyone was watching. "Could you help me with something outside?" he asked.

The boy asked him what he needed help with.

"Just something outside," the man said.

In an instant, the boy took note of the young man's ear-length, straight blond hair and slight moustache. The smell of stale beer and cigarettes was undeniable. The youth was instantly on guard. He glanced over his shoulder to see inside the store where his mom was shopping. She was in the checkout lane. Something wasn't right.

"No," he said quickly, and he walked away.[27] He turned around as he walked toward the Kmart and saw that the man continued to watch him. He stepped up his pace toward the store, and he knew the man had turned around because he could hear the squeaking sound in the man's tennis shoes.[28]

As the boy hustled toward the store where his mom had just finished shopping, the man quickly left the building, walking briskly toward a Jeep.

—

27. Grantham, Daniel, "Bailey Exam Continuing Today," *Livingston County Daily Press,* December 11, 1985

28. People v. Ronald Bailey, 85-4447-FC and 85-4448-FC, Livingston County, 7, 180, September 9, 1986

As Ron Bailey pulled out of the Brighton Mall in his Jeep, he realized he needed more cigarettes. The cheap beer he had been drinking with his cousin provided a familiar buzz as he drove through Brighton on this beautiful Saturday afternoon. It was Labor Day weekend, and now he was angry. He was the predator, and he had just missed his prey. He wasn't giving up until he could satisfy his sexual appetite.

Just before making a turn to the south onto Whitmore Lake Road from Grand River Avenue, he passed a familiar-looking building on his left. The thirty-foot by forty-foot, two-story brick structure at the intersection was easily recognizable. Along with the State of Michigan seal, the fifty-year-old building had the words "Michigan State Police" engraved into the sandstone facade centered over the front door of the building. It was identical to the other Depression-era MSP buildings around the state that were built with government-infused money used to put the American people back to work just before World War II.

To hell with it, he thought to himself. He was still pissed off as he made the turn and headed south away from Brighton. It seemed everyone else had plans for the Labor Day weekend except himself. He had asked at least two co-workers from ARA if they wanted to go up north with him. They couldn't. He had asked his seventeen-year-old friend who had helped him fix up his apartment, but his mom wouldn't let him go. He had asked if his twelve-year-old cousin could go; he was told no. A babysitting job kept his so-called girlfriend from going. He asked his sister and she couldn't go. He asked his brother. Another no. It seemed like he was the only one without any plans for the holiday weekend. As he aimlessly drove around, he stopped briefly to buy more booze—schnapps, whiskey, beer—and some ice, then smoked a joint. It was supposed to have been a great weekend, and he didn't want to go up north alone.[29] Now angry, Ron Bailey's one desire was to find his next victim.

Up ahead he could see the Pump and Pantry convenience store on his right as he drove along Whitmore Lake Road paralleling US-23. He would get his cigarettes there. Instead of an entire carton, maybe he would just buy a couple packs.

At the Pump and Pantry, a woman walking into the store passed a teen boy walking out. He was polite as he gave her a soft smile and said "hi" when they passed each other. She noticed the can of A&W root beer in his hand.

Ron Bailey scanned the cars as he came to a stop in the southeast corner of the parking lot facing Whitmore Lake Road and US-23. With the bright sunshine and a temperature near seventy degrees, he noticed a teenage boy sitting by his bike near the parking lot. The teen was thin with his blond hair parted down the middle. The man walked inside and bought his cigarettes. He stood near the door and gave a quick smile to a nearby customer, but he looked away as he wrung his hands together and looked around as if to see if anyone was watching him.

Not realizing he had already made a purchase, the woman standing nearby wondered why he wasn't in the checkout line. She bought her own pack of cigarettes and, as she left the Pump and Pantry, she didn't pay any attention to where the teenager had gone.

Ron Bailey watched the boy intently from inside the store. He was reminded of himself ten years earlier. After Bailey left the store, he continued watching the boy while he lit a cigarette inside his Jeep. As he exhaled, a cloud of smoke swirled and slowly fogged the interior before gently flowing from his open window.

---

29. Dr. Harley Stock to Mr. Frank R. Del Vero and Mr. Charles A. Murphy, June 23, 1986

In his own mind, the boy was much like the others. To Bailey, the teenager looked lonely, and the ravenous urge to take him was overwhelming. Once again, he envisioned himself showing the boy some things he had learned about sex.

In all, there had been perhaps fifteen others before him, but Bailey had lost track of exactly how many.

Only a minute or two passed as he stalked the slim, blond teen dressed in gray jogging shorts and a beige short-sleeve shirt. *He's the best looking of them all*, he thought to himself as he inhaled from the newly lit cigarette.[30] He wondered if he should ask the kid if he wanted to have some fun because, much like Bailey himself, the teen looked like he didn't have any place to go.

He watched as the boy sat on the curb by his bike, sipping the A&W root beer.

With the Brighton Amoco gas station across from the Pump and Pantry, the intersection was too busy for him to make his move. He would surely be seen. He would wait for the boy to leave and see which direction he was going, then he would choose just the right spot to make his move. He was determined not to let this one get away.

He put his Jeep in "Drive" and drove slowly out of the lot, stopping briefly at the Lee Road intersection before continuing south on Whitmore Lake Road. He watched the boy in his mirror. He was short of breath with anticipation. He could feel his heart pounding inside his chest. Two hundred yards south of the intersection, he stopped and backed the Jeep into a parking area near a roadside fruit stand. He could still see the parking lot of the Pump and Pantry, and he waited to see which direction his next victim would be heading.

---

30. Douglas, John and Olshaker, Mark, *Journey into Darkness*, Pocket Books, New York, NY, 1997

Ron Bailey was in luck. The teen got on his ten-speed and, after waiting for traffic, he headed south on Whitmore Lake Road. With his Jeep parked perpendicular to the road, Bailey watched the boy pass in front of him, then disappear around a slight bend in the road. The man slowly pulled out of the fruit stand and headed south too. As he rounded the slight curve on Whitmore Lake Road, he could see the blond teenager he had just admired riding his bike up ahead.

The Jeep came to a stop along the west gravel shoulder of Whitmore Lake Road. Bailey jumped out and called to the thirteen-year-old bicyclist a short distance ahead of him.

"Hey, I want to talk to you."

Shawn looked over his shoulder while trying to steady his bike. Not knowing what to do, he slowed his bike as the man caught up to him.

In Bailey's mind, the teen was depressed and lonely. He asked Shawn if the road they were on went to Ann Arbor. As Shawn spoke, Ron Bailey's demeanor changed in an instant, and he said, "Come with me! I've got a knife."[31] In reality, Bailey had forgotten his knife. It was in the Jeep, but Shawn had no way of knowing that.

Terrified now, Shawn struggled to keep from being forced toward the Jeep as the man put his left arm around the teen's shoulder, grabbed his arm, and impelled him back toward the vehicle.

—

Ronald Moncman had a lot on his mind. As he drove southbound along US-23, all he could think about was his ten-year-old daughter. The helicopter had airlifted her from the family farm near Vassar, east of Saginaw, to the University of Michigan Hospital in Ann Arbor after a

31. Douglas, John and Olshaker, Mark, *Journey into Darkness*, Pocket Books, New York, NY, 1997

farming accident. Moncman and his fiancée, Kathryn Perez, knew she was in good hands, and they were making their way to the hospital as quickly yet as safely as they could.

Moncman had the cruise control on his '85 GMC pickup set at 60 mph. He knew that his daughter would likely need surgery, so with his camper on the truck, the two intended to stay at a campground near Ann Arbor to be close to the hospital. With his mind on the tragedy that had unfolded at home, he wasn't paying attention to his exact location as he traveled along US-23.

There was only moderate traffic on the highway, and Moncman was making good time. After briefly noting the I-96 interchange, he passed the Lee Road exit. He casually glanced to the service road running alongside the highway, and something caught his attention. First it was the rear of a vehicle parked alongside the road, and then he noticed a man and a young boy just to the south. They were on the west side of the road and facing to the north. Moncman could see the man had grabbed the boy's arm with his right hand, and his left hand looked like it was in the center of the boy's back. It looked as if the man was twisting the boy's arm behind his back, but he couldn't be sure. The two were walking at a quick pace back toward what Moncman thought was a pickup truck.

But something didn't seem right. It looked as if the boy was being manhandled. The boy was struggling and stiffening his legs as if to keep from being forced to move toward the truck. He was crying.

The look of terror on the boy's face told Moncman there was something wrong. "Look, look," he said to Kathryn as he hit his brakes hard enough to disengage the cruise control on his truck.[32]

---

32. Supplemental Report, Detective Ed Moore, Livingston County Sheriff's Department, 7995-85, September 1, 1985

Moncman only got a fleeting glance. His first impression was simply a father disciplining his son but in the back of his mind, something told him there was more to it. His mind shifted from the worry for his daughter to the terrified boy. In a split-second decision, the GM security guard knew he had to get to the next exit and try to circle back onto the service road. Something was definitely wrong. Mr. Moncman was going to try to get a license plate number.

As he sped back up to get to the next exit, he watched along the service road for anything he might be able to use as a landmark to find his way back. He noticed two brick fences that lined a driveway to a business about a half mile to the south, and he noticed two lawn care workers near the road.

He could see the next exit coming up. It was Silver Lake Road. He took the exit and easily found Whitmore Lake Road just west of the highway. Driving north now, he saw just two vehicles coming southbound, one following the other. The first was a station wagon, and he couldn't recall the second car, but it was smaller than the first. As he neared the area where he had seen the man and the boy struggling, he became even more concerned when he slowed down and saw a ten-speed bicycle lying on the west shoulder of the road. Moncman never stopped. He instinctively knew he had to find the police.

At the next stop sign, he couldn't believe his luck; a police car was facing him on the other side of the intersection.

—

At just eighteen years old, Sherry Huey lived in South Lyon at the southeast corner of Green Oak Township and attended Eastern Michigan University in Ypsilanti. Whenever she drove to Brighton, she took Whitmore Lake Road rather than US-23 because there was much less traffic. As the afternoon sunshine cascaded across the pavement between the trees lining the edge of the road, she crossed the Maltby Road intersection and continued her drive northbound on her way to her sister's house in Brighton.

She was just seven miles from home when she slowed slightly as a young boy on a bicycle pedaled southbound, appearing unsteady. He was on the west edge of the pavement, and the front tire of his bike was wobbling back and forth as he looked over his shoulder while trying to maintain his balance. He wasn't very big, and the boy had a genuine look of fear on his face. Beyond him, Sherry could see a man walking hurriedly toward the boy. As she passed the boy on the bike, the man looked down but continued his walk toward the teen. Beyond them both, she noticed the Jeep. Her boyfriend had one just like it.

5
The Investigation Begins

It was between 3:15 and 3:30 p.m. when Dave Ostrem, a patrolman with the Green Oak Township Police, stopped by Paul's Towing on Whitmore Lake Road north of Lee Road. The day before, Ostrem's 1980 Ford Mustang had thrown a timing chain in Ann Arbor and had to be towed to a Ford dealership. He wanted it repaired back in Brighton, so he asked the local towing company to pick it up and bring it back. It was a quick five-minute conversation and, as he left, he turned onto Whitmore Lake Road and headed south in the unmarked Dodge Grand Fury.

Without any overhead lights, the blue lenses covering the inside headlights and the spotlights mounted at the bottom corners of the windshield made his car instantly recognizable to oncoming traffic.

Ostrem had lived in Brighton for thirteen years. Born in Detroit, he moved with his family to Redford Township when he was three and then to Brighton in 1972. The youngest of three, his brother was thirteen years his senior, and his sister was eleven years older.

After graduating from Brighton High School in 1976, Dave Ostrem started his collegiate career at Michigan State University in mechanical engineering while working in the Brighton hardware part-time. He considered himself more of a physics guy, and he changed his major to criminal justice after some ride-along programs with local mid-Michigan police departments. He quickly realized his love of police work. While he did an internship with the Pontiac Police Department, he was hired as an uncertified reserve officer with the Green Oak Township Police Department. His tuition for the police academy was paid by the department and in 1981, he graduated from the Oakland County Police Academy. After graduation, he took a part-time position with the Brighton Police Department until a full-time position opened with Green Oak Township. He returned briefly to the Brighton Police after a short layoff from the township before being hired back. It had been five years, and he loved what he was doing but there were simply no opportunities for advancement. He was looking for more chances to further his law enforcement career.

It was a busy summer for the Green Oak Township Police, and to Ostrem, it seemed as if the angel of death was along for the ride. There had been a myriad of calls involving death, including a suicide at the juvenile detention facility, a motorcycle crash, and the crash of a United Parcel Service cargo plane in the township.

Ostrem became interested in the specialized investigators at the crash scenes. National Transportation Safety Board investigators were at the plane crash, and he watched as their investigation progressed. It looked like a fascinating job, and he also thought auto crash investigation might be interesting. With a chop shop in the township, he thought he might like to be assigned to the Detroit Auto Theft Unit. There were so many possibilities out there.

The young patrolman was frustrated. With only five officers, a chief, and a handful of reserve officers, the Green Oak Township Police Department was small. Deep down inside, he knew there was so much more to his career than chasing taillights. Earlier in the day, he'd had lunch with his former chief and discussed other career opportunities that might be available to him. After lunch, he headed toward

Paul's Towing. The only call he'd had all day was to swing by his chief's new home to check a license plate he had found in the house.

Ostrem worked the day shift. No cop ever liked to work on a holiday weekend, and he had evening plans with his fiancée. He didn't anticipate anything major in the remaining forty-five minutes of his shift. The previous night, the driver of a stolen car had crashed into one of the Green Oak Township police cars and fled. The car was recovered on Ostrem's shift by a neighboring police department and Al Steinaway, a Livingston County Sheriff's detective, was helping out Ostrem by processing it. Other than that, it had been a very quiet day.

As Ostrem headed south on Whitmore Lake Road, he hesitated at a stop sign at the intersection of Lee Road. Intent on turning left, he glanced in both directions for cross traffic and refocused his attention to a pickup on the opposite side of the intersection. Seeing no turn signal, the young officer assumed the truck would be going straight through, so he waited to give the driver the right-of-way. As he paused, the headlights on the pickup truck began to flash on and off rapidly. Ostrem immediately knew what that meant: the driver was trying to get his attention. To any cop who ever wanted to get off their shift on time, it was the kiss of death.

"What does this guy want? My shift ends in twenty minutes," he mumbled to himself as the thought of his fiancée and their evening plans lingered in the back of his mind. He made another quick glance to the left and right before driving across the intersection while thinking to himself, *Why are you doing this to me?* He was certain the driver was going to report a woman with a flat tire on the highway. He stopped next to the pickup and rolled his window down. "What's the problem?" he asked.

"I need to talk to you. I think I just saw some kid being abducted,"[33] the driver said in a hurried tone.

Ostrem's adrenalin was suddenly rushing, and he instantly forgot about his evening plans as he suggested they pull into the Amoco station parking lot.

The driver, Robert Moncman, wasted no time in telling the Green Oak Township Police officer that he had been driving southbound on US-23 when he and his fiancée saw a man and young boy on foot along the road that ran parallel to the highway, and the man appeared to be forcing the boy back toward a vehicle. Moncman estimated the two were about fifty to one hundred feet south of a pickup truck that was parked along the side of the road facing south. Moncman was so concerned about what he had seen, he told Ostrem that he got off at the next exit so he could backtrack along the side road to try and get a license plate number. All that remained was a ten-speed bicycle lying on the side of the road.

Moncman did his best to describe exactly what he had seen. He described the boy as ten to twelve years old with blond hair and wearing light-colored clothing. He went on to describe the man as thirty-five to forty years old. He thought the man was about five feet eight inches to five feet ten inches tall. The man appeared to weigh around 155 pounds and was wearing a light-colored shirt and some sort of green hat with a visor.

Moncman tried his best to describe the vehicle he thought he had seen alongside Whitmore Lake Road. He was certain it was a light-colored Chevy or GM pickup truck with a dark-colored cap on the back, and he thought the year of the truck might have been from 1980.

Dave Ostrem listened intently, hurriedly scribbling notes as Moncman described what he had seen. He took note of everything Moncman said. As the young officer listened,

---

33. Dave Ostrem, Interview by author, December 2, 2022

he thought Moncman seemed very credible and paid close attention to detail. He never doubted the description of the vehicle. After all, Moncman worked at GM and was familiar with GM products.

Ostrem grabbed his radio and relayed the information to the dispatcher, including a description of the vehicle Moncman had described.

Neither Ostrem nor Moncman knew that while he had correctly described what he thought might be a kidnapping, one key piece of critical information was wrong, and it would send the search for Shawn Moore in the wrong direction for the next two days.

—

Detective Ed Moore[34] was trying to make a little extra money. His normal duties as a detective with the Livingston County Sheriff's Department usually involved working in a suit and tie with normal business hours from 8:00 a.m. to 4:00 p.m. Monday through Friday. During Labor Day weekend, he was back in uniform working marine patrol. With over 160 lakes in Livingston County, the marine patrol was kept busy in the summer, especially on holiday weekends.

Moore had started his law enforcement career thirteen years earlier as a cadet with the sheriff's department. With seventy-six employees, the Livingston County Sheriff's Department didn't require a deputy to be certified through the State of Michigan and in 1974, the young cadet was hired part-time. The sheriff's department had their own dispatch, and Moore worked not just as a dispatcher but also on the road patrol and in the jail. Three years passed, and after his graduation from the police academy, Ed Moore began his career as a full-time deputy.

---

34. Detective Ed Moore was no relation to Shawn Moore's family.

Moore's assignment for the 1985 Labor Day weekend was to take boating complaints from residents along the lakeshores. One or two other marine patrol officers were actually trailering boats to different lakes and enforcing boating laws on the water.

Assigned to a sheriff's department pickup for marine patrol, Ed Moore was driving along Grand River Avenue near the MSP post in Brighton when he heard a radio broadcast from the state police. The Green Oak Township Police had a possible kidnapping with a vehicle description. Moore knew he was just a mile or so away and reached for the police radio. "Have you been to the scene yet?" he radioed to Ostrem. The Green Oak Township officer hadn't. He was still taking information from the witness reporting it. Moore headed south on Whitmore Lake Road to check the area.

The detective stopped as he reached the intersection of Lee Road. He could see Ostrem at the Brighton Amoco taking information from the witness. Moore continued south, watching for either a pickup truck or a ten-speed bicycle lying alongside the road. Just north of Maltby Road, he could see what Robert Moncman was describing to Ostrem; the silver-and-red Huffy ten-speed bicycle was lying in the gravel along the west shoulder of the road.

As Moore slowed, he could see tire tracks in the gravel to the north of where the bike lay. Not wanting to disturb any potential evidence, he stopped short of the spot where the tire tracks left the roadway and radioed to Ostrem. He had found the bike.

Ostrem let Moncman know the bike had been found, and he also knew Moncman still had to get to the hospital in Ann Arbor. The young officer made sure he knew that Moncman was going to the hospital at the University of Michigan and how to contact him, then he and his two witnesses met with Detective Moore. Moncman confirmed that it was the spot where he had seen the man forcing the teen along the road near the ten-speed bicycle, but he couldn't wait any longer. He had to get to the hospital.

The two officers knew if this was an attempt to kidnap a teen, there was a chance the boy might have escaped and could be hiding in the area. A quick decision was made between the two officers to request a tracking dog.

With a canine trooper from the MSP Brighton post on the way, Ostrem asked Moore if the sheriff's department would process the crime scene. Ed Moore knew his colleague from the sheriff's department, Detective Al Steinaway, was the on-call detective for the weekend and was already processing the stolen car that had been recovered in South Lyon, so he radioed him and asked that he head back to Whitmore Lake Road.

Ostrem had all but forgotten his evening plans. As the two officers waited, he had gotten word that his fiancée was waiting for him at the police department. Knowing she was going to pick him up because he didn't have a car, he asked that she stop by the scene briefly so he could explain to her why he wasn't sure what time he would be getting off work. In the back of his mind, he knew this was the biggest case of his career thus far.

It had been a little over an hour since Ostrem had been flagged down when a state police trooper with the tracking dog arrived. Steinaway was already there with the sheriff's department crime scene van, and he decided it was best to wait until the dog had done a sweep of the area before he began collecting any evidence and processing the scene. Detective Moore searched the neighboring fields along Whitmore Lake Road south toward Maltby Road and beyond with the trooper and his dog. There was no sign of anyone or anything related to a kidnapping.

—

Dave Ostrem was assuming the worst, yet still hoping for the best. The three officers were still unsure if there had been a kidnapping, or if it was simply the case of a parent disciplining a child. Steinaway began to process the scene by taking photographs, then measurements of the tire marks in the gravel, noting the location of the bike with the A&W root beer can wedged between the bicycle seat and top frame rail.

Ostrem had already notified his chief.

At 5:25 p.m., now two hours after Moncman had reported what he had seen, the officers were finishing their initial investigation on Whitmore Lake Road and were still no closer to knowing exactly what they were dealing with. By that time, another Livingston County detective, Bob Bezotte, along with Ostrem's chief, had shown up at the scene.

—

Even as Livingston County's chief law enforcement officer, Frank Del Vero was still doing what he loved to do. He was coaching ninth-grade football in Hartland, north of Brighton.

Del Vero had only been out of high school for two weeks when he began his collegiate career at the University of Michigan. He graduated in 1965 with a bachelor's degree in history and a minor in physical education. He wanted to be a football coach, and the minor helped him learn the theories and principles behind coaching. He was hoping for a coaching job at some point after being hired as a teacher.

After graduating from the U of M, he took a teaching job at a junior high in Roseville, where he became the baseball coach while also volunteering as a coach for the football team. The following year, he was made the assistant coach of baseball and football.

Del Vero's wife was from Brighton, and while they were both teachers in Roseville, they decided to return to her hometown, where they found new teaching jobs.

From 1967 to 1975, Frank Del Vero worked as a history teacher at Hartland High School, making $5400 per year. He also coached junior varsity football and seventh- and eighth-grade basketball while teaching night school for people trying to complete their high school education and earn their GED. Over time, he began to wonder if it was something that he wanted to continue doing.

Del Vero's brother-in-law had gone to the Detroit College of Law, and Frank decided to take the Law School Admission Test. He did well enough to be accepted to the Detroit College of Law. They offered night classes twice each week.

After four years of classes, he graduated in 1975, and he took the Bar exam in August.

He received his passing results in November, and he retired as a teacher at Christmas that same year. In January, he started as an assistant prosecuting attorney in Livingston County.

There were only three prosecutors in Livingston County at the time, and it was an election year. By April, Tom Keiser, the prosecuting attorney who had hired Del Vero, decided he wasn't going to seek re-election. Del Vero had no intention of running for office, but he was approached by several people who wanted him to put his name on the ballot, and he was the only candidate who lived inside Livingston County. He had established himself in the community with an unblemished record, and he had a great reputation in the Hartland area. In August 1976, he won the primary election. He won the general election in November as a Republican, and he took office on January 1, 1977.

During Frank Del Vero's time in office, his staff grew from three prosecutors to seven. They moved to larger offices on two occasions as the office expanded and by

1985, his office had started their victim/witness advocacy program in Livingston County. By that time, he was also in a mostly administrative position, while his chief assistant and the other assistant prosecutors were handling the trial work.

On August 31, Frank was at football practice. Hartland High School needed two freshman coaches, and they wanted Del Vero as one of them because of his experience in coaching. It was a scrimmage Saturday. Frank Del Vero never expected to see a state police trooper on the sidelines asking for him. After a quick conversation, he knew the scrimmage would have to continue without him.

—

It was around 5:00 p.m. when the Moores noticed Shawn hadn't returned. Scott was going to look for him and bring him home for dinner. He got into his Volkswagen Rabbit and started driving north along the same route he had taken on his bike when he was a teenager. Not long after leaving the subdivision, he noticed police cars stopped along the side of Whitmore Lake Road. As he neared, he saw his brother's bike. There was no doubt in his mind because he could see the black foam padding he had added to the handlebars on his little brother's ten-speed. The can of root beer under the seat told him Shawn had made it to the store. Scott stopped next to a trooper, told him the bike belonged to his brother, and asked what happened. The trooper told him he should speak with Officer Ostrem.

In the two hours that had passed, several people on Whitmore Lake Road had slowed or even stopped to see what was going on as they drove by the scene, so it wasn't unusual when another car slowed. The driver stared at the bike and the officers, spoke briefly with the trooper, then got out and walked up to the Green Oak Township officer.

Scott Moore was under the impression there had been an accident.

"What accident?" Ostrem asked him.

He told Ostrem the bike belonged to his brother, and there must have been an accident.

Dave Ostrem asked, "Why do you think there was an accident?"

"Well, my brother went out to get a can of pop. He hasn't come home, and here's his bike."[35]

Dave Ostrem's worst fears were true. They quietly took Scott Moore aside and told him there hadn't been an accident, and a witness had reported seeing a teen being forced toward a vehicle. Scott Moore remained stoic as he came to the realization that his little brother had been abducted.

Shawn Moore's older brother seemed pensive. There wasn't a lot of emotion displayed when Ostrem explained what had happened. As Officer Ostrem started to gather information about the man's younger brother, he suddenly realized who he was talking to. The two men had graduated from Brighton High School together. The missing teen's brother was Scott Moore, and the victim was his younger brother Shawn.

—

After talking with Scott Moore, Ostrem, Steinaway, and the other officers were now convinced that thirteen-year-old Shawn had been kidnapped, and Steinaway radioed Ed Moore. He asked him to return to the scene. Steinaway told him to head for Ann Arbor and track down Mr. Moncman. He wanted an even more detailed statement but by the time Detective Moore got to the hospital, Moncman had already left for the evening. Moore stayed until 8:00 p.m., hoping

---

35. Dave Ostrem, Interview by author, December 2, 2022

that he might return, but he didn't. No one at the hospital knew where Mr. Moncman and his fiancée were camping, so the detective knew they would have to try and catch him at the hospital the following morning.

—

Horizon Hills subdivision was just a mile south of Maltby Road. With only one way in and out, by all accounts it was virtually crime free. The Green Oak Township Police Department seldom responded to any calls there. The neighborhood was literally on the other side of US-23 across from the Green Oak Township Police Department and was made up of upper middle-class, white-collar families living in split-level and tri-level homes.

Scott Moore lived with his parents and his teenage brother in the subdivision on Twilight Lane. At twenty-six years old, Scott was much older than Shawn and had just graduated from Eastern Michigan University with a master's degree in economics.

By the time Scott had shown up at the scene, two more Green Oak Township officers had started the evening shift and were checking with hospitals in the area to see if a young teen boy had been admitted, thinking one possible scenario was that he could have had an accident of some sort. After Scott was told about his brother's kidnapping, the two Green Oak Township officers accompanied him back to the family home in the Horizon Hills subdivision. Along with Scott, they would have to tell Mr. and Mrs. Moore that their youngest son had just been abducted.

While Steinaway was processing the scene, he discovered partial shoe impressions along the shoulder of the road. One impression was simply the outline of a heel, while the other was a small portion of sole. They weren't of any value. The only substantial evidence found was Shawn's bike and the A&W root beer can.

When Ostrem and Steinaway finished their work on Whitmore Lake Road, Ostrem headed for Twilight Lane. The two evening shift officers had been there for about thirty minutes with Scott when Ostrem finally arrived, and they had already given the news to Shawn's parents.

To Dave Ostrem, it was one thing to see Shawn's ten-speed bicycle lying on the side of the road. It was another thing to see Shawn's parents after they had just been told their young son had been kidnapped, and Ostrem was very empathetic. *What just happened here?* he thought to himself.[36]

While no one had any idea where Shawn was or if he was safe, to the officers at the house, it was much like a death notification, and they knew the Moores' lives had just been changed forever. Shawn's parents were in shock and were trying to process the information that they had just been handed.

—

While details of the abduction were being broadcast by radio across the entire state of Michigan on the Law Enforcement Information Network, Trooper Tom Cremonte, working out of the Brighton Post, took it upon himself to start contacting various media outlets throughout southeast Michigan. He knew the sooner the information was publicized, the better the chance of finding Shawn.

It was after 9:00 p.m. when Detectives Steinaway and Moore arrived back at Shawn's parents' home. They were going to place a recorder on Bruce and Sharon Moore's phone but the suction cup on the phone recorder didn't always hold. Steinaway had to use Scotch tape to keep it

36. Dave Ostrem, Interview by author, December 2, 2022

in place. If the kidnapper called and demanded some sort of ransom in exchange for Shawn, the investigators wanted it recorded. The device was nothing more than a cassette recorder plugged into an electrical outlet. The microphone, attached with the suction cup, was placed near the earpiece on the phone, and all the Moores had to do was push the record button before answering. The recorder would capture the entire conversation. At the end of a conversation, they would have to remember to stop the recorder as well.

It was the next step in the immediate investigation, and the investigators agreed that they would all meet the following morning. It didn't matter that it was a holiday. Just before leaving the Moore home, Special Agent Jim Reilly from the FBI's Ann Arbor office arrived and offered whatever assistance the Bureau could in the investigation. As the men stood inside the Moore home, S/A Reilly noticed a postcard on the table. It read, "Sorry about last weekend."[37] The agent took note of it.

After finishing at the Moores' house, the investigators met back at the MSP post to formalize a plan for the next day.

It was almost 11:00 p.m., and the late news was just coming on television as Dave Ostrem was getting ready to leave the post and head back to the Green Oak Township Police Department. He was at fifteen hours and counting for his shift. Almost immediately after the story aired about Shawn's kidnapping, the phones at the Brighton post started ringing.

—

Early the next morning, Ed Moore arrived at the post for an investigative meeting about Shawn's kidnapping. On the

37. Officer D. Ostrem, *Supplemental Report*, Green Oak Township Police Department, 12-2437-85, September 2, 1985

first full day of the investigation, Dave Ostrem and Moore were teamed up together. By 10:00 a.m., Chief Snelling from the Green Oak Township Police, Detective Steinaway, and four MSP detectives were all there along with the MSP post commander. Moore and Ostrem were assigned to track down Mr. Moncman and re-interview him while more witnesses to the abduction started calling in.

The initial follow-up assignments for the others included re-interviewing the Moore family, interviewing two witnesses who had seen Shawn at the Pump and Pantry just prior to his abduction, and interviewing Shawn's sister, Kathy. They were also going to interview some of Shawn's friends and the employees at the Pump and Pantry.

While the case was being investigated by multiple agencies, it was still a Green Oak Township case, and Chief Snelling was going to fill out the tip forms and handle the media releases. One of the tips had been called in shortly after the story had aired the previous night and seemed promising. There was a witness who had been traveling northbound on Whitmore Lake Road and might have witnessed the kidnapping.

The one thing they were hoping for was the possibility of Mr. Moncman providing a description to a police composite artist. With that, Ostrem and Moore headed to the University of Michigan hospital.

When the two officers interviewed Moncman again, he was sure the vehicle he had seen alongside Whitmore Lake Road was a 1973 to 1980 GMC pickup. He was so certain that he described a homemade cap on the back of it. The two officers knew about the tip that had been called in the previous evening after the 11:00 p.m. news. They asked if he was certain, and he maintained that the vehicle he had seen was a GMC pickup.

When Ed Moore and Dave Ostrem interviewed Moncman's fiancée, Kathryn, she said she had seen the man and boy struggling alongside the roadside, but she hadn't noticed the vehicle.

She described her fiancé as being involved in the Community Watch program in Vasser, and as a security guard for GM, he was generally a suspicious type person. He always assumed the worst when he saw something but typically, as he looked into something, it normally didn't turn out to be as bad as he might have first assumed.

The two officers arranged for the Ann Arbor Police Department's composite artist to do a sketch of the suspect based on Moncman's memory. Ostrem and Moore knew the sketch would only be as good as Moncman's ability to recall what he had seen, but he seemed certain of his description of the suspect. After a two-hour session between the artist and Moncman, the two officers had a rendering of their suspect.

—

Moore and Ostrem returned to the Brighton post by early afternoon.

Following up on the original investigative plan, Moore was assigned to interview two of Shawn's friends who attended school with him. By 3:30 p.m., he was in the secretary's office on the second floor of the MSP post with Lucy Parks*.

Lucy lived in the same subdivision as Shawn, and she had known Shawn for seven or eight years. They even had band together, and Shawn's best friend was her brother, Danny*. They had gone on trips to Boblo Island Amusement Park together and, on occasion, Shawn had even spent the night at their home.

On August 28, two days before his abduction, Shawn was playing kickball during the evening with some other neighborhood kids. There was an argument about whether the ball was out of bounds at one point, and one of the neighborhood girls pushed Shawn. He pushed her back and in turn, she scratched him from the side of neck to his chest area and drew blood. After the argument calmed down, the kids all went their own way. It was the only time Lucy had ever seen Shawn involved in any type of an argument.

Lucy wasn't familiar with any of Shawn's other friends but mentioned that Shawn had a recent girlfriend he had been going with for about a month.

Moore wondered about any adult friends Shawn might have. Shawn had a friend by the name of Rich. He was twenty-six years old and lived next to Shawn's brother-in-law.

The detective wasn't ruling anyone out. Shawn liked to tease some of his teachers, and the band director got along with him very well, but there was one teacher Shawn didn't get along with. It was his shop teacher. Shawn had confided to Lucy that the shop teacher was mean and acted really weird toward him. Shawn never really mentioned to her what he meant by "weird."

Shawn didn't get along with the gym teacher either. He confided to Lucy that the gym teacher was mean to him, and he felt the things kids were asked to do in gym class were stupid.

There was also an older boy at school whom Shawn didn't get along with, and the kid always tried to pick a fight with him, but that student had moved away on August 27, four days before Shawn went missing.

There was one more person Shawn didn't care for, and it was his school bus driver. He always teased Shawn and called him a munchkin. There were times when he would make Shawn sit in the front seat of the bus for no apparent reason.

Lucy felt close to Shawn and was certain no one had ever approached him with any type of sexual advances because Shawn had never mentioned anything like that.

Danny Parks was interviewed by Ed Moore right after Lucy. Danny considered himself Shawn's best friend and had been for at least the previous five years. The two boys did several things together throughout the summer, and Danny knew about the girl Shawn had been going with for the previous month. The two had met through the Catholic church they attended together.

Like Lucy, Danny knew who Shawn's adult friends were. He also felt Shawn's brother-in-law was one of his close adult friends, along with his own brother, Scott.

There were a few neighbors in the subdivision whom Shawn didn't care for but none who gave him any real problems. The only kids Shawn hung out with in the neighborhood were Danny and his sister, Lucy.

Ed Moore asked Danny if Shawn had ever mentioned being approached by anyone for anything. Shawn had told him that about six months earlier, he felt he was being followed along Whitmore Lake Road. Shawn might have mentioned to Danny that the vehicle was a pickup truck. There was a trail near the subdivision entrance, and Shawn cut off on the trail and lost whoever he thought was following him.

After interviewing Danny, investigators met at the Brighton post for another investigative meeting the following day. No one had any idea that a new tip was going to completely change the direction of the investigation.

6
The Jeep

"Where the hell is your chief?" Ostrem heard someone shout. It was Lt. Bill Pertner from the MSP Brighton post. Ostrem had no idea where his chief was. Pertner continued, "The media is here and they want a statement. This is your department's case, so you get out there."

The boyish-looking young officer hesitated for just a moment. "How do I look?" he asked Pertner.

"You look like a tired, overworked cop. Get out there."[38]

Everyone knew that the kidnapping of Shawn Moore was going to require more resources than what was immediately available. Ostrem's chief had assigned him and a second township officer to the newly set up task force. Having barely slept, he showed up on the second day of the investigation in plain clothes at the MSP post for the initial investigative meeting. He was exhausted and it showed. The second officer, Scott McGonigal, was assigned to track and record more tips that were starting to come in while Ostrem would be out on the road following up on them.

Dave Ostrem understood the complexities of the Shawn Moore case and the need for cooperation from several police agencies across mid-Michigan. He also recognized the need for leadership from his own small department. He expected

---

38. Dave Ostrem, Interview by author, December 2, 2022

Chief Snelling to be there, and he was frustrated when the chief didn't show. Although he knew he would be working on the case, he had never asked to be put on the task force. With that, he walked outside and began to update the media in his chief's absence.

—

On Labor Day, as investigators began to gather at the post, tips that had been phoned in were assigned to the officers working on the case. While helicopter searches were going on in the Brighton and Green Oak Township area, Ed Moore and Dave Ostrem had re-interviewed Mr. Moncman. Afterward, Ostrem was going to track down the two men Moncman had seen working alongside the road as he raced to get to the next exit after seeing Shawn's kidnapping.

Ostrem spent the early afternoon trying to find the names of the men and, after interviewing them, he discovered they only remembered seeing one vehicle pass them as they were landscaping near the edge of Whitmore Lake Road. It was either a pickup or a van with a loud exhaust.

Ostrem was given another tip: A college student from Eastern Michigan University might have information related to the kidnapping. She had called in a tip, and he was assigned to track her down because she lived in Green Oak Township. He was disappointed when he discovered she wasn't home, so he left a business card hoping she would return his call. Her name was Sherry Huey.

It was late in the day when Moore and Ostrem finally headed home for the day, knowing there would be more tips to follow up on the next day. Shortly after they left the post, Sherry Huey called. Detective Sergeant Beaupre took the call, and he asked if she would come to the Brighton post for an interview.

Sherry Huey was much more detailed in her description. At the time, she didn't think anything more of the boy she had seen on his bike or the man who seemed to be following him. Later that night, the college freshman became concerned. She had seen the story of the young teen abducted on Whitmore Lake Road. She knew she had information that could help the police.

The bike Shawn was riding had some red on it, but she couldn't recall the make of the bike. The man following the teen had straight, light-colored hair, and it fell forward as he looked down when she passed him. Most of his hair fell to the right side of his head, so she thought he may have parted it on the left side. He seemed a little overweight, but he wasn't fat. He might have weighed 180 pounds or so, and he was in his mid-twenties. His cheeks were full, and he had a sort of rounded chin. He was wearing a light-colored t-shirt and blue jeans.

Beaupre switched his line of questioning to the vehicle she had seen. She was certain it was a Jeep. It could have been a CJ-5 or CJ-7 model, and she thought it was white. Huey described light blue printing along the side of the hood that read "Renegade" and told Beaupre the Jeep appeared to her to be clean with normal-size tires.

Beaupre knew if her description was correct, investigators had been searching for the wrong vehicle over the previous two days. He showed her a vehicle identification book, and as she thumbed through it, she stopped at a 1982 Jeep CJ-5 and CJ-7. One had a soft top while the other was a hard top. To Beaupre, it was looking more and more like Moncman had been mistaken on the type of vehicle he had described.

The detective wanted to verify the spot where she had seen Shawn being followed. He took Huey with him and drove down Whitmore Lake Road from the post. They neared the area where Shawn had been abducted, and she pointed it out to Beaupre without being prompted. The man following Shawn had been about two car lengths behind him, and the Jeep was about another two car lengths behind him.

Her story was looking more credible with each passing minute. The detective headed to the local American Motors Corporation Jeep dealership. Huey knew what the detective was doing. He wanted her to see if she could find a similar Jeep to the one she had seen. As the detective pulled into the dealership, she got out and walked immediately to a hard-top CJ-7 with the word "Renegade" printed across the side of the hood. She was certain of it.

Beaupre had been assigned a second tip. There was another witness who had come forward after the story aired in the media. An instructor from the Bio-Physics Department at U of M was traveling southbound on US-23. He was likely just ahead of Mr. Moncman when he saw a man running toward a teen on a bike. He verified Sherry Huey's description of the vehicle. It was, indeed, a Jeep.

A fourth witness traveling southbound on US-23 saw the man and the teen walking back toward a Jeep too, and he described the man as having his left arm around the boy's shoulders with his right hand on the boy's arm. The man was gently pushing the boy, and while he thought it odd, he talked himself out of believing there was any foul play involved. When he saw the news coverage, he knew he had to come forward with the information.

After the numerous witnesses who identified the vehicle used in Shawn's abduction as a Jeep, a former colleague from Bruce Moore's employer, the *Ann Arbor News*, went to the AMC dealership and photographed the Jeep that Sherry Huey had identified. Copies of the photograph were made and given to media outlets reporting on the abduction.

Beaupre immediately had a flier made up with the composite sketch, a photo of the Jeep CJ-7 with the word "Renegade" across the side of the hood that was provided by the *Ann Arbor News*, and a description of Shawn. It was distributed to law enforcement agencies and media outlets across the state. Time was of the essence.

7
A Task Force

Because Dave Ostrem knew Scott Moore and had a rapport with him and the rest of the family, he went to their home on Tuesday morning to interview them.

Ostrem told them about the new information about the Jeep. Did it sound familiar? The Moores didn't know anyone with a vehicle like that.

Bruce Moore told Ostrem about the post card with the apology lying on the table that was seen on the night of Shawn's disappearance. It was from their daughter, Kathy, who was living in Seattle. She'd had a disagreement with her husband, Rick. Because of the argument, she was going to fly back to Michigan and have Bruce pick her up at the airport. At the last minute, she changed her plans. She had sent the postcard to apologize for the inconvenience to her dad.

Scott offered Ostrem some background about his sister. He thought Rick Miller might have been married before his marriage to Kathy, and he might have had a child from that marriage. He was pretty sure his sister didn't know about his previous marriage or the child. Kathy and Rick were married in the summer of 1984, and three months after their marriage, they got harassing phone calls at the Moore residence. One caller threatened Rick Miller's child from his previous marriage. Miller told the Moores that the calls were likely pranks and offered little additional information.

Besides the calls in 1984, other calls had been received just a few months earlier, and there was no conversation when they answered their phone.

In June, Kathy's husband took a job in Seattle, so she moved home briefly with her family before moving to Seattle with her husband the following month.

Sharon Moore offered more information about the harassing phone calls. The family had received suspicious calls in June and July. The calls were between 1:00 a.m. and 3:00 a.m., and Bruce answered the phone each time. Each time, a young male would ask to speak to Kathy. There was never any other conversation. Bruce would keep the line open and after a few minutes, the caller would hang up first. Bruce was the only one to ever answer the phone in the middle of the night. Kathy only answered the phone once out of the four or five calls they received, and she told the caller that if he called again, she would call the police. They never received another call.

Dave Ostrem knew the Moores had received a couple strange calls on Monday, just a day after Shawn's abduction. There was one call at 10:30 a.m. and a second call at 1:50 p.m. The line was kept open on the first call for about six minutes until the line went dead. There was no sound on the call and no conversation. When the second call came in, they left the line open for ninety minutes but eventually just hung up.

After Ostrem finished the interview, he drove back to the task force office and ran a criminal history check on Rick Miller. He filed the information as a tip in case they needed the information for some later part of the investigation.

Later that afternoon, Officer Ostrem was speeding back toward the Moore home, but it was too late. The Moores had a caller on the line, but he had already hung up. Bruce Moore had answered the phone. The caller said his name was John Finnerty, and he had information about Shawn's whereabouts but would only speak to Det/Sgt. Arnold Phillips from the state police post in Livonia. Finnerty said he feared for his own safety but trusted Phillips.

Lieutenant Hughes from the task force called Phillips and relayed the information, hoping the caller was legitimate. Maybe Shawn was safe.

Phillips did some quick checking because the name Finnerty sounded familiar. He had come across a man named Finnerty a few years before when the man's car was broken down on I-94. He had helped him out, and Finnerty appreciated the officer's efforts.

By 4:30 p.m., Phillips was calling the number but was told Finnerty had just left and wasn't expected back until 7:00. A surveillance was set up on Finnerty's house before Det/Sgt. Phillips made the call back to him at 7:00.

Phillips made the call at 7:15. The two men spoke at length about Shawn Moore's disappearance and what information Finnerty might have about it. Phillips listened intently as the man on the other end of the line said he had gotten information about Shawn's disappearance through "other than human resources." Finnerty said he had psychic powers, and they were on record with, "Bill Webster in Washington."[39] He was referring to William Webster, the director of the FBI. He told Phillips that he had spoken with Webster in Washington about what had happened.

Phillips was disappointed. He had legitimately thought Finnerty might have useful information but the more he spoke with him, the less believable he became. Phillips thought that everything Finnerty had told him had already been released to the media, but there was more. Finnerty told the trooper Shawn was alive in an apartment, and he was being fed and taken care of. Finnerty wanted to meet face to face with the trooper.

---

39. William Webster, director of the Federal Bureau of Investigation

After the phone conversation, Phillips spoke with Lt. Hughes, and both men agreed that any information Finnerty had would be suspect at best. Finnerty lived in River Rouge near Detroit, and Phillips checked with the River Rouge Police. They considered Finnerty a nut. Phillips decided not to make the meeting, and the tip was closed out.

No one realized how accurate some of John Finnerty's information really was, and none of the information was investigated.

Later that afternoon, Bruce Moore made an impassioned plea for his son's safe return. In front of scores of reporters, Shawn's dad pleaded, "Please return him, and there will be no questions." He continued, "I'm worried about one thing. Shawn is dressed very lightly. Should he catch a cold, sometimes he has asthma that could require medication."[40]

With all of the witness accounts of the kidnapping, police revised their description of the suspect and described him as a White male, approximately twenty-four years old, five feet nine inches tall and weighing about 180 pounds.

Tracking dogs worked throughout the day on Tuesday searching in and around Green Oak Township and southern Livingston County with no success.

Dozens of volunteers and officers from all over lower Michigan searched from the point where Shawn was abducted outward in an effort to find him.

Now addressing the media, Lt. Pertner described how the new suspect vehicle information came to light. He described the new witness northbound on Whitmore Lake Road when she saw a boy "...peddling away and looking over his shoulder back at the man a couple car lengths behind him."[41]

---

40. AP, "Captor Description Altered, but Police Still Stymied," *Battle Creek Enquirer*, September 3, 1985, p 11

41. AP, "New Witnesses Change Police View of Livingston Teenager's Abduction," *Detroit Free Press,* September 3, 1985, p 2

As Pertner answered questions, a television reporter mentioned that there were similarities between the abduction of Shawn and another abduction and murder in Ferndale. Kenny Myers had been kidnapped and murdered the previous year. Pertner wasn't trying to hide anything. The media had been a great asset to the investigation thus far because they were publishing updated information as soon as it was released. When the reporter mentioned Kenny Myers's murder, Pertner said the Wayne County Sheriff's Office had been contacted on September 1 about similarities between the two cases.

—

There was an immediate request for MSP detectives from around the mid-Michigan area to help track down leads in Shawn's kidnapping. The request was sent to MSP First District Headquarters in Lansing, and Lt. Lynn Knuth, nearing the end of his career with the state police, drove to Brighton to assess just how many detectives were needed. Some started arriving on Tuesday, and by Wednesday morning, there were as many as fifty to seventy-five MSP detectives and other officers assigned to the task force, including Detective Don Brooks, a fourteen-year veteran of the state police. Brooks was relentless as a detective and was a familiar face to many of the others assigned to the task force. He had been a detective since 1980 and had spent the previous four and a half years working with the Michigan Attorney General's office on a cold case. After his initial assessment, Detective Brooks knew they could use more help so the Lansing post sent their best—including John Boggs, Bob Kowalski, and Dale Welton.

With so many detectives in the small MSP post, it was clear they needed a bigger workspace. Across the street stood an abandoned bank, which would be perfect for the task force to work from. After making arrangements with the building owners, investigators moved the task force operations across the street. All of the follow-up to Shawn's kidnapping would be done from the temporary task force office. A computer was added in a back room, and a data base was started that included known sex offenders in the area, along with information provided by AMC about Jeep owners. The computer crashed within days with no backup.

The MSP mobile command post was sent from Lansing and set up in the parking lot outside the building because it had a phone bank in the trailer, and temporary phone lines were also installed inside the building. Phone wires hung loosely like vines from under the ceiling tiles over desks as detectives in white shirts and ties began to work tirelessly collecting tips. The task force was a collective of officers from Green Oak Township, the Michigan State Police, the Livingston County Sheriff's Office, the Brighton Police Department, and the FBI. New tips were starting to add up.

The task force was set up on Tuesday, September 3, day three of the investigation. Lt. Roger Bittell, assigned to the Livonia post in charge of narcotics, was sent to initially assist Lt. Knuth. Knuth supervised the detectives in Lansing, but he was nearing retirement. Bittell had once been assigned to the Brighton post. During that time, he fostered relationships with many of the law enforcement agencies in and around Livingston County, and he was the natural choice to run the investigation with nineteen years under his belt.

Bittell was an army veteran who had served from 1963 to 1965 before joining the state police in 1966. His first assignment was at the East Tawas post along the Lake Huron shoreline, and he was instructed early in his career to never speak with the press. Everyone was on a "need to know" basis, and he was also told to never divulge anything about an investigation until he absolutely had to.

By the early seventies, Bittell was assigned to the Ypsilanti post when serial killer John Norman Collins was arrested in 1969. From the sidelines, the young uniformed trooper watched and made observations early in his career. He took note of the things that held investigations back. One of those was the propensity for various departments involved in an investigation wanting to be identified as the lead investigating agency and to enjoy the spotlight and publicity that goes with that. In the Collins case, detectives were closed-fisted about any information they had, and the uniformed troopers were left out of the loop. Bittell was certain that the guys working on the road could be a huge help if they knew what was going on in the investigation.

When Roger Bittell received word from MSP Inspector Sam Hutchins about Shawn's kidnapping, he and Hutchins discussed how the case should be supervised. The men had mutual respect for each other as investigators and as friends. Roger Bittell vowed, in the interest of solving Shawn Moore's kidnapping, that any agency involved in the massive investigation would get equal billing, and he didn't care who got what as long as the case was solved.

Each day, Bittell had briefings with the assembled agencies involved in Shawn's abduction. On the first day, lasting impressions were made when he stood in front of the task force members and said, "I don't care which agency you work for. I don't care how many years you've been a police officer. If you have any ideas, any suggestions, I want to hear them."[42] He made sure everyone was up to speed and each officer knew where the investigation was going. It was an impressive stance.

—

The task force began fielding tips in Shawn's abduction, and a number of FBI agents were assigned to help out. The detectives turned to the FBI in hopes of creating a profile of

42. Don Brooks, Interview with author, January 5, 2023

Shawn's abductor. The Behavioral Sciences Unit at the FBI was relatively new, and agents were collecting data from predator cases around the country in hopes of understanding how a predator thinks and what type of person might fit into that category.

Special Agent Jim Harrington, the FBI's Detroit field office profile coordinator, was asked to gather all the information that might help in creating a profile of Shawn's abductor. Once Harrington collected the data, he called Special Agent John Douglas. Together, the two collaborated over the details of the abduction.

Initially, there were two possibilities. The first was that Shawn was the victim of a stalker, perhaps someone who had been watching his every move for weeks prior and had finally struck. The second possibility was that a family member could be involved, and while the idea of someone in Shawn's family being implicated was an uncomfortable thought, the agents knew, as did every other officer involved in the case, that sometimes parents kill their children. They knew they had to at least consider the possibility because some of the investigators involved in the investigation felt that Bruce and Sharon Moore weren't responding appropriately to the abduction of their son. Red flags were raised when it seemed the Moores weren't grieving like some felt they should over the kidnapping.

When Harrington met with Bruce and Sharon, he found strong-willed, loving parents. The Moores impressed each and every law enforcement officer they came into contact with throughout the ordeal with their personal strength and optimism.

The idea of a stalker striking along a busy roadway on a holiday weekend didn't make sense to the FBI either. There were too many other less obvious ways that he could have kidnapped Shawn. Both Harrington and Douglas came to the conclusion that Shawn Moore's kidnapping was committed by a stranger who had found the perfect opportunity to grab him.

Whoever kidnapped Shawn wasn't someone just passing by. He knew the area. To kidnap a thirteen-year-old during daylight hours on a busy stretch of roadway, let alone a holiday weekend, led the two agents to believe the suspect was likely using alcohol or drugs. It would lower his reticence.

Whoever had kidnapped Shawn had low self-esteem. He would be trying to compensate for that all the time in ways such as having a masculine vehicle of some sort. He might also brag about hunting and fishing, but everything would be a mask to hide his desire for young boys. If he had a girlfriend, she would serve the same purpose. It was nothing more than an ideal relationship to disguise himself as normal.

Rather than being comfortable with people his own age or older, this suspect's real relationships would be with younger males. He might even use money or gifts to keep those young males interested in him, and even with the abduction of a thirteen-year-old, he had chosen Shawn because he was small and easy to intimidate.

The kidnapper wasn't someone with a college education but likely graduated from high school. He wouldn't be highly skilled and would simply have a blue-collar job.

Harrington and Douglas believed that the suspect felt emboldened by the use of alcohol or drugs and had experience in kidnappings. The two special agents told investigators they should be looking for someone with a history of sex crimes and at least some history of similar abductions. As a result of those charges, the person might have been imprisoned or hospitalized, or maybe even both. Whoever was responsible, he had a specific location in mind to take Shawn that would provide some sort of privacy.

There was no doubt the kidnapper had a troubled relationship with his parents, but the profilers also felt he was probably living with a family member; therefore, he couldn't bring Shawn back to his house. Thinking that the suspect hunted or fished, they felt he might take Shawn to someplace in the woods where he knew no one would come to, or maybe to a cabin within an easy drive that might belong to a friend or family. It might even be abandoned.

Bruce and Sharon Moore were very optimistic their son would be found, but Harrington and Douglas felt that if Shawn wasn't released in the first day or two, his kidnapper likely had no intention of releasing him at all, and eventually, the thirteen-year-old's body would be found near wherever the kidnapper had taken him.

The profile was specific, although they were still unsure about the suspect's age. The two agents were confident in their profile, and they told police that there was someone out there who fit the profile, and law enforcement might have already talked with the person.

Shawn's kidnapping, according to the profile, was the result of a precipitating event, or what was referred to as "other stressor," likely related to either the suspect's job or personal relationships. Since the abduction occurred on a holiday weekend, it was more likely that it was related to a relationship issue. Suspects involved in abductions were often frustrated, depressed, and lonely on holidays. It was possible the kidnapper needed to vent. Whoever rejected the suspect was someone he perceived to be very much like Shawn. Shawn was a stand-in and a displacement for anger and rage against whoever the suspect felt he had lost.

With the two agents' profile of the suspect in hand, investigators began to focus their efforts on the type of person described, and they gave greater weight to the witness report of a blond or light brown-haired man in his twenties driving a Jeep. The FBI was certain the kidnapper lived somewhere in the area, and there couldn't be too many people who matched the description.

It was Ron Bailey's first day back to work after the Labor Day weekend. He was unusually quiet, and it appeared he might be hung over. He pulled into the parking lot at ARA Services in Livonia. His Jeep was covered in mud that looked as if it was still damp. Tall grass was stuck in the fenders. He told a co-worker he was going to take the Jeep back to a carwash to get it really clean. In passing, he mentioned that he had gone to the same spot to go four-wheeling that he had been at the previous week.

Bailey had always left work at lunchtime. His co-workers noticed that on this particular Tuesday, he spent his lunch hour cleaning his Jeep. He drove inside the warehouse, which was unusual, and using a Shop-Vac from ARA, he vacuumed the entire interior of the Jeep, then cleaned all the windows. He used Armor All to wipe down the entire interior. His co-workers had never seen him do anything like that on his lunch hour and thought it was odd he wasn't cleaning the outside of the vehicle. When one of them asked why, Bailey told them he was going to a wedding the following day, and he just needed the inside clean, yet he had told a different co-worker he was taking it to the car wash to get it really clean. The co-workers wondered who would get married on a Tuesday, and Bailey never mentioned a wedding again.

—

As the task force came together, Ostrem was asked to be a liaison between law enforcement and the Moore family during the evenings. He spent each day following up on tips, and during the evening, he met with the Moores and briefed them on the day's investigative activities. Detective Al Moffatt from MSP was also assigned to be the liaison during the day. For twelve to fourteen hours a day, Moffatt was with the family to help with anything they needed, working much like a victim advocate.

The subdivision was closed to anyone who didn't live there, and the media, desperate for any updates, were circling like vultures.

By Tuesday's investigative meeting, everyone agreed they were now focusing on a mid-eighties Jeep Renegade rather than a GMC pickup truck. Fliers were being sent out with the updated information.

8
The Tips

There were at least fifty task force members from local, state, and federal jurisdictions working on Shawn's abduction by Wednesday, September 4, and over 500 tips were phoned in by that time. Searches continued throughout the day.

Lt. Jack Smith from the state police had already made a phone call to the National Center for Missing and Exploited Children asking for help in publicizing Shawn's kidnapping and requesting any other resources they could provide to help in the investigation.

Detectives in Wayne County had already taken note of the glaring similarities to the unsolved abduction and murder of the teenager from Ferndale the year before. Both boys bore a striking resemblance to each other and both were riding ten-speed bikes when they were kidnapped.

Wayne County Sheriff's Detective Ray Allen, who was investigating the Kenny Myers murder, said he didn't know for sure that the cases were connected but they were very similar. "You take the time of day, daytime, a kid on a bicycle, same age, same description, the clothing descriptions were similar…" he said. The Wayne County Sheriff's Department contacted MSP the day after Shawn's kidnapping and even searched Edward Hines Park for Shawn, the same place Kenny Myers's body had been found.

Even Marie Edenstrom noticed the similarities and was very thankful there had been some witnesses in Shawn's kidnapping. "I'm hoping it's the same man, so he can be caught and stopped," she told reporters.[43]

Bruce Moore was frustrated and angry when he spoke with the media about Shawn's abduction, yet he still found some comfort knowing how much effort was being put forth by law enforcement. "God, I know they're doing all they can, they're putting out a tremendous effort, but this is my son. No one can know how I feel. People say they do, but they can't know." He continued, "The nights are the worst. When all the neighbors and friends have left and it's just Sharon and me, it gets bad. Real bad."[44] Moore had once said that he had lost faith in humanity, and that was why he decided to move from Ann Arbor to Green Oak Township. After the outpouring of support when Shawn was kidnapped, it renewed his faith in humanity. "In this darkest moment, people have come to us, offering support and giving everything they have to help us find Shawn. You expect that from family and close friends, but most of these people we've never must. They just care."[45]

Shawn's dad was hopeful in the face of his ultimate fear. "Maybe when you write this story, the man who took my son will read it." He continued, "Please let him know how precious our son is to us. Write it so he knows how much we love Shawn." Bruce Moore would do anything to get his thirteen-year-old back. "Tell him he can walk away free

43. Kresnak, Jack, "Police Flooded by Tips in Kidnap Case; Reward is Offered," *Detroit Free Press*, September 4, 1985

44. Gallagher, Mike, "Parents Grieve for Missing Son," *Lansing State Journal*, September 4, 1985

45. Gallagher, Mike, "Kidnapping of Son Offers Silver Lining for Mich. Father," *Courier-Post*, September 5, 1985

if he lets our boy come home to us." Fighting emotions, he whispered, "Please, please bring him back safely to us."[46]

The Moore family was inundated with cards, letters, and phone calls from people they had never met, all offering their support and prayers for Shawn, with many containing cash and checks. They were overwhelmed. One heart-wrenching letter read:

> *I am an eleven-year-old girl who lives in Yale. I heard about Shawn missing. It's probably a real bad feeling not knowing where your son is. I really hope he is found safe and sound. I have a thirteen-year-old brother who rides his bike three miles from here to his friends. I can't imagine if this were to happen to him. I hope Shawn turns up and he is unharmed. You might hear from me again. I'll pray for you.*

Under the girl's signature, she wrote:

> *An eleven-year-old girl in Yale who is hoping Shawn is found soon.*

—

The WeTIP program was set up through WXYZ in Detroit, and when calls were made to the 1-800-73-CRIME phone number, they were answered in Ontario, California.

At 1:35 p.m. in California, the WeTIP phone rang. An anonymous tipster was reporting that a man named Ron Bailey might be a suspect in the abduction near Brighton. The caller described Bailey and his Jeep. The caller also knew where Bailey worked. The tip sheet read:

---

46. Gallagher, Mike, "Shawn's Father: Help Renews His Faith," *Lansing State Journal*, September 5, 1985

He lives off of Farmington Road near School Craft.
He has been said to have been in areas of other
kidnappings. He was driving a station wagon during
the time of one kidnapping. The license plate number
on the silver Jeep is 984-NTL.

Two hours after the tip was phoned in, it was passed on
to the task force in Brighton.

Five hours after the first call was made, the WeTIP line
in California rang again. Another caller was reporting that
a man named Ron Bailey resembled the composite sketch
that was shown on TV in Michigan. The tipster also knew
Bailey had been arrested in Florida, and that he was using
two social security numbers. The second tip read:

(Crime profiled on WXYZ-TV on 9/3/85) #1 looks
like the composite drawing shown on tv of the
suspect being sought in connection with this missing
child: It is said that #1 was arrested about 2 years
ago (unk city in Florida), for child molestation-
details unknown. #1 is also supposed to be using
two different social security numbers (those #'s not
known).

Within the hour, the information had been passed on to
the task force.

—

Residents in and around Brighton tied yellow ribbons
to trees, lampposts, and buildings as media outlets and
reporters from across Mid-Michigan and beyond were
reporting on the investigation into Shawn Moore's
abduction, including a young reporter from Channel 7 in
Detroit. Chris Hansen had interned with the station while
attending Michigan State University. He had covered the

story of Kenny Myers's abduction and murder, and now he was covering the abduction of Shawn Moore around the clock. The kidnapping was getting a lot of attention because Shawn's dad worked for the *Ann Arbor News*. Bruce Moore knew how to get the story out, and Channel 7 felt compelled to cover it. Chris Hansen felt it was his responsibility to get the story right and hold whoever had taken Shawn Moore accountable.

The *Brighton Argus* and the *Livingston County Daily Press* were two papers affiliated with each other. There were two editors, but both publications used the same reporting staff. Nicole Robertson covered the Brighton area and Green Oak Township area while Dan Grantham handled the news in the Howell and Fowlerville area. Both of the papers were part of a larger chain that covered the suburbs of Detroit, including Milford, Novi, South Lyon, and Northville. Grantham, a recent college graduate, had only been with the paper for five months and had just started building his list of sources he could go to for information. When he first heard about Shawn's kidnapping through the larger media outlets, he knew he would be involved.

Across the Brighton business district and beyond, Wanted posters were in windows of restaurants, on doors, on store counters. Each poster described Shawn's kidnapper. Lt. Pertner was having trouble keeping up with the demand for the posters and reached out to a local printer. By Tuesday afternoon, 15,000 copies were waiting for MSP with 50,000 more expected. There was no charge. Domino's Pizza was expecting thirty thousand of the Wanted fliers, which would be given out with each pizza order.

—

Within days of the abduction, a letter was sent to the White House in Washington, DC. It was a letter from the students at Scranton Middle School in Brighton. Like many other kids in the mid-Michigan area, they were terrified—not just for Shawn, but for themselves. They wanted to do their part to help find Shawn, and they were hopeful that the President of the United States might be the answer. Their letter read:

Dear Mr. President Reagan,

Something terrible has happened in Brighton, Michigan, Saturday, August 31. One of our classmates and friends, Shawn Moore, was kidnapped by a stranger while riding his bicycle in town. There were several witnesses who were able to describe the stranger and his vehicle. The police used this description to draw up a wanted poster, which we are enclosing.

The police are trying very hard to find Shawn and the stranger, but so far have not had any luck. We are all very nervous about our own safety as well as Shawn's. By now it is possible that the stranger could have driven Shawn to any location in the United States, making the job of finding him much more difficult.

Kidnapping is a growing tragedy which affects everyone in the United States. If you could share this poster on one of your news conferences, you might be able to save Shawn's life and the lives of other kids that might be victims of this stranger. Your concern for kids like Shawn also discourages other kidnappers. Please help us bring Shawn back.

Respectfully, The Students of Scranton Middle School.

—

Police were averaging twenty-five tips per hour by Thursday, and the reward had grown to $46,000 after $20,000 was donated by two companies in Ann Arbor. Sadly, some of the tips were perverts calling in to tell police what they were doing to Shawn and then hanging up, but police estimated that about ten percent of the legitimate tips were of some value.

As tips poured in, each was assessed and assigned to a team of investigators to follow up, even if it sounded far-fetched. One of the first tips handed to Brooks and Ostrem sounded good. A woman in Detroit called in to say she had seen a Jeep in Detroit with a young boy matching the description of Shawn given out by the media. On Friday, September 6, the two task force members met with the tipster and took the information. She was a local prostitute. They listened to her describe what she had seen and decided to meet her on Saturday morning in Detroit to have her sit down for a composite sketch with a police artist. Maybe she would be able to verify some of the information she was reporting.

On Saturday morning, September 7, she didn't show. With a surveillance team in tow, Brooks and Ostrem headed to her apartment in the Cass Corridor, one of the roughest parts of Detroit. Prostitution, drugs, and other crimes were commonplace, and it was known as Fire Alley because it had the reputation of being Michigan's arson capital.

Four unmarked police cars sat down the street as Ostrem and Brooks watched the front of the woman's apartment. Several dopers sat around the front stoop smoking weed. When the prostitute showed up and went inside, the four unmarked cars converged on the front of the building as the now wide-eyed locals tossed whatever they had. The surveillance team entered the building, but Brooks stopped short. "Can you guys do us a favor and watch our cars for us?"[47] It was the ice breaker they needed. The group of men burst out laughing as Brooks headed inside with Ostrem.

Inside the run-down building, the surveillance team kicked in the prostitute's apartment door. Brooks and Ostrem interviewed the surprised woman again, and she eventually admitted that she had been lying and had made up the story of seeing the Jeep in Detroit. She was hoping for part of the reward.

—

A key part of the ongoing investigation centered around the American Motors Corporation. Jeeps were manufactured by AMC, and with the incredible detail that Sherry Huey was able to provide, the corporation was contacted to obtain a list of all Jeep owners in Wayne County, Oakland County, and Macomb County. The list was in the form of vehicle identification numbers, so the investigators ran the VINs through the Law Enforcement Information Network (LEIN) for the names of the owners. They took those same names and checked criminal history records that might be associated with them. The list of owners was divided up between investigators for them to begin cross-checking the names of the registered owners with known sex offenders. Brooks and Ostrem received their list of owners to check on. One name on their list of Jeep owners was a man named Ronald Bailey. Because Bailey was a juvenile when he was arrested for the 1975 kidnapping and attempted murder in Livonia, the criminal history from that arrest didn't show up when they checked his name.

Brooks and Ostrem headed to an address on Scone Street in Livonia to talk with Ron Bailey. Alfred Bailey and his wife were very cordial to the two men when they arrived. Ron wasn't there but he would be back later in the day. The

47. Don Brooks, Interview with author, January 5, 2023

Baileys never mentioned their son's past criminal history of kidnapping and sexually assaulting young boys. They did show Brooks and Ostrem where Ron slept in the house. It was a large, open basement area. There was nothing more than a bed and dresser there. Brooks started taking photos of the area, including a yellow blanket that was folded nearby. He left a business card with Mr. and Mrs. Bailey and asked that when Ron returned, he call the post so someone could interview him.

Late on the afternoon of September 10, the phone rang at task force headquarters.

Bailey was interviewed by members of the task force in the early evening. He was very clear about what he had been doing on the day that Shawn Moore was kidnapped. Knowing nothing about his past, the investigators only knew that Ron Bailey had a Jeep Renegade, and he was one of hundreds on the list provided by AMC to the task force.

Caseville, Michigan sits on the shoreline along the east side of Saginaw Bay in Michigan's thumb area. Ron Bailey told investigators from the task force that it was where he spent August 31. He said he had woken and showered at his parents' home around 8:00 a.m. and begun packing for a fishing trip he had planned. He and his friend, Mike Slavin, had planned the trip for a couple days. The night before, he said he had dug some worms from the back yard, and on Saturday morning, after packing, he sat around the house until noon, then loaded the Jeep and headed out. On his way to pick up Slavin, he stopped at a party store at Eight Mile and Farmington and grabbed some beer. After he picked up his friend, the two of them headed to Caseville. Bailey said they got there at around 2:30 p.m., dropped their bags off, then got on the twenty-four-foot Thompson boat, complete with a cabin, canopy, and downriggers. After two hours without any luck, he said the two of them came back in. They sat around listening to the stereo, drinking beer, and partying for the rest of the night.

On Monday night, September 2, he said he got back home at around 10:30, and his dad was still up. Bailey said his dad told him the police were looking for a Jeep that was similar to his, and he told his dad not to worry because he had been with Mike all weekend.

The investigators scribbled notes as Ron Bailey detailed his activities during the time of Shawn's abduction. They knew they would have to check his story, but it was late in the day. They would continue to follow up on it tomorrow. At that point, they had no idea that Bailey's story about being with Mike Slavin in Caseville for the entire weekend was about to collapse.

—

Jess Lopez, a special agent with the FBI, was assigned to the Brighton task force and was working the afternoon shift. Lopez was assigned with three other agents from four to midnight, and they were doing interviews with people who might not have been at home during the day when task force members tried to contact them. He was part of the FBI's Violent Crime/Major Offender Program (VCMOP), and he had heard of the Kenny Myers abduction and murder just a year before but hadn't worked on it.

Prior to joining the FBI, Lopez had no law enforcement experience. After high school, he served in Vietnam, then attended Southern Illinois University, where he received his bachelor's degree in accounting. He was working on his master's degree when his own brother was murdered in Chicago. Not wanting others to endure what his family had endured, he joined the FBI so he could go after killers himself.

Late in the evening, the task force phone rang. It was an officer from the Livonia Police Department, and he said he knew a guy in Livonia by the name of Ron Bailey. Bailey had a similar Jeep, and in the seventies, Livonia Police had Bailey on charges of kidnapping, sexual assault, and attempted murder.

The officer said, "You've got to look at this guy. We've had him in before on these sexual fixations with young boys and he sounds just like the guy you're describing."[48] He thought Bailey had been cleared in the Moore investigation but wasn't sure. "Hey, if you've got time, drive out here and we'll go to Bailey's house," he told Lopez.

Lopez wasn't waiting until the next day. He and his partner, Det/Sgt. Doug Smith, headed out to track down Ron Bailey. At 10:30 p.m., Alfred Bailey answered the door on Scone Street.

Ron wasn't home. He was at his friend Mike Slavin's house on Eight Mile near Farmington. Lopez asked Mr. Bailey if he knew where Ron was for the weekend, and he said that Ron had gotten back on Monday evening after a weekend fishing with Slavin in Caseville.

Lopez was the first task force member to learn about Bailey's criminal past, so he asked Alfred Bailey why he hadn't mentioned it earlier when officers had been at the house.

Mr. Bailey didn't want to bring it up because his son had been out of town for the weekend, and it might have caused problems. Ron's dad was sure he would be home by 11:30 or midnight, and Lopez told him they would be back.

Livonia Police had an address for Mike Slavin on Bridgeman Street in Farmington Hills. Two Livonia officers were assigned to watch the Bailey home in Livonia in case Ron arrived back home.

When Lopez and his partner arrived at the home on Bridgeman, they saw Bailey's 1985 Jeep Renegade parked in the driveway with several other cars, and they called for

48. Douglas, John and Olshaker, Mark, *Journey into Darkness,* Mindhunters, Inc., New York, NY, 1997

a uniformed officer as a backup unit. While they waited, someone got into the Jeep and pulled out of the driveway. When the Jeep was stopped by a uniformed officer, Ronald Bailey was behind the wheel.

FBI Special Agent Lopez told Bailey why they stopped him, and Bailey instantly became agitated and defensive, waving a business card from an MSP detective in front of Lopez and telling him that he had already been cleared. Lopez didn't care if he had been cleared or not. Bailey agreed to come back to the Livonia Police Department to clear up the alibi he had given to the task force members earlier that evening. They stopped back at Slavin's residence, and Slavin said he would come down to the Livonia Police Department and give a statement to the investigators.

Ron Bailey's Jeep was towed away and would be processed at the MSP crime lab in Northville.

—

He had heard them before and he knew it was a formality, so he feigned interest as the detective Mirandized him. He didn't have to say anything, and he knew if he did it would come back to haunt him, so the idea of having an attorney there was becoming more and more appealing. As he silently mediated his options, the voice of the FBI special agent dragged on like white noise. Of course, he understood his Miranda rights. He had been questioned umpteen times over the past several years by the police. He quietly acknowledged his understanding and signed the printed form labeled FSD-22. He knew that by signing it, he wasn't admitting to anything. It was simply a piece of paper indicating he understood what the detective had read to him. He knew if he changed any of the story he had told a few hours earlier to task force members, they would have him.

Now the FBI and MSP wanted to question him again, so he made the decision not to say anything else.

Ron Bailey sat in the small interview room with Lopez and Smith, and his animosity was obvious. Lopez smoked menthol cigarettes, and he offered one to Bailey. Bailey declined the offer; he didn't smoke menthols. When Lopez tried to question him, Bailey said he had already given a statement as he pointed to the paper one of them was holding. In silence, he hoped they wouldn't check his story, yet deep inside he knew they would.

The detectives were certain he was their guy. He owned a Jeep, and he had a history of molesting young boys. Jess Lopez told Bailey that his earlier story to investigators hadn't been verified, and that was the reason they wanted to question him again.

Bailey finally agreed. He recounted the story he had told earlier to MSP about going fishing in Caseville with his friend, Mike Slavin. He said the only other person who could verify his story was a store clerk he had seen in Caseville on either Saturday or Sunday. He mentioned the part of his alibi where his dad had mentioned that police were looking for a Jeep similar to his and how he told his dad not to worry because he had been with Mike all weekend.

Lopez asked him about his past. Bailey didn't want to talk about it. He described it as his black past. "It's a fucking nightmare that affects my entire life."[49]

At the same time Jess Lopez and his partner were interviewing Ronald Bailey, two officers from the Livonia Police Department were interviewing Mike Slavin. Slavin told them that he wasn't with Ron Bailey during the Labor Day weekend, and he wasn't in Caseville. Ron Bailey had asked the Slavins to lie for him. Bailey had come to the Slavin home on September 7. Michael was at work. Ron Bailey was in a slight panic as he spoke with Michael's

---

49. Lopez, Jess, Supplemental Report, 12-4872-85, September 10, 1985

wife. The state police had been at Bailey's home earlier and were questioning him about the abduction in Brighton because he had a similar Jeep. Bailey told Mrs. Slavin that he had spent the weekend of the abduction camping with an underage boy, and he didn't want to get in trouble for it. His dad, Alfred, had already told the police that his son was in Caseville on August 31, so Ron needed the Slavins to back up his story about being in Caseville.

Lopez and Smith sat back down with Bailey knowing they had the key piece of information they needed. They had caught Bailey in a lie. Smith asked Ronald Bailey if he wanted to recant his statement. Bailey refused. He said he had told the story just as it had happened, and he wasn't changing anything in it. He said he never lied. Bailey grabbed one of the menthol cigarettes lying on the table.

"Hey Ron, I thought you said you didn't lie," Lopez said.

"I don't."

"You said you don't smoke menthol cigarettes, and you just took one of mine."[50]

Bailey glared back at the agent.

Smith leaned forward in his chair, his hands clasped together, and in a soft tone told Bailey that he probably needed help, and they could provide it for him. Bailey refused and said his story wasn't going to change.

Lopez was certain that Bailey was on the verge of breaking down and confessing. He called Lt. Reed at task force headquarters in Brighton and told him about Bailey's lie. Reed contacted Det/Sgt. Beaupre at home. Beaupre headed for Livonia.

When Beaupre met with Lopez, Smith, and Det/Sgt. Krease, Lopez told him they had just finished interviewing Ronald Bailey. He had been read his Miranda warnings, and they were sure he was ready to make a statement.

---

50. Lopez, Jess, Interview with author, September 18, 2023

Beaupre sat down across the table from Ron Bailey. He seemed cooperative and said he understood his rights, adding that he was willing to make a statement, but when Beaupre zeroed on his whereabouts for August 31, Bailey said he refused to answer any more questions. He wanted an attorney.

The detective knew what that meant. The interview was stopped. Since Bailey refused to say anything else, the detectives took a different approach. They took Ron Bailey into custody and drove him back to the Michigan State Police Post in Brighton, where he would be introduced to a public defender.

Thirty minutes later, he was in Brighton at the task force headquarters. It was almost 3:00 a.m. They took all of Bailey's personal property from him before he met with the attorney.

Bailey was introduced to his public defender, and the two conferred quietly in a conference room for the next two hours. While the suspect and his attorney discussed their options, Detective Lieutenant Mike Smith from the Livingston County Sheriff's Office set up a stand-up lineup that met with the approval of the defense attorney.

It was late morning by the time the first witness was brought in. Ron Bailey stood shoulder to shoulder with five other men ranging in height from between five feet seven to five feet ten inches. Bailey was nervous and desperately hoped that whoever was looking at the group of men he was standing with wouldn't recognize him.

Ron Bailey was placed in position number two. The first witness to view the lineup was Sherry Huey. The public defender watched her. She stared intently as her eyes scanned every feature on every face. After much consideration, she resigned herself to the fact that she just couldn't be sure. "The only one that really looked like him was the last one;

the way his face was full," she said.[51] Two more witnesses were brought in separately. Much to the disappointment of the detectives, neither of them could identify Bailey.

While the lineup was going on, Roger Bittell made a phone call to the MSP Flatrock post and spoke with Det/Sgt. Don Hoder. Bittell told Hoder that Special Agent Jess Lopez would be doing some follow-up in that area, and he asked Hoder to help out Lopez.

The investigators knew they had no other option now. Ron Bailey would have to be released and driven back to Livonia. The focus of the investigation had narrowed to Bailey overnight. They were certain he was the man responsible for kidnapping Shawn Moore, but they needed more. Before they released him, they would have to return the property they had taken from him when he arrived at task force headquarters. This included his driver's license, two shoelaces, a Byron wristwatch, some matches, a Bic lighter, some loose change, and his wallet. The investigators noticed several papers in his wallet, including a towing receipt. Everything in the wallet was photographed before it was returned to Bailey. There were two things that weren't returned to Bailey: his Sergio Valente belt with the buckle, and his 1985 Jeep Renegade. They were held as potential evidence.

Bailey had been with the police all night. It was now past noon. He was hungry and didn't want to go home, so he asked the detectives to drop him off at the intersection of 5 Mile Road and Farmington Road because he wanted to get something to eat.

What Ron Bailey didn't know was that the FBI and Michigan State Police had already assigned a surveillance team to watch his every move.

---

51. Record of Lineup, Livingston County Sheriff's Department, September 11, 1985

Jess Lopez called Hoder at 8:00 a.m. and filled him in. Bailey was still being interviewed at task force headquarters in Brighton, and Lopez had a promising lead. A towing company receipt found in Bailey's wallet while he was being interviewed was from John's Garage in Flat Rock. The receipt was for Ron Bailey's Jeep. It had been stuck somewhere around Flat Rock. Maybe Shawn's body was in the Flat Rock area. The two men stopped at John's Garage, and one of the owners at the garage remembered the tow. It was a Jeep Renegade, and he had towed it on Sunday, September 8. The wrecker driver remembered the driver of the Jeep was a White male, and he recognized the passenger as Deb Chesney, one of the Chesney daughters. A quick computer check showed that Deb Chesney lived in the Flat Rock area.

The two investigators still had no idea where Shawn was when they sat down with the heavy-set woman with glasses at her home and read her Miranda rights to her. They told her they were there because Ron Bailey was a suspect in the kidnapping of Shawn Moore, and she had been with Bailey on September 8 when his Jeep was towed after getting stuck. Chesney seemed surprised. She hadn't heard anything about a kidnapping, and she was certain there was no way her boyfriend was capable of something like that.

Chesney told Lopez that she and Bailey had been out the previous weekend four-wheeling, and Ron's Jeep had gotten stuck so they called John's Garage for a tow. There was nothing more to it than that.

Deb Chesney told the two men that Ron Bailey was her boyfriend. The two had met when they were both at the Hawthorn Center. Ron never told her the truth about why he was there. He simply said that he didn't get along with his parents. After they were discharged from Hawthorn, they stayed friends until Ron moved to Florida. They reconnected when he returned to Michigan and had been intimate with each other at one point, though she did have a four-year-old boy by a different man.

She denied knowing Ron Bailey was gay but when she was told he was in custody while the interview was being done, she finally admitted that she did know about his sexual preference, but she didn't know anything about his criminal background.

Before the four-wheeling excursion when her boyfriend got his Jeep stuck, she had seen him on Wednesday, August 28, just before the holiday weekend. Bailey told her he was planning on going up north to the Chesney family cabin in Gladwin County with Mike Slavin. He had already gotten the keys to the cabin from her brother, Fred. Bailey said he was planning on cutting the grass at the cabin. He asked her to go along, but she would be working and couldn't get away.

The next time she saw Bailey was a week later, on September 4. She asked him if he had gotten the lawn cut at the cabin. The only thing he said was that something happened to the mower, and he could only cut half the grass.

Now Special Agent Jess Lopez knew where Bailey had gone on Labor Day Weekend. It was all starting to come together. Lopez needed to know where the cabin was. Deb Chesney thought her brother could explain the location better than she could, so she called Fred. After getting a description of how to get there, Deb described the cabin to Lopez as blue and white. There was no driveway, and there were neighbors on one side with the last name of Knope.

When Jess Lopez told Deb they would have to check the Chesney family cabin because there was a possibility that Ron had taken his victim there, she offered her consent to search the cabin and signed a form to allow them to do it. Lopez also received verbal consent over the phone from Fred Chesney.

Along with two more FBI special agents and three MSP detectives, Lopez headed for Gladwin County in northern Michigan on an FBI plane. The six were picked up by two troopers at the Gladwin County Airport. One of those troopers was a canine handler.

Deb Chesney had given them an excellent description of the family cabin on Ridge Road. The cabin was white with blue trim, a blue door, and a blue roof. There was a fifty-five-gallon oil drum on the east side of the cabin. They noted an outhouse about thirty feet behind the cabin. The canine trooper did a cursory search around the cabin and across the road but didn't detect anything. It was 3:30 p.m.

—

Tony Guerra was the program coordinator at the Hawthorn Center where Bailey had spent some of his time prior to being admitted to Northville Psychiatric Hospital.

Guerra had met Bailey at Hawthorn in June 1983. He knew Bailey was there because of some sexual situation involving another boy, but he thought the patient seemed like a nice boy. During Bailey's entire time at Hawthorn, Guerra would see him while making his rounds, and Bailey would always smile and say hi.

After Ron Bailey's discharge from the Hawthorn Center, Guerra didn't see him again until after he returned from Florida. It was a chance meeting at the Winner's Circle Bar in Northville when the two crossed paths again. After that, they would occasionally meet at other bars in Northville, like the Wagon Wheel and Riffle's.

It was 3:30 p.m. on September 11 when Tony Guerra's phone rang. It was Ron Bailey, and he was calling from Five Mile and Farmington. It had been at least a year since the two had seen one another, and Bailey told him he needed a ride to pick up his car and meet some friends in Northville.

Guerra already had plans to meet someone at Riffle's, and he invited Bailey to come along.

It was just after 5:00 when Guerra arrived at The Bench Bar and walked inside.

As the two men talked, Bailey, without any specifics being mentioned, said the police had questioned him about some sort of investigation going on at Northville. He also told Guerra that he was on vacation, and he might head out of town.

—

With their consent to search, the six officers at the Chesney address in Gladwin County entered the cabin. It was a brief search for anything obvious that might point to Shawn Moore having been there.

Several items were found and taken as potential evidence. The items included an empty Red White & Blue beer can, .22 caliber ammunition, a coffee cup, two Benson & Hedges cigarette butts, a Marlboro cigarette butt, a wooden match, and a plastic six pack holder. Outside the cabin, they found some spent .22 caliber shell casings, a .410 shotgun shell casing, and a target. Several photos were also taken inside and outside the cabin.

By 6:35 p.m., the team of investigators were back at the airport in Howell.

—

A new five-man surveillance crew had taken over. They relieved the previous team near the Bench Bar, where their suspect had been dropped off a few hours before. They watched and waited patiently.

Forty-five minutes later, one of the team members moved in closer to see if he could spot Bailey still inside.

He couldn't, but five minutes later their suspect walked out. He wore a beige shirt and faded blue jeans, and his blond hair was short, straight, and unkempt. His light-colored moustache was barely visible. He was with an older man who looked like he could be in his fifties. The two got into a 1974 cream-colored Ford Thunderbird and left the parking lot. The team followed the car to Riffle's. After the two left Riffle's, the T-bird drove to the Manufacturer's Bank in Northville, where their suspect used the 24-hour teller and withdrew $180.00. After the withdrawal, there was a quick stop at Spragg's Party Store in Northville. The driver came out with a bottle of brandy and a Pepsi. As the car left the parking lot, the surveillance team followed along Six Mile to a Comerica 24-hour teller at Newburgh Rd. Bailey got out and made a balance inquiry, then withdrew $220.00. After the transaction, the two men parked behind Black's Hardware in Northville and walked to the Starting Gate Lounge nearby.

As the surveillance team watched and waited, a black Ford taxi pulled up to the bar. Ron Bailey walked out, alone now, and got into the cab. The team tailed the cab as the driver headed toward Detroit Metro Airport.

—

Odell Powell was working for the Plymouth Cab Company when he was dispatched to pick up a passenger at the Starting Gate Lounge in Northville. He picked up a White male matching Ron Bailey's description and was told to head for Detroit Metro Airport in Romulus. The man in the back seat mentioned that his father was sick. Powell assumed he was going to visit his father because he noticed the man didn't have any luggage with him. If the man had been heading out on vacation, he normally would have had luggage. When they reached Metro Airport, it was 7:55 p.m., and the man directed the cab driver to stop at the American Airlines Terminal.

Ron Bailey got out and walked inside to the ticket counter. The two-man surveillance team followed at a distance. They had no idea where he might be heading.

Using an alias of Michael Ledesma, Bailey paid cash for his ticket, then headed to the bar for a few drinks before finding his gate. The surveillance team checked with the agent at the counter where he had purchased the ticket. At 5:51 p.m., he had bought a one-way ticket to Orlando. Flight 807 was scheduled to depart Detroit at 8:25 p.m. with a short layover in Atlanta. It was the last flight to Orlando for the evening. In Atlanta, their suspect would change to Flight 567 and depart for Orlando at 11:04 p.m. His arrival was scheduled at 12:05 a.m.

While Bailey sat in the bar, the surveillance team was busy making phone calls. A law enforcement colleague had some connections. Tom Monaghan, the founder of Domino's Pizza and owner of the Detroit Tigers, offered his private jet. Monaghan's pilot would ferry the surveillance team to Florida and tail the commercial jet carrying Ron Bailey.

Jess Lopez had been up all night interviewing the prime suspect in Shawn's kidnapping, sat through several hours of lineups in Brighton, been to Flat Rock to interview the suspect's girlfriend, then flown to Gladwin County to check out a location where Bailey might have taken Shawn. He was exhausted. He had just gotten home when his phone range. "Get out to Willow Run Airport. You're going to Florida," he heard his boss say. Before leaving, he met with his supervisor, who handed him $5,000 and said, "I don't care if you spend all of it. Just don't come back without him."[52]

Lopez had no idea he would be spending the next several days in Florida as he sped to Willow Run Airport,

52. Lopez, Jess, Interview with author, September 18, 2023

where Monaghan's jet was waiting for him and the rest of the surveillance team. He boarded wearing his suit and tie. None of the team had any clothing with them other than what they were wearing. They dined on Domino's Pizza during their flight.

A call was made to Orlando to ensure that FBI agents would be on standby at the airport when the flight arrived to pick up the surveillance.

As the two men watched their suspect at the airport in Detroit, he walked to a Comerica 24-hour teller and withdrew $10.00, then walked to a Federal Express 24-hour teller and withdrew another $40.00.

The surveillance team followed him to the gate and watched him board the plane.

A second surveillance team boarded Monaghan's private jet at Willow Run Airport. It was faster than the commercial airline, and Bailey's flight had a layover in Atlanta. The surveillance team arrived in Orlando before their suspect did.

9
Up North

The uneventful commercial flight to Orlando touched down in heavy rain on schedule after the Atlanta layover. It was just after midnight, and the man being tailed by the FBI and MSP paid cash at the Days Inn near Orlando International Airport under the false named he had used at the airline counter.

Jess Lopez and his team watched the suspect's room for the rest of the night.

The next morning, still under surveillance, Ron Bailey waited for a Greyhound bus. One team member, Al Moffatt, who had been one of the two law enforcement liaisons with the Moore family after Shawn's abduction and was now a part of the surveillance team, waited for the bus too, unbeknownst to Bailey. He boarded the bus with Bailey and planned on following him to wherever he was going while the surveillance team arranged a rental car.

Without any rain gear, they would be soaked if they ended up tailing Bailey outside of the car. With just the clothes on their backs, they bought a package of large garbage bags and cut holes in the bottom and sides of them, then put the bags over their heads. The trash bags would have to serve as temporary rain gear until they could buy some cheap clothing the next day.

The only rental car available was a Lincoln Continental. In one of the team members' briefcases was a small, blue rotating light they threw on the dash. Before they got the car, Bailey and Al Moffatt had already boarded the bus and were gone. They had lost the bus with their suspect and Det/ Sgt. Moffatt but found out their destination by checking with the bus company. At his first opportunity, Moffatt called the surveillance team to let them know where the bus had stopped. The surveillance team and their rented Lincoln Continental sped off to catch up with their team member and the killer.

After a two-hour-long ride, the bus rolled to a stop in Ocala. Bailey got off the bus, and so did Moffatt. Bailey still had no idea he was under surveillance, and Moffatt watched him from a distance until someone picked Bailey up. The surveillance team grabbed Moffatt and continued following the car that had picked up their suspect.

Near the town of Belleview, Florida, ten miles south of Ocala, the team quietly followed their suspect to the Big Ridge Acres Trailer Park near the Ocala National Forest. They were certain their suspect was staying at a friend's trailer in the small trailer park. It was small enough that at sunrise, any attempts at surveillance would be obvious in the trailer park. With their suspect now at a fixed location and likely to spend the night there, they changed their surveillance to a limited capacity.

—

It was almost noon on Thursday, September 12 when Don Brooks and Dave Ostrem drove to the Bailey home. With Ron Bailey fleeing to Florida, they were assigned to let the Bailey family know their son's name would likely be released in a press conference about the abduction of Shawn Moore.

When the two officers spoke with Alfred Bailey, he offered the names of some of his son's friends, including George Soper, whose mother owned the trailer in Florida where Ron had lived before returning to Michigan. After Brooks and Ostrem left, they met with Detectives Deering and Chambers from the task force. Deering had interviewed Ron Bailey's cousins in Fowlerville, and during those interviews, the relatives had mentioned seeing a .22 caliber rifle and a 12-gauge shotgun in Bailey's Jeep on the day Shawn was kidnapped.

Late in the afternoon, Brooks called Alfred Bailey and asked if his son had any guns. The senior Bailey said his son had both a shotgun and a rifle, and they were kept in gun cases in the basement where Ron slept. He added that there was a box of ammunition for the guns kept there too. Mr. Bailey had recently checked both guns to make sure they were unloaded.

Brooks wanted those guns as possible evidence in Shawn's abduction. After he spoke with Alfred Bailey, he had a surveillance set up on the Bailey home in Livonia to ensure no one left the house with either of the guns. While the home was being watched, Brooks met with Livingston County Assistant Prosecutor Robert Detweiler and drew up a search warrant for the guns that were in the Bailey home. By 8:30 p.m., Livonia Judge Robert Brzezinski signed the warrant, and at 9:00 p.m., Brooks, Ostrem, Deering, and Chambers were back at the Bailey home.

Mr. Bailey took the detectives to the basement and pointed out the two cased guns that were near the stairwell leaning up against some hanging clothes. The box with the ammunition was under a table in the northwest corner of the room. The guns were taken to the crime lab in East Lansing the following morning.

—

As the surveillance team in Florida watched the trailer park from a distance, members of the task force, along with other law enforcement officers from around mid-Michigan and northern Michigan, were preparing for a search in Gladwin County the next day.

It was Thursday, September 12. Shawn Moore had been missing for thirteen days. Investigators from the task force in Brighton planned to have personnel from the crime lab search the cabin for trace evidence. Normally, the MSP crime lab in Bridgeport would have been the lab assigned because the cabin was in Gladwin County, but a request was made to have the lab in East Lansing process the cabin. The East Lansing lab had done most of the analysis on other items that had already been submitted in the case. By 1:00 p.m., three scientists from the East Lansing lab had arrived in Gladwin. Roger Bolhouse from the micro-chemistry unit, Ed Busch from the latent print unit, and Robert Cilwa from the firearms and tools unit were all set to start processing inside the cabin. They hadn't been in the cabin very long when task force headquarters in Brighton asked the crime lab to vacate the cabin and stand by. The decision had been made to get a search warrant rather than relying on the Chesney family's permission for the search. The new plan was to have the search warrant ready to go on Friday, September 13, and the lab personnel could search the cabin then. Everyone was set to meet at 7:00 the following morning.

At task force headquarters in Brighton, MSP Inspector Sam Hutchins attended a briefing about the plan to search for Shawn's body the next day. Hutchins, a veteran investigator, but now in an administrative role with the state police, wasn't supposed to get involved in the day-to-day operations. With his knowledge as a veteran investigator, it was hard to keep him away.

Roger Bittell was busy making assignments regarding who would head to Gladwin the following morning. He paused, thinking that the troopers he was sending up north wouldn't have a clue where they were going. He saw Hutchins standing in the back of the room, and he knew Hutchins had served at the West Branch post, just thirty minutes north of Gladwin. Hutchins was very familiar with Michigan's northern country.

"Sam, your first post was West Branch, wasn't it?" he asked.

"Yeah."

"You're familiar with the Gladwin area," Bittell continued.

"Very familiar with it." Hutchins knew what was coming next, and Bittell knew he didn't have to ask but did anyway.

"Would you go up to Gladwin and run the search for the body?"

"Yeah, I'll be glad to," Hutchins replied.[53]

The next morning at 7:00 in Gladwin County, Det/Sgt. Heikkila and Det/Sgt. Janiszewski met with Livingston County's Chief Assistant Prosecutor David Morse, who had joined law enforcement in the search for Shawn, drew up an affidavit for a search warrant for the cabin. Gladwin County Prosecuting Attorney Douglas Jacobson signed it, and Judge Jean Behnke, 80th District Court Magistrate, authorized the warrant by signing it too.

Thirty troopers and FBI agents, along with Morse, were briefed by Inspector Hutchins at the MSP Gladwin post on the search for Shawn Moore. They had several maps of the area in hand, each with a grid drawn on it. There would be several teams of two, and each team was assigned a grid to search. When the search for Shawn finally got underway, Morse stayed behind in case an additional search warrant was needed and, if that were the case, he would need a phone. In rural Gladwin County, the phone company tapped into a phone line along the side of Ridge Road, ran a new

---

53. Bittell, Roger, Interview with author, September 28, 2023

phone line from there to a small table alongside the road, and attached it to a phone. Morse sat there as the crews dispersed to begin the search while an FBI plane with infrared heat-seeking technology circled overhead.

It became clear that information about the case had leaked to the media. Without naming Ron Bailey, the media was reporting that a man had been questioned and released in the investigation, and his vehicle fit the description of the Jeep used in the kidnapping. The media also mentioned that the man's Jeep was being processed by the state police. The following day, newspapers and media across the state were reporting that the man questioned in connection to Shawn's disappearance had fled the state. It was clear the media knew Bailey's identity even though MSP refused to give it. News stories were already mentioning Bailey's criminal past both in Michigan and in Florida.

—

Livingston County's Chief Assistant Prosecuting Attorney David Morse was a graduate of Central Michigan University. He had his teacher certification in secondary education and initially began teaching fourth, fifth, and sixth grades for a small school district near Cadillac. He taught for several years both in Michigan and Atlanta, Georgia. He wanted to be a better teacher than he felt he was, and gratification in that field was pretty much delayed. He wanted something more immediate.

While living in Atlanta, he worked briefly as a paralegal for a highly respected law firm before going to work for a Fortune 500 company in industrial relations for their corporate office. He knew if he wanted to advance, he would have to move around, but he didn't want to do that.

Morse had always wanted to go to law school, and he had a very good friend at the University of Michigan. At thirty years old, he decided to go, and he attended Thomas M. Cooley Law School.

After graduating, he began working as an assistant prosecutor for Livingston County and after a year and a half, he had a chance to work for the Calhoun County Prosecutor's Office. He had been there for a year and a half when his former boss, Frank Del Vero, called him to let him know his chief assistant prosecutor was leaving. He wondered if Morse wanted the position.

—

The search for Shawn Moore wouldn't be easy. The entire area had a few cabins here and there. The rest was a vast expanse covered in a heavy forest and swampland with large ferns growing in the sand along the roadside and extending into the woods along both sides of the road. There were troopers from several different posts around the state who were there to help find Shawn. Two of those were Det/Sgt. Paul Bowers and Trooper Richard Margosian, both from the Pontiac post. Their search area was three and a half miles east of the cabin in Section 32 of the township. As the pair got out of their car, they noticed tire tracks leading back off the road through some sand. Overhead, Margosian noticed large birds circling. He asked Bowers what kind they were. Bowers told him they were buzzards, and the two started walking back into the underbrush.

The search for Shawn had barely begun when, at 10:45 a.m., there was a radio transmission. Shawn Moore's body had been found.

The entire area was quickly sealed off. Overhead, news helicopters circled, trying to get their shot for the 6:00 news. A quick phone call was made by the FBI to the FAA, and the airspace over the crime scene was closed.

David Morse and Frank Del Vero already knew they had enough to charge Bailey in the kidnapping, but they would have to wait for a positive identification before murder charges could be filed. His office was already typing the warrant for the kidnapping while Lt. Beaupre was on his way to tell Bruce and Sharon Moore that a body had been found in Gladwin County.

Beaupre, Roger Bittell, Dave Ostrem, two FBI agents, and a family priest all met at the Moore home. The group sat in the Moores' living room. Mr. and Mrs. Moore, along with Scott, had already known there was a likelihood that Shawn's body might be found in Gladwin County. Even without a positive identification, they already knew.

"We found a body. We're sure it's Shawn."[54]

Hearing the worst news they could ever imagine, Shawn's dad was the most emotional, though there were no hysterics. That, alone, exemplified the way the Moore family had handled everything since Shawn's disappearance.

—

By 11:00 a.m., the media in Brighton were told there would be a 1:00 p.m. news conference. The intention was to announce the discovery of a body in Gladwin County and the arrest of Ron Bailey.

An assistant prosecutor in Livingston County was typing the arrest warrant for Bailey, and Lt. Beaupre would be signing it. A call was made at 11:20 to Judge David Gee. The prosecutor's office would have a kidnapping warrant for him to sign before noon, and he should wait at his office to sign it before leaving for lunch. Gee knew how that went. If he waited for the prosecutor's office every day, he would never get his lunch in. If they didn't have it to him before noon, he figured it wasn't his problem. At noon, he walked

---

54. Ostrem, David, Interview with author, December 2, 2022

down to the prosecutor's office and asked if the warrant was ready. By that time, there weren't any attorneys in the office, so he told them where he would be having lunch.

Beaupre was delayed. He had been with the Moore family delivering the devastating news. He didn't get to Judge Gee's office in Howell until 12:15 p.m. Gee had already left and was having lunch with the Livingston County Public Defender. He was at the Elks Club.

At the same time Beaupre was at the prosecutor's office, Gee and the public defender walked into the Elks and sat down with Dan Grantham and Nicole Robertson, two local reporters. Lt. Beaupre and Sheriff Dennis DeBurton walked into the club and asked the judge if he would come back to his office to sign the warrant. He told the lieutenant that he had been waiting for the warrant but it wasn't ready, so he left for lunch.

Sheriff DeBurton emphasized the importance of the warrant, telling Gee it involved the kidnapping and murder of a thirteen-year-old boy. Gee refused, and the discussion became more heated. As the two continued their back-and-forth, each accused the other of not cooperating. The judge finally gave in, asking the sheriff if the warrant was done and if Beaupre had it. It was done, but the sheriff didn't know if Beaupre had it with him. Gee told him to have Beaupre bring it to the club and he would sign it there.

At 12:40, another assistant prosecutor walked into the Elks Club with the warrant in hand. Judge Gee, DeBurton, and Beaupre moved to another table, and after a few questions of Beaupre, Judge Gee signed the warrant charging Ron Bailey with the kidnapping of Shawn Moore.

—

George Soper's trailer in Belleview, Florida had been under limited surveillance since the previous night because it was too obvious to maintain constant watch. Roger Bittell was working in the command post with the other surveillance team members as the FBI kept an eye on the trailer. With word there was a valid warrant for Ron Bailey in the kidnapping of Shawn Moore, law enforcement moved in.

The inside of the trailer was nauseating. The stench from dog feces was overpowering, along with open bags of dog food for the animals to eat from. The trailer was filthy, and Ron Bailey was nowhere to be found.

—

There were thirty-five or so reporters and other media people outside task force headquarters anticipating a press conference in the kidnapping. They were told again and again that it would be delayed for fifteen or twenty minutes, and they were getting anxious. What they didn't know was that investigators were waiting for word from Florida that Ron Bailey was in custody.

Since Shawn's kidnapping on August 31, the relationship between law enforcement and the media had changed. In the beginning, the constant news coverage generated hundreds of tips. Some of those tips revealed crucial details in the investigation but as police narrowed their search to Ron Bailey, the media focused exclusively on him. Various media outlets and reporters had been barred from task force headquarters, and some of the investigators were heard referring to the news media as vultures waiting for the news.

When the press conference finally began at 3:00 p.m., eight key task force members stood before the media to announce that a body had been found in Gladwin County, and warrants were being prepared for Ronald Bailey's arrest. No positive identification had been made yet, but law enforcement justified the kidnapping warrant for Bailey based on his resemblance to a composite sketch given by a witness to the kidnapping. The media was told he owned a Jeep Renegade that he had recently purchased, and it was the same as the vehicle described in the abduction. Law enforcement officials released other information that was relevant, including that Bailey had been in Livingston County just an hour or so before the kidnapping, and witnesses in Gladwin County identified Bailey as being in the area of the cabin approximately three hours after Shawn's disappearance. With a body being found matching Shawn's description, they felt they had enough to charge him with the kidnapping. "Because of the similarities in age, sex, and body size, we felt we had Shawn Moore," Frank Del Vero said.[55] Once a positive identification was made, he would add an additional charge of murder.

Channel 7 interrupted their regular programming and were carrying the news conference live. Their lead reporter on the Moore kidnapping, Chris Hansen, already suspected that Ron Bailey had fled the state, but there was no official word from law enforcement yet. Representatives from Green Oak Township, Livingston County Sheriff's Department, Michigan State Police, the FBI, and the Livingston County Prosecutor's Office were all there. For many, it was an unforgettable live-TV moment when Hansen, referring to murder suspect Ron Bailey, asked, "Is it true that he escaped and is on the run now partly because the judge wouldn't come back from lunch to sign the warrant?" Frank Del Vero blamed part of the delay in starting the news conference on Judge Gee leaving for lunch and refusing to wait for detectives to arrive with the warrant for Bailey. He conceded that it was simply a matter of unfortunate circumstances. It infuriated many in the community.

Hansen finished his live shot on the 6:00 news. Both his sound man and camera man were friends of his. They had

---

55. AP, "Body Found, May be Abducted Boy," *Battle Creek Enquirer*, September 14, 1985

first met when he was doing his internship with Channel 7 while attending MSU. Hansen looked at them, and one of them said, "I know it's your birthday, but I guess we're going to Florida."[56] They were on a plane later that night.

—

Two weeks in the state forest had taken its toll on Shawn's body. The thirteen-year-old was nude and in an advanced state of decomposition. He was lying on his back with his hands above his head, his legs bent and pulled up toward his torso. Shawn's chest cavity was torn open, and two ribs had been broken off by wildlife chewing on the body. Shawn's entire face had been chewed off down to his skull, while his lower jawbone had been dragged off and was lying ten feet away.

—

The Gladwin County Medical Examiner was called to the scene to view Shawn's body as all of the search teams returned to the command post. As they filtered back, David Morse overheard some discussion that MSP would likely request a murder warrant for Ron Bailey in Gladwin County because it was clear the murder had occurred there. Morse grabbed the phone and called Frank Del Vero in Howell. Del Vero wasted no time in calling Michigan Attorney General Frank Kelley. Within a few hours, Kelley called back and said he was designating Livingston County as the venue for the case to be tried.

David Morse had contacted the Gladwin County prosecutor after the discovery of Shawn's body. There was no doubt the murder had happened in Gladwin County, but

56. Hansen, Chris, Interview with author, September 16, 2023

there was no sense in trying two different crimes in two different jurisdictions. It was clear that Gladwin's prosecutor differed in his opinion but ultimately, they agreed to charge Ronald Bailey in Livingston County for the murder of Shawn Moore.

Since the prosecution of Bailey would be in Livingston County, Det/Sgt. Bob Kowalski accompanied Shawn's body to the morgue at Sparrow Hospital in Lansing. There, forensic pathologist Larry Simson would conduct an autopsy the following morning.

Two of the crime lab scientists who were set to execute the search warrant at the cabin were redirected to the location where Shawn's body had been found. They would process that scene first, then do the cabin.

At 4:00 p.m., they were back at the cabin and ready to conduct the search. Meticulously, they went through the cabin spreading fingerprint powder on anything that had a smooth surface. By 6:00, they were done. All of the evidence they gathered from inside the cabin was taken back to the crime lab in East Lansing.

—

"Up north" is a term used loosely to describe the northern half of Michigan. No one agrees on where it begins. Some argue that it begins when a vacationer passes Clare County, while others argue that it begins at the 45th parallel that runs from the South Manitou Island Lighthouse on Lake Michigan across and through Gaylord, then on to Alpena on the coast of Lake Huron. Some would even say it begins when you cross the Mackinac Bridge and enter Michigan's Upper Peninsula. Everyone's definition is different. To Ron Bailey, Gladwin County was up north.

Gladwin County lies an hour northwest of Saginaw. It encompasses 516 square miles, and in 1985, the population was just over 20,000 people. With fifteen townships, there are just two cities in the county: the city of Gladwin and the city of Beaverton. It is the second smallest county in the state and is largely made up of state forest land.

While some locals called it Ridge Road, to most it was known as Mosquito Alley Truck Trail. Along the trail, small summer cabins sat near the Chesney cabin, and investigators were doing interviews to see if any of the neighbors had seen anything that could help in the investigation.

Police had already received a tip from a woodcutter in the area. George Bartels lived on Three Rivers Road and worked closely with another woodcutter. They had both been over to a friend's house on the night of September 11. The three men talked about the police being seen at the Chesney cabin and the flier that had been delivered by police to the cabins in the area showing a composite sketch and the Jeep police were looking for. When *The Bay City Times* ran the story of Shawn Moore's kidnapping, Bartel's friend, Chris Searfoss, said, "For God's sake, that Jeep was right back there!"

Eighty-five-year-old Chris Searfoss was retired and living with his wife on Three Rivers Road just to the north of Ridge Road. On Sunday, September 1, at about 6:50 p.m., he was riding with his son-in-law when they passed the Chesney cabin and Searfoss saw a light-colored Jeep parked next to it. He knew the cabin was used mostly during deer hunting season in November, so he made a casual comment that someone was there, but his son-in-law didn't pay any attention to it because he was driving. Searfoss could see the vehicle was covered with mud, almost as if it had been just pulled from a mud hole. He was sure of the time because his wife was going to church that night, and she left ten minutes before the service to get there on time. After she had left, he went for a ride with his son-in-law, Alvin Onweller, and they passed the cabin.

Michael Garner and his wife, Dawn, left their Carlton home at around 2:00 p.m. on August 31, headed to Gladwin for a short Labor Day weekend getaway. They were going to stay with Dawn's grandmother, Lillian Knope. Mrs. Knope, who lived in a retirement community in Taylor, owned a cabin on Ridge Road. Dawn Garner's parents, Lonny and Judy Allen, had recently purchased the cabin next to Mrs. Knope's cabin, and they were on their way to Gladwin too. On the other side of the Allens' was a cabin owned by Fred Chesney. On their way to Gladwin, the Garners stopped at the Exit Stop Restaurant in Birch Run before continuing on and finally arriving at around 5:30 or 6:00 p.m. The Allens arrived around 11:00.

The Garners were going to spend Sunday morning fishing, and in the afternoon the entire family was going to clean out the recently purchased Allen cabin.

Mrs. Knope wasn't home, but the Garners knew she kept a key in the root cellar. Michael Garner's attempt to retrieve the key to the Knope cabin was unsuccessful when he was chased from the cellar by a swarm of wasps. He and his wife, thinking better of their choice to retrieve the key, decided to wait for Mrs. Knope, hoping she wouldn't be too long. While the Garners sat in their car, they chatted about getting bait from a marina the next day and going fishing. After fifteen minutes or so, they noticed a silver Jeep Renegade driving down Ridge Road. The Jeep stopped just beyond the common area between the Chesney cabin and the Allen cabin. Garner watched as the Jeep backed up about ten feet, and since there was no drive, drove across what could only be described as the front yard between the two structures. The driver steered toward the Chesney cabin, and Garner casually noticed two figures in the Jeep.

Pine trees and brush blocked his view of the Jeep as it came to a stop, and he never gave it another thought.

On Sunday morning, as the Garners drove by the Chesney cabin, they noticed the Jeep was facing Ridge Road and parked at an angle within a few feet of the southeast corner of the cabin. The Jeep blocked the view of the front door.

When they got back around noon, they had breakfast at Lillian Knope's, then everyone walked next door to the Allens' cabin to begin cleaning it out. While they were cleaning, there was a horrible odor, and when they removed a patch from the ceiling, they discovered bats inside. Chaos ensued as the women couldn't help but scream and laugh as they ducked and ran from inside the cabin.

Garner and his wife's two cousins, who were also there helping to clean out the Allen cabin, had taken a couple shots at the bats with a BB gun when they heard someone say, "You can shoot better than that." They turned to see a man walking toward them from Fred Chesney's cabin with a beer in his hand.

Lillian Knope saw the good-looking young man with blond hair and asked, "Are you Freddy?"

"No," he said.

"Well, I can see you aren't because you're too small for Freddy."

He told her his name was Ron, Freddy's sister's husband.[57] "We have bats too," he said. As Ron Bailey introduced himself to everyone, Lonny took him in the cabin for a minute to show him where the bats had come from. It was a casual conversation between Bailey and the small group, and he used the word "we" a second time when he mentioned wanting to come north for some pheasant hunting. He said he was up there with a friend.

---

57. People v. Ronald Bailey, 85-4447-FC and 85-4448-FC, Livingston County, 8, 115, September 16, 1986

Bailey asked the small group of family members if they wanted him to bring over his .22 caliber rifle to help them get rid of the bats. They politely declined, fearing holes might be shot in their roof.[58]

While Ron was talking with Judy's husband, she and her daughter were chatting nearby when Dawn saw someone come out of the Chesney cabin. "Oh, look. There's someone over there with that guy. He just came out of the cabin," she said.

Right after Dawn said that, Ron left and walked back to the Chesney cabin. Within a few minutes, he came back out with a gun and fired it toward the road without saying a word. It seemed strange to the small group of family members.

Judy said, "I guess he wanted us to know he had a gun."[59]

On Monday afternoon, Mrs. Knope was in her cabin and she could see the Jeep parked at the Chesney cabin. She noticed Ron Bailey packing the Jeep. He carried out a small roll of carpet and put it inside. She couldn't see much more than that. The Jeep was still parked as close to the cabin as it could be. She watched him on and off until she heard the door slam and saw the Jeep drive across the front lawn. Instead of turning toward Three Rivers Road, Bailey drove east on Ridge Road toward the forest. A few minutes later, Mrs. Knope's daughter got to the cabin and noticed the Jeep was gone. She said something to her mother about it.

"Yeah, he just drove out," Lillian said. It was just ten minutes after seeing him leave when Mrs. Knope and her daughter saw him again, this time driving west past the cabin toward Three Rivers Road. It was the last time they saw him.

---

58. Lam, Tina and Cohen, Janet, "Bailey Seen Driving Near Body Site," *Ann Arbor News*, September 18, 1985

59. People v. Ronald Bailey, 85-4447-FC and 85-4448-FC, Livingston County, 8, 134, September 16, 1986

10
On the Run

At twenty-four years old, Ray Cassar, thin and soft-spoken, had only been practicing law for one year, and just a very small part of his new career was in criminal law. From a very early age, he knew he wanted to be an attorney. More than that, he wanted to be a defense attorney.

As a boy of eleven, one of Ray's hobbies was launching model rockets. Ironically, that is what convinced him to become an attorney. Cassar and a small group of friends had their complex tube-like device loaded with combustibles and ready to launch from the front yard of his home in Garden City in the early seventies. They were convinced that after the launch, it would likely travel a huge distance, maybe as far as Dearborn, and they were excited. In fact, they were so enthusiastic that they wrote their names on it in the hope that someone might find it and let them know how far it had traveled. Sadly, their hopes and dreams were quickly shattered when the projectile shot across the street and blew up with a loud explosion under the neighbor's awning. The neighbor was furious and threatened to call the FBI on them. After all, it was a federal offense to blow things up. They knew they were in trouble.

With his friends in a state of uneasiness, Ray calmly looked at them and said, "I can handle this."[60]

He went to his neighbor's door, and he quietly explained that he and his friends had no intention of blowing up the rocket or doing any damage to the neighbor's home. They were just kids, they realized that what they did was wrong, and they didn't have any intention of hurting anyone. Cassar's neighbor decided not to call the police. It was that one incident that convinced Ray Cassar he wanted to be a defense attorney. Looking back at that day years later, the future attorney considered it his first win.

Coming from a Catholic family, Ray Cassar's dad wanted him to become a priest. There was no way he was going to become a cleric. He loved women too much to go into the priesthood. He graduated in 1981 from the University of Michigan and in 1984, he graduated from the University of Detroit Law School. Cassar had interned for Charles Murphy, a defense attorney in Farmington Hills, while he was in law school, and when he passed the Bar, Murphy offered him office space. Cassar figured he would at least have an office to work from.

In the beginning, as a young, soft-spoken defense attorney, Ray Cassar didn't have a lot of clients. He was on the assigned-counsel list, and it was a sort-of training ground for new attorneys. He also worked as an adjunct professor at Oakland Community College, teaching business law one night each week. He had been offered a job early on in a prosecutor's office, but he would be assigned in the paternity unit. Cassar wanted no part of that, so he turned down the offer. Now, as a defense attorney, he figured that if it didn't work out, he could always teach. He loved his students and they loved him.

There was a young woman in his business law class, and she came to Cassar after class one night and explained

---

60. Cassar, Raymond, Interview with author, February 27, 2024

that her brother was in big trouble. She didn't know if her professor had heard about the Shawn Moore case. The young defense attorney and part-time professor had heard about it but hadn't made the connection between Ron Bailey and her. She was Ron Bailey's sister. Ray Cassar agreed to meet with her father.

After Ray Cassar met with Alfred Bailey, he made the decision to defend Ron but felt he needed some credibility since he had only been practicing law for one year. His experience in criminal law was limited. He had never represented anyone in a homicide case or an extradition, so he brought his colleague, Chuck Murphy, on board because Murphy had been practicing law for the previous ten years. Murphy was a large, pretentious lawyer who lived part-time in Florida, and he loved to talk about some of the big drug cases he had been involved in. In contrast to Cassar's scholarly image, Chuck Murphy was boisterous and to some, he seemed argumentative.

After agreeing to take the case, Ray Cassar began to have cold feet. Every time he turned on the television there was something about Ron Bailey, who was now on the run in Florida. He started to second guess himself and his ability as a very young attorney. He worried that if he was defending someone like Ron Bailey, then he must be a bad guy himself, and he became concerned about the safety of his mom and dad.

On Saturday morning, while the media was covering the manhunt for Bailey in Florida, he stopped over at his parents' home. By taking Ron Bailey's case, Ray was worried about what other people might think of him and what someone might do to his parents because everybody hated Ron Bailey. Ron Bailey was the number one wanted guy. After Ray Cassar talked with his dad, he was relieved to hear him say, "Raymond, you went to law school to learn how to represent people's rights, not to judge them." His dad's words of encouragement were a huge relief, and Ray considered those words as a gift from his own father. He knew he didn't have to worry about representing Ron Bailey.

"You're right, Dad. My job is to represent their rights and not to judge them."

Ray was still concerned that someone might throw a rock through his parents' window or do something else simply because of who he was representing, and he knew people in the Catholic Church would probably say things to his dad about Ray defending Bailey.

"Don't worry about us," his dad said, trying to calm the worry in his son. "We're fine. No one's going to harm us." As the two talked, the young attorney realized what a great inspiration his dad truly was.[61]

—

Ronald Bailey was on the run—or was he? With limited surveillance, the Marion County Sheriff's Office and the FBI both said they couldn't keep an eye on the trailer the whole time. Their presence was too obvious. They had gotten word there was now a valid Michigan warrant for kidnapping and a second federal fugitive warrant for unlawful flight to avoid prosecution. After moving in for the arrest and discovering Bailey wasn't in the trailer, they began to search the park and the adjacent woods. At 4:00 p.m., a man identifying himself as Ron Bailey called the police and said he was at a bar in Oklawaha, about ten miles southeast of Belleview. Police converged on the bar but Bailey wasn't there. They searched all the bars in the area, but still no Bailey. It seemed he was taunting them.

At 8:00 p.m., after spending a considerable amount of time in the Oklawaha area searching for their suspect, two FBI agents returned to the trailer to continue their surveillance when they spotted Bailey. All of their earlier

61. Cassar, Raymond, Interview with author, February 27, 2024

focus had switched to Oklawaha, and no one realized the suspect had returned to the trailer. At some point, as agents were preparing to move in and make an arrest, their suspect quietly slipped out a back door a second time, leaving behind a khaki shirt he had been wearing. Frustration and anger set it. Inside the now empty trailer they found a police scanner.

—

From Ocala, Belleview, Florida is about ten miles southeast and settled around what is known as Lake Lillian. When the city was founded in 1884, Lake Lillian was known as Nine Mile Pond because it was located roughly nine miles from Ocala.

In late August and early September 1985, heavy rains and high winds battered the central part of Florida when Hurricane Elena caused downed trees and power lines across much of the region. After the category three storm, locals in the normally quiet small town were eager to put it behind them and looked forward to the grand opening of a Kmart store in October.

On the northwest fringes of Belleview, the Big Ridge Acres Trailer Park was home to George Soper and his returning roommate, Ronald Bailey. The people who lived there were used to a quiet and serene setting against a backdrop of ten square miles of dense forest. It seemed the biggest thing residents had to worry about in the quiet town of Belleview was whether or not another hurricane might move inland during the storm season.

Highway 301, running between Belleview and Ocala, was a sort-of eastern border to the large, forested area west of the highway. At the intersection of 95th Street, the Belleview-Santos Elementary School sat with the Britt's Grocery Store nearby.

When FBI agents realized Bailey had eluded them a second time, police swarmed the entire area. Overnight, thirty deputies were set every 500 feet or so in order to contain the area and prevent Bailey's escape. It wasn't easy. The forest was covered with dense underbrush, mosquitoes, snakes, lime rock pits, pasture, and the occasional modest home.

A helicopter with search lights buzzed overhead. Deputies on the perimeter held their positions as others searched through the trailer park and into the woods while heavy rain set in.

At 3:00 a.m., a mobile command post pulled into the Belleview-Santos Elementary School parking lot. After a quick clean up from the recent heavy rains and winds caused from Hurricane Elena, it was brought to the scene of the manhunt with communications gear and other resources that were needed.

There were ten roadblocks set up around the area where police felt Bailey was hunkered down, and every car moving in and out of the Big Ridge Acres Trailer Park was checked.

Reporters covering the story were staged at the small convenience store near the elementary school. They were exhausted, and during the night, they tried to squeeze in short rounds of sleep inside their cars.

By daybreak, the number of law enforcement personnel had swelled to over 200.

The sound of helicopter blades whirling overhead and planes circling, along with police radios blaring and law enforcement officers in both uniform and plain clothes, seemed to be everywhere. Police on horses were searching the area along with bloodhounds from a Florida prison. Officers on three-wheeled ATVs were moving through the woods in an effort to root out Bailey.

A news helicopter, enlisted by law enforcement, was also circling the area, trying to spot him.

Bob Vinson lived in the Big Ridge Acres Trailer Park near where his mother lived. It wasn't a typical quiet Saturday morning. Police were everywhere, looking for the murder suspect from Michigan. Vinson got distracted as he was getting something out of his shed, and he unwittingly locked his keys inside. His mom lived nearby and had an extra key, so he started walking across the field to her home. As he drew close, he noticed the dog was acting strange near his mom's white aluminum shed. When he opened the door, he was surprised to find the man police had been looking for all night. Ron Bailey was curled up on a pallet of blankets that were setting on top of a freezer, and he looked rather comfortable. Ironically, the shed was only seventy-five feet from the trailer where Bailey had fled.

Vinson slammed the door. He tried to snap the lock shut on the shed but the lock was broken. He ran for a phone to call the sheriff's office. He knew the man in the shed was the murder suspect the police were looking for. By the time Vinson got back to the shed, he found the door open and Bailey gone.

Ron Bailey had eluded capture for a third time.

—

Chris Hansen and his news crew had arrived in Florida and were covering the story along with several other media outlets. Satellite technology was relatively new to the media, and there was only one satellite station in Marion County. Hansen jokingly referred to it as "Satellites-R-Us."[62] Channel 7 in Detroit was considered a powerful and wealthy ABC station, and they bought twelve hours of

---

62. Hansen, Chris, Interview with author, September 16, 2023

satellite time in Marion County to cover the story. Other news outlets couldn't get their stories out about the hunt for Bailey. Hansen was in it for the long haul, and he covered the story the entire day.

—

Residents in and around central Florida, and especially in the Belleview area, had been watching the continuous news coverage of the hunt for the killer. They had seen the photos of Shawn Moore that were now being broadcast across their state. The owner of Britt's Grocery, just a few hundred feet from the trailer from which Bailey had fled, carried a chrome-plated pistol in his back pocket. Bailey had been in his store before, and the owner thought he was odd. He wasn't taking any chances.

Many were glued to the news as the story about the manhunt for a child killer from Michigan spread across the country with live coverage. Others were disgusted by the coverage. In Michigan, a real estate broker said, "I was just about disgusted that the media came on and said, 'We're bringing it to you first.' I thought, 'Could you please be a little more tasteful—the poor child is dead.'"[63]

There was sympathy across Marion County and central Florida, and it was as if they considered Shawn Moore one of the kids next door. At Britt's Grocery, one of the clerks said, "They showed his picture last night on TV. Such a pretty little boy." Another area woman said, "Give our sympathy to the family. We all feel terrible about what happened."[64]

Anger among law enforcement turned to determination as the now more than 250 local, state, and federal officers

---

63. Robertson, Nicole, "Death Brings Sadness, Fear, Anger," *Brighton Argus*, September 19, 1985
64. Smith, Amy, "In Florida, Tension and Sympathy," *Ann Arbor News*, September 16, 1985

on foot, in helicopters, in cars, on ATVs, and on horseback quickly organized and sealed off the ten-square-mile area of forest. The perimeter of the search area was tightened as over fifty police cruisers parked within eyesight of each other, while officers scanned the horizon in search of Bailey. Planes and helicopters continued to circle the search area looking for the suspect. The search area was bounded by US-301 to the east, SE 25th Avenue to the west, Redding Lane to the south, and County Road 328 to the north.

Neighbors in the area were frightened, and all eyes were on the media coverage while everyone waited for Ronald Bailey to make a mistake. "I don't like it. It's too close. Too close to home," said one resident in the trailer park where Bailey had been staying.[65]

A spokeswoman for the Marion County Sheriff's Office told reporters, "We received a call that he was hiding in a utility shed. By the time we arrived, he had escaped to the woods. But the description we received fit him perfectly."

The FBI also addressed the media, saying, "The suspect, Bailey, is believed to be in the wooded area, and there's a massive manhunt going on. I can't tell you if it's a firm sighting. We believe it was, and we're acting on it."[66]

As Saturday wore on with no sign of Bailey, law enforcement officials were getting frustrated. "Our belief is that he is under a tree out there somewhere covered with leaves or whatever, and he is going to wait until nighttime to make a move," said Sgt. Ken Ergle of the Marion County Sheriff's Department.[67]

Deputies began to walk shoulder to shoulder in a line-search pattern through dense woods by mid-afternoon.

65. McKinnon, John D., "Search Continues Near Ocala for Kidnapping, Murder Suspect," *St. Petersburg Times*, September 15, 1985

66. AP, "Manhunt on for Slain Boy's Abductor," *Fort Myers News-Press*, September 15, 1985

67. McKinnon, John D., "Search Continues Near Ocala for Kidnapping, Murder Suspect," *St. Petersburg Times*, September 15, 1985

—

While the manhunt continued in Florida, Dr. Laurence Simson was conducting an autopsy on Shawn Moore at Sparrow Hospital in Lansing. He noted Shawn's body was already in a bad state of decomposition with most of the face, neck and chest, and internal tissues of the face missing. Part of the remains were already skeletonized. Simson was able to retrieve tissue samples from portions of the liver, kidney, and spleen. They were the best of the specimens to be submitted for a toxicological analysis. With the aid of fingerprints lifted from personal items in Shawn's bedroom, along with dental records, Dr. Simson positively identified Shawn's remains, but because of the decomposition, he couldn't pinpoint a cause of death. In spite of that, he ruled Shawn's death a homicide.

An hour after the positive identification, with the paperwork already typed, Livingston County Magistrate Floyd Erdman signed a third warrant for Ronald Bailey charging him with open murder.

—

Jim Gabriel saw the news coverage of the hunt for Ron Bailey in Florida. Sitting in his Bay City, Michigan home, he knew he had to call the state police.

Over the Labor Day weekend, Gabriel and his eleven-year-old son, a fifth-grader, had been trail riding on three-wheel ATVs in Gladwin County. At thirty-three, Mr. Gabriel worked for Delco Manufacturing during the day and during the evening hours, he worked as a cameraman for Channel 49 in Saginaw.

On Monday, September 2, the two were riding from the cabin they were staying at on Ridge Road, heading to the west toward Three Rivers Road. They approached a curve in the road and Gabriel had to tell his son to move the three-wheeler over to the edge because of the sharp curve. There was a Jeep coming at them. The Jeep passed them heading east while they continued to the west. A short time later, they decided to return to the cabin they were staying at, and as they headed back to the east, they saw the same Jeep sitting on the north side of the road backed in to the edge of the forest. The driver was standing at the front of the Jeep, and to Gabriel, it looked like he might be waiting for someone while he whittled on a stick. He remembered the Jeep had a hard top and had the word "Renegade" printed on it. Since seeing the news reports of the hunt for Ron Bailey, he realized the person he had seen sitting on the front of the Jeep looked like Bailey. When Gabriel and his son spotted him alongside Ridge Road, he was wearing a white t-shirt, a faded, light blue plaid shirt unbuttoned all the way down the front, and blue jeans. He was certain it was around 11:30 a.m. From the time when they first saw the Jeep heading east to the point when they saw it parked on the north side of the road, about ten to fifteen minutes had elapsed.

Mr. Gabriel's son was interviewed too. Like his dad, he had seen the pictures of Ron Bailey in the news, and he recognized Bailey as the man he had seen in Gladwin County on Labor Day. He and his dad only knew that Shawn Moore's body had been found somewhere along Ridge Road. They had no idea exactly where the body was located.

After the interview with both of them, the investigators met Mr. Gabriel and his son at the cabin where they had been staying over the Labor Day weekend. Mr. Gabriel was asked to point out the spot where they had first seen the Jeep coming at them and where they had seen it parked on the north side of the road. The sharp curve in the road was about a mile and a half west of the cabin. They turned around and headed back to the east to a point where a trail, sometimes called Cherry Hill Road, crosses Ridge Road. It was where Mr. Gabriel was sure the Jeep had been parked.

His son disagreed. He thought it was farther to the east, so the investigator and the Gabriels headed east. Without being prompted, his son stopped at the exact location where Shawn Moore's body was found just off the roadway. From the point where the younger Gabriel remembered the Jeep being parked to the point where Shawn's body had been found was a matter of about fifty feet.

—

In Farmington Hills, Alfred Bailey was meeting with Ray Cassar and Chuck Murphy at their office. His plan was to appeal to his son to turn himself in. The Bailey family had already abandoned the Livonia home where they had lived for fifteen years. Carrying suitcases, clothes, and blankets, the senior Bailey said, "I'm very, very sorry for [the Moore family]. If my son is charged with this crime, I will be even more sorry than I have ever been in my life."[68]

—

In Florida, desperate to keep the killer contained in the ten-square-mile area, off-duty police and corrections officers from Marion County were volunteering to assist in the search for Bailey. Marie Craven, a three-and-a-half-year corrections deputy with the Marion County Sheriff's Department, was one of those volunteering to help in the search. Her normal duties at the jail included booking and transporting prisoners, but on this day she was in the field trying to help catch a killer.

At 7:37 p.m., there was still no sign of Bailey, and the sun had dropped below the horizon. By 8:00, police had

68. Pepper, Jon, "Shock and Sorrow at Suspect's Home," *Detroit Free Press*, September 14, 1985

to use flashlights, and they were anticipating another long night. They weren't giving up.

Many believed that Ron's dad and brother were going to head to Florida in an attempt to get Ron to turn himself in, but Alfred Bailey, now in front of television cameras back in Michigan, said, "I just want to appeal to my son Ronald to either call me or give himself up to the authorities in Florida and do whatever he can to come home." He was hoping the plea would be seen by his son on CNN in Florida. "I think he's running scared right now."[69]

—

Marie Craven was on her perimeter point near the intersection of County Road 328 and US-301 on the north fringes of the search area as the sun dropped farther and farther below the horizon. At 8:17, with complete darkness fast approaching, she shined her flashlight across a shadowy figure standing by a nearby cattle fence. It was a man with his arms draped across the barrier. As soon as the beam from her flashlight hit him, he threw his arms into the air. "I'm Ronald Bailey. I'm tired of running. I'm hungry, and I give up," he said.[70]

The radio squawked, and news reporters heard someone over the radio say Bailey had been captured.

Ronald Bailey, taken into custody without any resistance in Florida, was under arrest for the kidnapping and murder of Shawn Moore in Michigan and the federal warrant for unlawful flight to avoid prosecution, was exhausted and covered with scratches and insect bites. He was taken to the Marion County Jail.

69. Lam, Tina and Cohen, Janet, "Murder Suspect Captured," *Ann Arbor News*, September 15, 1985
70. Lam, Tina and Cohen, Janet, "Murder Suspect Captured," *Ann Arbor News*, September 15, 1985

A short time after his son's arrest, Alfred Bailey stood before television cameras again in Murphy and Cassar's office. In the doorway of an inner office, he told reporters that his son was in custody. His voice cracked as he fought back tears. "I just talked to my son, in jail in Florida. I asked him to waive extradition so he can come home as fast as he can, and we can help him right here in Michigan."[71] Ray Cassar added that Bailey was calm, yet excited to talk with his father by phone.

Ron Bailey appeared before Marion County Circuit Judge Carven Angel for a hearing, where he waived extradition. It was an unusual hearing because it was late at night. He would be taken back to Michigan on Sunday.

On Sunday morning at the Marion County Jail, Ron Bailey ate boiled eggs, bacon, and hashbrowns for breakfast as the paperwork was readied for his transfer to MSP. Before his departure mid-afternoon, he ate baked ham, candied yams, green beans, and corn as the paperwork was finalized. When he had been booked the previous night, whatever property he had on him or in his pockets was taken from him. He seemed overly concerned about one particular item that he wanted given back: the Byron wristwatch he had been wearing.

At Ocala International Airport-Jim Taylor Field, security was tight for his transfer and departure.

---

71. Lam, Tina and Cohen, Janet, "Murder Suspect Captured," *Ann Arbor News*, September 15, 1985

11
Mr. Personality

Alfred Bailey spoke briefly with reporters on Sunday morning. "When I read the papers this morning, I was seeing things about a person that lived in my home that I never knew." He added, "We never talked at all since he got out of the hospital."[72]

In Florida, news crews stood in the glaring hot sunshine. A sudden loud buzzing and loud click from the heavy steel jail door startled the reporters as Ron Bailey appeared. He looked frail and frightened. He was physically exhausted. He stepped into the sunlight, briefly squinting from the glare as he and the deputies escorting him walked toward a waiting unmarked Marion County Sheriff's car. The ankle chains he wore made it difficult to walk. Bailey had spent Saturday night under special guard at the jail. Having waived his extradition, he was being returned to Michigan to face trial in the kidnapping and murder of thirteen-year-old Shawn Moore. As the unmarked car left the sheriff's office and headed down the two-lane highway, they passed the Vietnam Veterans' annual Country Fair Picnic. When they arrived at Jim Taylor Airport, they met a heavily guarded

72. Lam, Tina and Cohen, Janet, "Murder Suspect Captured," *Ann Arbor News*, September 15, 1985

plane, and Bailey was surrendered to the FBI and Michigan State Police on the runway.

The twin engine FBI plane took off from Ocala and had a planned stop in Louisville, Kentucky, for fuel. While refueling, there was a quick run to get McDonald's sandwiches while some of the surveillance team stayed with their prisoner on the plane. As the plane took off for Michigan, Jess Lopez sat behind Bailey. Bailey crumpled up the wrappers from his McDonald's sandwiches and tossed them over the back of the seat toward Lopez. It didn't matter. Lopez chuckled, knowing they had taken a killer off the streets.

Halfway through the flight back to Michigan, the pilot received word by radio of threats being made against Bailey, and the FBI wasn't taking any chances. As the plane neared Michigan, the special agent in charge from the Detroit FBI office radioed to Lopez and told him about the threats. Lopez was told to have everyone put on their bullet resistant vests and to put one on Bailey too. Lopez and his colleague should come off the plane first, followed by Bailey, and then Bailey would be followed by the two MSP detectives.

The plane touched down at the Livingston County Airport and rolled to a stop on the tarmac. Lopez looked at Ron Bailey and told him to go.

"What?" the puzzled killer asked.

"I said go."

"Your boss told you that you were supposed to go out first," Bailey said.

"I don't care what he said. You're not the president, and I'm not the Secret Service," Lopez shot back as he gave Bailey a push out the door.[73]

Reporters and television cameras were kept away as a small motorcade made its way from the airport for the short trip to the Livingston County Jail. At the jail, Bailey was

---

73. Lopez, Jess, Interview with author, November 7, 2023

taken through a back door, booked, and put into a maximum-security cell. Sheriff DeBurton didn't know of any direct threats against Bailey, but he had heard reports of some being made. He wanted to ensure that nothing went wrong.

The first order of business for Ray Cassar and Charles Murphy was the initial visit with their new client. They were already waiting at the Livingston County Jail when Bailey arrived from the airport. Murphy had a very engaging personality, and he was both funny and smart, but he didn't want to meet Bailey face to face. "You go in and meet him," he told his colleague.

Apprehension set in for Cassar. *What's he going to be like? He took a kid off a bike and killed him.* He looked at Murphy. "What do I say to him?"

"Just start talking to him. Find out what's going on."

Ray Cassar knew he would have to establish a rapport with Bailey immediately, and he knew they already had some sort of a bond. They were the same age. Bailey lived in Livonia. Cassar lived in Garden City. They were essentially five miles or so apart.

Ray Cassar was surprised when he first met his client. Ron Bailey looked as if he had been beaten, and he was covered with scratches and insect bites. "Did they beat you?" he asked.

"You mean the cops?" Bailey asked.

"Yeah, because you look horrific."

"No, nobody beat me. It was from running through the swamp."[74]

The counselor and his new client felt a little more at ease with each passing minute. Ron Bailey began to tell his complicated story to his new attorney, and over the next few meetings, Bailey confided to him about his treatment first at the Hawthorn Center, and then at the Northville Regional Psychiatric Hospital. Cassar already knew about

---

74. Cassar, Raymond, Interview with author, February 27, 2024

the witnesses to Shawn Moore's abduction and that his client owned a Jeep Renegade matching the description of the Jeep used in the kidnapping.

Over the next few meetings, Ron Bailey told Cassar about how long he'd had mental health issues. He hadn't just been receiving day treatment at Hawthorn; he had been living there and was being treated by Dr. Jose Tombo. Still early in his representation of Bailey, Cassar wasn't sure if his client was being truthful with him about some of the allegations he made.

The more Ray Cassar and Ron Bailey talked, the more Cassar's impression of him was that he was an immensely lost soul.

"Ray, I had no intention to kill him," Bailey told his attorney.

"What happened, then?"

Bailey described a sadist sexual practice he had used on Shawn by choking him. After he discovered Shawn was dead, he had to get rid of the body, so he left it in the woods.

Cassar knew then that nothing about the case was going to be easy. There was no doubt in the attorney's mind; Ron Bailey needed help, and Ray Cassar intended to give it to him.

Almost immediately, Ray Cassar began to think an insanity defense might be the best way to approach Ron Bailey's case. Everything Bailey had told him mirrored what Alfred Bailey had told him about his client's mental health. An insanity case was a long shot for anyone, with the exception of John Hinckley and his attempted assassination of President Reagan.

Ray Cassar still had to know one very important thing. "Are there other people?" he asked his client. He was referring to other victims Bailey had murdered. If there were, he needed to know.

"No."[75]

Cassar wasn't so sure.

—

Jess Lopez thought very highly of Shawn's dad, Bruce "Bud" Moore. In the short time he had known him, he knew Bud was in a lot of emotional pain, but he also knew that Shawn's dad still had a very strong will. As a result of Lopez coming to know the family, Bud Moore asked both Jess Lopez and Dave Ostrem to be pallbearers at Shawn's funeral.

On Monday, September 16, an all-night vigil at the Holy Spirit Catholic Church in Hamburg, southwest of Brighton, was held for Shawn. Open to the community as a whole, it was for those who had shared the Moore family's grief over the previous two weeks. Parishioners from the church signed up for half-hour time slots throughout the night to kneel at Shawn's casket and keep vigil until morning. Many of those same parishioners had a feeling of helplessness while police searched for Shawn, almost as if they were being held hostage themselves. Scripture services were scheduled for 7:30 p.m., and the vigil would conclude shortly before Shawn's funeral on Tuesday.

Speaking briefly with a reporter, Sharon Moore explained that the vigil wasn't something she had thought of doing. "People's hearts have gone out to Shawn. When so many people's hearts go out to you, it didn't strike me as something to do." Collectively, the Moores did think it would be the best way for everyone to share their own grief.

Reverend Charlie Irvin was a historian and minister to the tightly-knit congregation, and he said a vigil was a custom from Europe that had some elements of an Irish

75. Cassar, Raymond, Interview with author, February 27, 2024

wake but with a religious base. "It will be Shawn being with us for this time until the Mass of the Resurrection."[76]

Shawn had wanted to attend the Holy Spirit Catholic Church and had taken a religious education class there. Bud and Sharon, along with their family, had attended there for several years.

Sharon Moore told a reporter, "He was the neatest kid— Mr. Personality." She continued, "He was a young man, and it shouldn't be sad, sad." Part of the scripture service scheduled included a picture of Shawn's cat, Mr. Peabody, a cross that Shawn had made, his Scranton Middle School cap, and some of his favorite music.

Father Irvin delivered his sermon to the congregation. He spoke of the early release of inmates from prison and the relationship between violence and pornography. If kids were to ride their bikes to get a soda pop, then early release of inmates had to be addressed. "There's a whole industry that feeds violent sexual thoughts into our nature against women and against children, and it reaps enormous benefits."[77]

The murder of Kenny Myers a year earlier still remained unsolved. Even so, Marie Edenstrom was convinced in her own mind that Ronald Bailey was responsible for her son's death. While she was steadfast in her belief, she didn't want to sway the police investigation into her son's murder. "That's their job, and until they can determine one way or the other, I don't think I should make any comment."[78] She had followed the story of Shawn's disappearance and the eventual discovery of his body. She wanted to meet the Moore family and offer her condolences to them.

76. Lam, Tina, "All-Night Vigil for Shawn," *Ann Arbor News*, September 16, 1985

77. Lam, Tina, "All-Night Vigil for Shawn," *Ann Arbor News*, September 16, 1985

78. Wowk, Mike, "Mother of Boy Slain in '84 to Attend Rites," *Detroit News*, September 16, 1985

Since Kenny's murder, Marie had formed an organization called KENNY, an acronym for Kids Everywhere Now Need You. The organization's focus was to inform kids on how to avoid strangers and the importance of learning addresses and phone numbers. She had also testified at a congressional hearing earlier in the year that part of the four million dollars in the Missing Children's Assistance Act should be used to provide grief counseling for parents.

In Livonia, members of the Ward Presbyterian Church were praying for Alfred Bailey and his family in addition to the Moores. The Baileys were members of the church. The Reverend Bartlett Hess said, "For the Baileys, there is the added tragedy and sorrow that it was their son that caused such a tragedy for the Moore family." He added, "They are very sensitive people. They are really broken by this."[79]

—

Sharon Moore was a teacher at Farley Hill Elementary School in the nearby town of Pinckney. The school had closed for Shawn's funeral so teachers could attend. The principal knew the day would be too emotional for Sharon's colleagues.

At Scranton Middle School, the students were told about Shawn's body being found on Friday. Some of the students wept openly. The principal tried to soothe the fears of the students by telling them that only one percent of missing children's cases were kidnappings like Shawn's. It was simply a freak incident, and it could have happened anywhere. The superintendent felt it was important to let the kids know so they would have a chance to talk with teachers and peers before heading for home, possibly to an empty house. The school district also brought in a psychologist

79. Wowk, Mike, "Mother of Boy Slain in '84 to Attend Rites," *Detroit News*, September 16, 1985

as an advisor for teachers on how to deal with students' anxieties and fears. Kids were asking, "If it happened to me, what should I do?" or "Should I fight back? I'm smaller than Shawn was."[80]

—

A little girl with pigtails was close to Shawn's age. There was no doubt she was struggling to hold back her tears, her lip quivering uncontrollably as she waited her turn. When she got closer to Shawn's casket, she couldn't contain herself anymore. She stood by the casket for just a moment, tears streaming down her small face, then hastily left the church as tears filled the eyes of law enforcement officers while kids were hugged by their moms.

In front of the altar, Shawn's polished wood casket was draped with a white pall emblazoned with a red cross. It was surrounded with baskets of red and white carnations and his picture setting atop, with the framed picture of Mr. Peabody, Shawn's cat, nearby. A fabric cross Shawn had made in religion class was mounted on a wooden plaque. Flowers filled the vestibule and lined the walls of the sanctuary. To the right of the altar was a flower arrangement from the Detective Bureau at the Livingston County Sheriff's Department.

Shawn's teacher, Tom Mazzarese, was in tears as he carried Shawn's baseball cap that read "Scranton."

Six priests celebrated the Mass that included guitar and piano music. In his homily, Father Irvin began by reading an anonymous letter addressed to Shawn that read:

In two short weeks, you have brought an entire community to its knees. You have made a lasting

80. Robertson, Nicole, "Death Brings Sadness, Fear, Anger," *Brighton Argus*, September 19, 1985

impression. How proud we are to have had you in our lives.

As Shawn was laid to rest in the cemetery, Father Irwin spoke to each family member. He gave Bud a supportive tap on the cheek. Sunshine gleamed through the wooded cemetery, and there were smiles as Father Irvin's words resonated. "The goodness and innocence of little boys and girls shall overcome."[81]

Frank Del Vero was there, and he made a vow to himself that he was going to get justice for Shawn. He met Shawn's parents for the first time at the funeral. His sympathy for the Moore family was evident, and he told them he would do whatever he could for them, but he made no promises. He knew they were living every parent's worst nightmare.

Del Vero was running for election as a district court judge in Livingston County, and his campaign manager tried to talk him out of handling the case against Ron Bailey. He warned Del Vero that if he didn't win the case against Shawn's killer, his election campaign would be over. Del Vero said, "I don't care. I'm doing it."[82]

—

The threats against Ron Bailey weren't anything specific. They were vague and generic when they were phoned in. They were similar to "Have officers stay well back so they won't get hurt."

Arrangements were made with Sheriff DeBurton to have Ron Bailey arraigned on Tuesday in a small library at the Livingston County Jail rather than having it done in a public setting at the Livingston County Courthouse. The public

81. McGraw, Bill, "Sad Farewell to a Special Friend," *Detroit Free Press*, September 18, 1985

82. Del Vero, Frank, Interview with author, April 2, 2024

wouldn't be allowed in. Every measure was taken to make sure that neither Bailey nor any police officers were placed in any type of dangerous situation.

Dressed in green jail fatigues and black rubber sandals, Bailey entered the small room with his father at 11:20 a.m. With his hair disheveled, he looked as if he had been woken up to attend the hearing. Alfred Bailey had his arm around his son's shoulders, and the younger Bailey had tears running down his cheeks as he stared at the floor. He never said a word. The room was filled with twenty-five people including the media, county officials, defense lawyers, and law enforcement. The media presence consisted of fourteen newspaper, television, and radio reporters. Two were sketch artists.

As the four-minute hearing began in front of Livingston County District Judge Michael Merritt, Cassar spoke for the defense and said their client would stand mute to the charges. Judge Merritt entered a not guilty plea to both state charges of kidnapping and open murder, then referred Bailey to the State Center for Forensic Psychiatry for a mental evaluation. Both Murphy and Cassar agreed to waive the time constraint for the preliminary examination until Bailey was returned from the Forensic Center and a determination was made regarding his competency to stand trial. The judge set no bond. When deputies escorted Bailey back to his cell, Alfred Bailey gave his son a soft pat on the back.

—

It was known simply as the Forensic Center and had been set up by Michigan statute to examine people who claimed insanity as a defense. It included those who might have been incompetent to stand trial, and there were an estimated 2,000 evaluations per year. It also served as a maximum-security hospital for the criminally insane.

After the arraignment, Ray Cassar and Charles Murphy spoke with the media and mentioned that they would likely seek a change of venue to move the trial out of Livingston County. There was already intense publicity. When a reporter asked where they would like to have the trial held, Murphy jokingly said, "We'd like to take it to Brazil." He added that if the reports linking Ron Bailey to other unsolved child killings made it impossible for a fair trial, Bailey could avoid going to trial at all for Shawn's murder.

Murphy was concerned. If the media tried to connect Bailey to other unsolved cases across the state and beyond, it could cause problems. He told the press that time would tell whether Bailey was involved in other unsolved cases, but he also felt that the public could get a false sense of security with Ron Bailey in custody.

Ray Cassar was more diplomatic when he spoke in front of the media. As Ron Bailey's attorneys, it was their job to represent Bailey's rights. They weren't retained to try everything they possibly could to get Bailey off. When a reporter asked if Bailey being referred for a mental evaluation was a prelude to an insanity defense, Cassar simply replied, "No comment."[83]

It wasn't long after the arraignment when Cassar began to hear rumblings that he and Murphy were being criticized for defending Ron Bailey. It was clear that in spite of the viciousness of the crime, Bailey was still presumed innocent. Both Cassar and Murphy knew the prosecution's case was, at that point, strictly circumstantial, and there was nothing that directly linked their client to the murder of Shawn Moore. In their own defense, Cassar said, "We attorneys are doing our job representing people's rights to prevent [them] from summarily being convicted and hung."[84]

83. McGraw, Bill and McGee, Kevin T., "Bailey May be Quizzed in 2d Death," *Detroit Free Press*, September 17, 1985
84. McGraw, Bill and McGee, Kevin T., "Bailey May be Quizzed in 2d Death," *Detroit Free Press*, September 17, 1985

—

With Ron Bailey in custody, the task force had been cut from fifty or more investigators to around twenty. Roger Bittell, along with the remaining task force members, the Wayne County Sheriff's Department, and the Ferndale Police had already zeroed in on Bailey in the kidnapping and murder of Kenny Myers just a year before. There were too many similarities in the two cases. Both Shawn and Kenny were young, small in stature, and both were abducted off their bicycles by a White male. Everyone working on the two cases agreed there were too many similarities to simply ignore them.

On the day of Shawn's funeral, the media was reporting that Ron Bailey would likely be questioned in the kidnapping and murder of Kenny Myers. Cassar and Murphy took note.

12
Tombo

Alfred Bailey loved his son, and he didn't want to believe the things that were being said about Ron. It had always been that way. He simply couldn't believe the accusations, and he would be there to support him.

Ray Cassar and Charles Murphy were already preparing for their client's upcoming preliminary examination in district court, and the media was widely reporting that the two would be using an insanity defense for their client.

Three days after Ron's arrest in Florida, Alfred Bailey received a phone call from Dr. Jose Tombo, his son's treating psychiatrist. Tombo wanted to talk about Ron and the analysis that he had done on him, and to go over some of the information he had given to the Baileys when Ron was released from Northville. Mr. Bailey, still trying to process his son's arrest, couldn't talk to Tombo. Mr. Bailey asked if Tombo could come to their home to discuss it, but Tombo didn't want to be seen by the Baileys' neighbors. The suggestion was made to meet at Cassar and Murphy's office instead.

Cassar already knew his client had been treated by Dr. Tombo. He also knew that Tombo had checked his client out of the Hawthorn Center and taken him to Windsor, Canada in 1976. Cassar knew all of the details, including what Ron Bailey had already told him about being forced to perform fellatio on Tombo. Tombo didn't know that Cassar knew, and when he called Cassar to set up the meeting, he told the attorney he could help with Ron Bailey's case, especially the insanity defense.

The clandestine meeting took place at their law office in Farmington Hills, and at 8:00 p.m., Dr. Tombo, the little Filipino doctor, walked into the conference room. Alfred Bailey was already there. After introductions, Tombo, who spoke with a Philippine accent, said, "I can absolutely help you. I can help you with the insanity defense." He continued, "I treated him, and I can give you charts and show his digression and what was going on." The two attorneys were anxious to hear what Tombo had to say. Dr. Tombo said that Ron Bailey was clearly mentally ill and definitely insane at the time of the murder. Cassar and Murphy were encouraged, but there was a caveat.

"I can give you what you need; however, there has to be a deal here," he said.

"What kind of deal?" Cassar asked.[85]

Tombo showed the three men a newsletter that had been circulated at Northville Psychiatric Hospital by a group of current and former employees. In the newsletter, it detailed allegations of Tombo's sexual relationship with Ron Bailey. "This is all a lie," he said. He told them he didn't have a relationship with Ron, other than a day trip to Canada.[86]

"I'm going to give you as much information as you want, but I do not want any reference of me taking him to Windsor."

Mr. Bailey had known Tombo for a long time. Tombo was the only doctor his son ever had at Hawthorn and Northville. Mr. Bailey and his wife used to participate in hour-long counseling sessions with his son and Tombo,

85. Cassar, Raymond, Interview with author, February 27, 2024
86. Kresnak, Jack, "Bailey's Ex-Doctor Shifted Amid Allegations," *Detroit Free Press*, October 6, 1985

and the psychiatrist would share a lot of information about Ron. Tombo had told Mr. Bailey that he was partly at fault for Ron's problems, that his mother was too cautious with him about relationships, especially with girls. Ron Bailey's attitude began to slowly change, but any information about his sexuality came directly from Dr. Tombo.

Now, as Ron's dad sat in the conference room with Cassar, Murphy, and Dr. Tombo, he couldn't believe what he was hearing. Alfred Bailey was a big man and towered over Tombo. "What?" he said, more as a statement than a question.

"I think it would be perceived wrong, so we want to leave that totally out of it," Tombo told him. "I took my day trip to socialize him and get him out of the hospital. We don't want the Windsor thing to come up, and that's got to be the agreement."[87] Tombo knew that if the truth came out about what had happened in Windsor between Bailey and him, his credibility would be at risk. He claimed it was a treatment goal between Bailey and him. If the Windsor trip did come up at trial, they could argue it was his way of socializing Ron Bailey, but he never said anything about any sort of sexual activity with him.

Tombo had taken a liking to Ron Bailey in 1976 at Hawthorn and when he began treating him at Northville Psychiatric Hospital. After Bailey had turned eighteen, Tombo checked him out on a day pass, and they went to the races at the Windsor Raceway in Windsor, Canada. Bailey had told Cassar that at the time he and Tombo took the day trip, he was in a position where he would do anything to get out of the hospital, and he simply saw it as a way out. While the two were in Windsor, things began to take a sexual turn, and Tombo forced him to perform oral sex on him.

When Bailey first shared the story with Cassar, he wasn't sure if his client was being truthful with him. He thought to

87. Cassar, Raymond, Interview with author, February 27, 2024

himself, *What the hell? Is a treating psychiatrist abusing Bailey?* Cassar could see the grief on his client's face as he described what had happened between the two of them.

Alfred Bailey had heard the same story from his son, but like Ray Cassar, he didn't want to believe it either, so he kept it to himself.

In a split second, Alfred Bailey was on his feet and moving toward the small psychiatrist. He had realized everything his son had told him about having sex with Tombo was true. The normally even-tempered man yelled obscenities at the doctor as he moved closer to him, and Tombo, fearful now, started to move backward. Cassar and Murphy jumped to their feet in an instant, stepping between Mr. Bailey and Tombo. They knew that if Alfred Bailey got to Tombo, he would beat him to a pulp. "No, no, no. Now is not the time," Cassar said as they tried to calm Mr. Bailey down. Both attorneys were stunned at the revelation.

The two attorneys managed to stop the impending assault, and Tombo knew it was his cue to leave. As he was getting ready to go, he said, "We have to have that understanding; otherwise, I can't help you, and you're going to need my help."

"I don't think we can do this," Cassar said. "But you're going to need to come forward as a witness and explain." Tombo was ready to walk out. "It's not my interest to hurt you. It's my interest to help [Ron]," Cassar said quietly. Dr. Jose Tombo had let the cat out of the bag, and as he turned to leave, Ray Cassar knew it was last time they would see him.

Alfred Bailey was stunned. He'd had his suspicions, but he didn't want to believe that it was happening to his son. Tombo had just confirmed everything. He stood in the conference room with his hands on his head saying, "I can't believe I didn't believe him. I didn't believe my own son."

Cassar, still trying to reassure him, said, "Al, we're going to figure this out."

Ray Cassar looked at Murphy, and Murphy returned the stare. "Oh, my God, this is crazy," Murphy said. "We've got to tell the story because if we don't, we have no chance."[88] Ray Cassar knew they would need Tombo to testify. After the meeting, he realized he wasn't simply handling a murder case. There was sex involved, and now he believed that it wasn't consensual. He was convinced that Tombo was the start of Ron Bailey's problems because now he knew, according to Bailey, that the sexual abuse had started while he was at the Hawthorn Center. If the two attorneys were going to get any sympathy from the prospective future jurors, they would have to let the public know.

—

Dr. Jose Tombo became an American citizen in 1982 after coming to America nine years earlier. He was hired at the Northville Regional Psychiatric Hospital after completing his psychiatry residency in Ontario, Canada, and at Northville he seemed to be well-liked by his colleagues, arriving every day to work by 7:00 a.m. and staying until 4:30 p.m.

Over the next several years, he had built his reputation at the hospital, and in the mid-eighties, his service rating read:

Shows strong leadership as a unit director and excellent work habits. His service is very much appreciated.

Earning a salary of $80,000 per year, he put much of it into a deferred retirement plan.

With a positive work ethic, he seemed committed to his patients. He felt they deserved more attention from

88. Cassar, Raymond, Interview with author, February 27, 2024

doctors and more recreational activities. Overcrowding was a constant problem at Northville, and with over forty adult male patients with a host of mental problems, Tombo worked hard to lower the number of patients to twenty-five. "When you put a big crowd of mice in a small space, they start fighting and killing each other," he said.[89] He was referring to the psychiatric wards. When patients are living in overcrowded conditions and they don't see a doctor on a regular basis, they become a danger to staff, other patients, and themselves.

To his colleagues, Tombo was a clinician who had a "remarkable combination of human caring and concern" to his job. Besides his specialty in psychiatry, he seemed to have a good knowledge of medicine in general, and a loyalty to commitments with his patients, though he wasn't always diplomatic, and that, coupled with rumors of his sexual preferences, seemed to be the basis for most of the problems he was having.

—

The task force had been looking for Ron Bailey's old Buick station wagon—and they found it. A nineteen-year-old Wayne State University student was using it. It had been purchased from an auto dealer in Hamtramck near Detroit by the college student's uncle. His uncle had loaned him the car so he could get back and forth to school. When it was purchased, the grill was still missing, and the dents were still in the fenders, though the front seat had been re-covered. When the car was found, it was at the boy's grandmother's home, and she signed a waiver to allow the state police to search it for any evidence that Kenny Myers had been in the car. If anything tying Kenny Myers to the inside of the car

89. Kresnak, Jack, "Tombo Wants to Return Soon to Northville," *Detroit Free Press*, November 16, 1985

was found, Ron Bailey would be certain to face charges in Kenny's murder.

Investigators had looked at the photos taken by Don Brooks inside the Bailey home showing the area where their suspect slept in the basement. There was a photo showing a yellow blanket, and Ferndale police had evidence of yellow fibers being found on the Velcro tennis shoes worn by Kenny Myers when his body was found. On September 20, MSP and the Ferndale police went to the Bailey home on Scone Street with a search warrant in hand. They were looking for two blankets.

Alfred Bailey answered the door. The two investigators explained the search warrant to him and told him the blankets had been in the basement when they had been photographed. Mr. Bailey took the two men to the basement to find the blankets, which hadn't been moved since the photos were taken by Brooks. Alfred Bailey got some garbage bags so they could put the blankets inside. The two investigators left the Bailey home and headed for the MSP laboratory in Northville.

—

When word circulated of Shawn Moore's body being discovered in Gladwin County, people in and around Brighton weren't simply shocked and saddened; they were angry. Kathy Cameron, a Livingston County mother, took it upon herself to call school superintendents, township officials, newspaper editors, and politicians. She knew it sounded like a cliché, but she was angry, and she wasn't going to take it anymore.

For years, Oakland County's Prosecuting Attorney, L. Brooks Patterson, believed that criminals were thoughtlessly returned to society. When Cameron called him, he accepted her invitation to address the murder of Shawn Moore at a public forum she was organizing. Her hope was for judicial reform and for Patterson to provide the motivation for it. He would be the keynote speaker. Cameron's ultimate goal was to change legislation so that teens who committed violent and heinous crimes could be tried as adults.

L. Brooks Patterson, a native Detroiter and a Republican, was tough on crime. With a twin brother and one sister, his father was an autoworker at Chrysler. After earning a bachelor's degree at the University of Detroit, he taught briefly at Detroit Catholic Central High School and eventually earned his law degree from the University of Detroit in 1967. When he took a job as an Oakland County assistant prosecuting attorney in 1969, there was no doubt that he would be tough on crime. When he criticized the plea deals that were made by the prosecutor's office, he was let go. He then set up his private practice in Pontiac.

In 1972, he was elected as Oakland County's prosecuting attorney with his "tough on crime" stance. Across the state of Michigan, some considered L. Brooks Patterson a dominating yet likeable man with a gregarious personality, while others considered him a "dangerous demagogue and menace" because of his law enforcement style.

Kathy Cameron was hoping that Patterson would draw a huge crowd at the forum. She was furious when she learned that Ron Bailey had only received five years of probation for the 1975 sexual assault of a young boy.

Just one week after Shawn Moore's funeral and Ron Bailey's arraignment, 750 people poured into the Brighton High School Auditorium. Some carried posters that read "Stop Killing Our Children" and "Bring Back Capital Punishment."

Patterson received an enthusiastic welcome from the crowd as he stood at the podium and said that he wasn't there to try Ronald Bailey from the podium. He was working the crowd when he continued, "And I certainly don't want to spark an angry riot where we storm Sheriff DeBurton's jail, although that idea does have some appeal."

The Oakland County prosecutor told the crowd that he was forming a statewide association called Friends of Shawn Moore, and he asked that the crowd's anger and frustration at the system shouldn't fade and could be focused on judicial reforms. He agreed that some of the problems within the system were the fault of the legal system itself, but most of the problems were the result of the legislature and the corrections division. In true form, L. Brooks Patterson didn't hold back. "We have a legislature that sits around finding ways to let them out early. We spend hours and hours trying to figure out how to get those poor boys out of prison and into the community." He continued, "We're literally being raped and robbed and murdered by the same hardcore felons. So, I hold the legislature ultimately responsible for a lot of the problems."[90]

Patterson presented a $1,000 check to cover the initial start-up of the new association, and he told the packed house that they should push for capital punishment for first-degree murder, mandatory serving of minimum sentences, increasing severity for repeat offenders, abolishment of early parole for violent crimes, and abolishment of the insanity defense. "Let me tell you about the insanity defense. It doesn't belong in a court of law. Are there people that are insane? Sure. But that ought not to excuse the crime."[91]

When Patterson called for the State of Michigan to reinstate the death penalty, there was thunderous applause and a standing ovation.

There was no doubt about Oakland County's prosecutor. Patterson was passionate about his beliefs. He had already told the media, "Any defendant that gets five years'

90. Grantham, Daniel, "Don't Let Anger Die, Patterson Urges," *The Press*, September 25, 1985

91. Grantham, Daniel, "Patterson Urges Crowd to Back Death Penalty," *The Brighton Argus,* September 25, 1985

probation for an attempted murder, assault, and kidnapping has got to laugh his way out of the court. That individual has just beaten the system." He was referring to Bailey's previous arrests. Speaking of Shawn's case, he said, "I think a crime of this magnitude, of this brutality, is so outrageous that it ought to invoke the death penalty," adding, "I think rehabilitation is the biggest god-damned joke forced down the public's throat."[92]

On the same day the public forum was held, Scott Moore issued a statement for his entire family asking that his brother's name not be used in connection with the newly formed association. The Moore family was asking that donations be made to Michigan's Children's Trust Fund. Thousands of dollars were being donated in Shawn's memory. In two days, they had received over $3,000. The State had received hundreds of calls from people wanting to know more about the Trust Fund before they donated. The Fund, which received money from the state income tax checkoff system, had seen slow growth. The checkoff system on the taxes was scheduled to continue until $20 million had been received and the Fund became self-sustaining through interest income. The previous year, over six percent of Michigan residents had donated $686,000. Michigan ranked second in donations from around the county. In 1984, the Fund made grants totaling $300,500 to locals that funded programs like latchkey children, drop-in centers, coaching for new parents, and sexual abuse prevention. If they'd had the $20 million in the Trust Fund account, they would have been able to issue grants totaling over $2 million per year.

Beyond the forum, the whole idea of rehabilitation became the hot topic. With Patterson calling for capital punishment to be reinstated, others felt differently and supported Judge Bohn's decision to give Bailey five years

---

92. Davies, Andrea, "Jail or Cure for Mentally Ill Criminal," *The Brighton Argus*, September 18, 1985

of probation after his guilty plea in the seventies. Like Judge Bohn, many believed that he had a better chance of turning his life around at the age of sixteen while confined to a psychiatric hospital rather than in a prison setting.

Thomas DeLoach, the communications director for the Michigan Department of Public Health, spoke about the rarity and the tragedy of Shawn's abduction and murder. In 1985, with 50,000 people being admitted to public and private psychiatric hospitals, the only means to keep them there was whether the person was a danger to themselves or to others, and whether they had the ability to care for themselves or others. If the person was charged with a crime, it was a matter for the courts, but the person's mental health was another matter. "This is obviously the worst possible time to discuss this. This is a great tragedy," he said.[93]

The nineteen-year-old boy who had been kidnapped behind his home in Dearborn Heights by Ron Bailey ten years earlier was angry too. When he heard police were searching for Bailey, he had called MSP to see if he could help in some way. As a victim, he felt Bailey should have been jailed after he kidnapped, drugged, and molested him.

———

Ray Cassar admitted that the case against his client looked bad, but he maintained the prosecution still had to have a good case in order to prove Ron Bailey's guilt. Cassar knew that Dr. Simson, the pathologist at Sparrow Hospital in Lansing, hadn't been able to pinpoint a cause of death, though he labeled the death a homicide. He also knew that his client didn't match the original description of Shawn's abductor, and Bailey's Jeep was silver-blue in color, not

93. Davies, Andrea, "Keep Criminals Off Our Streets," *Livingston County Daily Press*, September 18, 1985

white as described by some. There was no direct evidence pointing to Ron Bailey as the killer.

Frank Del Vero wasn't going to get into a debate with Ray Cassar about the merits of the case against Bailey. With no cause of death listed in the autopsy, Del Vero was still waiting on testing of tissue samples taken at Shawn's autopsy. He was hoping the microscopic evaluation might provide some answers. He knew it was a difficult case, but he also knew it would take time. Even with pieces of the puzzle missing, he was hopeful the judge and jury would still see the big picture at trial. There was no doubt he would be relying on strong circumstantial evidence.

Although Dr. Lawrence Simson couldn't determine the cause of death, he was able to opine that it was a homicide based on the entire set of circumstances. It presented technical problems, and he admitted that. He first looked for evidence of injury or disease along with any evidence of drugs or toxicological materials. While Del Vero was hopeful, Simson knew the microscopic examinations probably wouldn't be helpful to the case. Even without a cause of death, the pathologist could give an opinion as to the manner of death. By that, he would take into consideration whether it was a natural death, an accident, a suicide, or a homicide. For Frank Del Vero, the manner of death was the most important. All he had to show was that Shawn's death was unlawful and that it was caused by another person.

Cassar spoke to the media about the case, and he was asked if the speech by L. Brooks Patterson might hurt Bailey's chances of having a fair trial in Livingston County. "Without a doubt. Pretrial publicity is bad enough, but to have Brooks Patterson out there discussing capital punishment."[94] In spite of that, he still felt the Brighton community was giving his client a fair shake.

---

94. Grantham, Daniel, "Attorney Says Convicting Bailey Won't be Easy for Prosecution," *Livingston County Daily Press*, September 25, 1985

L. Brooks Patterson was taking some heat for his appearance at Brighton High School and was being accused of exploiting the Shawn Moore case. Attending the Republican Party's biennial leadership conference on Mackinac Island, he said he was hurt by that accusation. "I'm a prosecutor with years of experience. I've got four kids, and I identified with that Brighton audience." He went on to say that people didn't trust politicians and didn't feel politicians could be motivated by good causes. It was rumored he would be entering Michigan's gubernatorial race. "I don't want to be considered, don't want to be rumored, because the next time I speak on behalf of the criminal justice system, the reforms that are necessary, people will know that I'm sincere."[95]

—

While the investigation had shifted to the murder of Kenny Myers, at the Livingston County Sheriff's Department in Howell, police set up a lineup on September 25. Thirteen witnesses viewed Bailey in a lineup in the hope they could identify him. Eleven of those thirteen witnesses picked him out.

When pressed about the results, Det. Ray Allen from the Wayne County Sheriff's Department said he couldn't comment on it.

Frank Del Vero confirmed to the media that there was, indeed, a lineup held in the Shawn Moore abduction and murder, but he refused to say whether any of the witnesses in the Myers case viewed it. There were legal considerations on whether or not they should have it, but he said the police wanted it so they went ahead with it.

Ray Cassar and Chuck Murphy felt it was unfair to Ron Bailey because there had been so much pretrial publicity.

95. Parks, Chris, "Thinking of Brooks," *Petoskey News*, September 25, 1985

"Our feeling is if you had shown a picture of Conan the Barbarian on TV for as many nights in a row as Mr. Bailey was out there, that all the witnesses would've picked Arnold Schwarzenegger as the suspect," Chuck Murphy said.

Cassar said, "With all the publicity, how could they not pick him out? It comes as no great surprise."[96]

Murphy felt that Bailey appearing in the lineup may have tainted potential testimony from witnesses, and he planned to challenge that potential testimony at trial.

Ron Bailey was in custody, and he wasn't going anywhere, so Wayne County was intentionally taking their time to cover all the bases before any charges were brought in Kenny Myers's murder.

—

Scott Moore had asked that the new organization titled Friends of Shawn Moore, announced by L. Brooks Patterson during the forum at Brighton High School, not use Shawn's name in their title. The new group was likely going to lobby for tougher punishments for criminals, and the Moores didn't want that to jeopardize Ron Bailey's right to a fair trial. After much consideration and discussions with the police and attorneys, they chose to remain unaligned politically.

In a statement to the media, the Moore family announced that they would sponsor an educational forum to discuss missing and exploited children. The date was set for October 15, and the intent was to provide information about the abduction of children and discuss things that the community could do to prevent child abductions.

The group that had formerly called themselves the Friends of Shawn Moore changed their name and dropped

96. Kresnak, Jack, "Lineup Reportedly Links Bailey to '84 Kidnap-Killing," *Detroit Free Press*, September 27, 1985

capital punishment from their agenda. Under their new name, Friends of Reform for Criminalized Victims Everywhere (FORCE), they would seek reforms in sentencing and judicial practices. By dropping capital punishment as one of the previous reforms they had been seeking, it allowed community members who didn't support capital punishment to be a member of the group. Things such as mandatory minimum sentences, increasing severity for repeat offenders, abolishment of early parole, and abolishment of the insanity defense would be topics for reform.

PHOTOS

Crime Scene looking to the north showing Shawn Moore's ten-speed bicycle lying on the west side of Whitmore Lake Road. Tire tracks from Ron Bailey's Jeep are visible alongside the roadway too. (Courtesy Livingston County Prosecutor's Office)

Crime Scene showing the A&W Root Beer Shawn Moore had just purchased before he was abducted. (Courtesy Livingston County Prosecutor's Office)

Crime Scene looking south along the west shoulder of Whitmore Lake Road showing Shawn's bicycle. (Courtesy Livingston County Prosecutor's Office)

Shawn Moore. (Courtesy Livingston County Prosecutor's Office)

Ron Bailey's 1985 Jeep Renegade.
(Courtesy Michigan State Police)

WANTED

SUSPECT VEHICLE

The suspect vehicle is a light colored Jeep—possibly white. It has either "RENEGADE" or "CHEROKEE" printed on the sides of the hood. The words appear to be a medium burgundy color. The interior contains high back bucket seats. The Jeep is believed to be a hard top, but a canvas top can not be eliminated.

SUSPECT

At approximately 3:45 p.m. Saturday, August 31, 1985, SHAWN MOORE was abducted while bicycling on Whitmore Lake Road 1/4 mile South of Lee Road, Green Oak Twp., Livingston County.

SHAWN is 13 years old, 4 ft. 10 inches, 85 lbs., blond hair and hazel eyes. He was last seen wearing a tan T-shirt, gray jogging shorts and blue tennis shoes.

It is believed that SHAWN was taken by a white male 24-25 years old, 5 ft. 8 inches to 5 ft. 9 inches, 180 lbs., described as "chubby"; light brown – straight hair, med. in length – just over the ear.

SHAWN MOORE

Any person with any information please call

313-227-1051

Any person wishing to make an annonymous call can
telephone the Silent Observer Hot Line at
313-227-1414

Wanted Poster with composite description of Shawn
Moore's abductor, a similar Jeep, and a photo of
Shawn Moore. (Courtesy Michigan State Police)

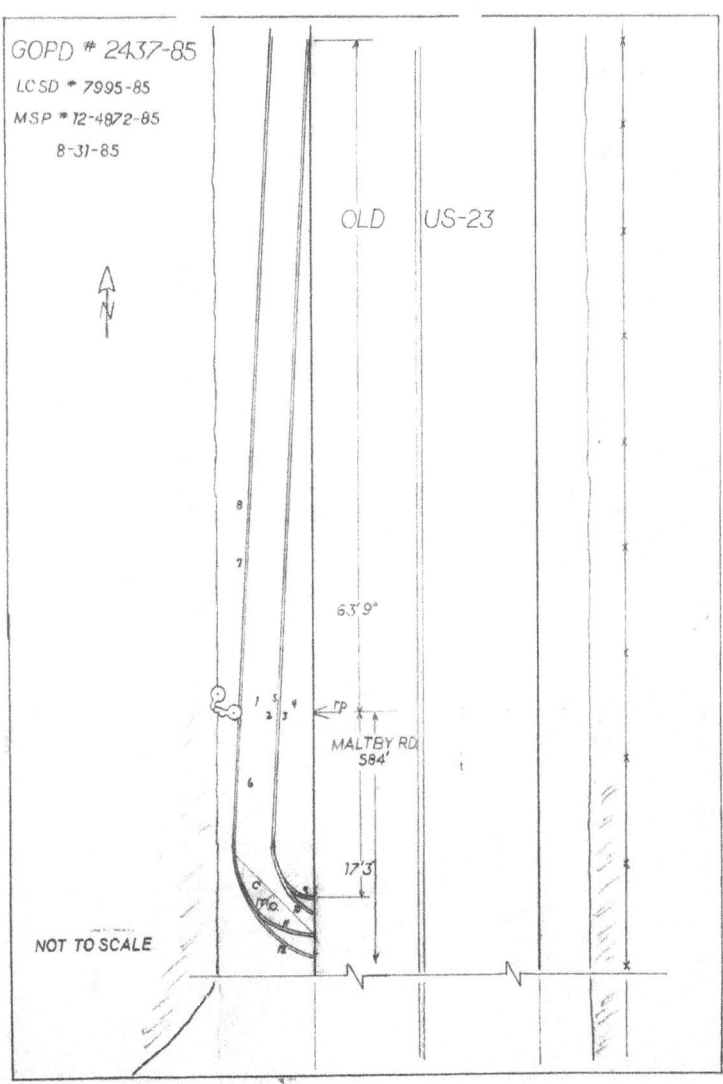

Crime Scene diagram prepared by police showing the location of Shawn's abduction. (Courtesy David Ostrem)

Ron Bailey's Buick Station Wagon that he used to abduct Kenny Myers in 1984. (Courtesy Cory Williams)

Rear view of Ron Bailey's Station Wagon that he used to abduct Kenny Myers in 1984. (Courtesy Cory Williams)

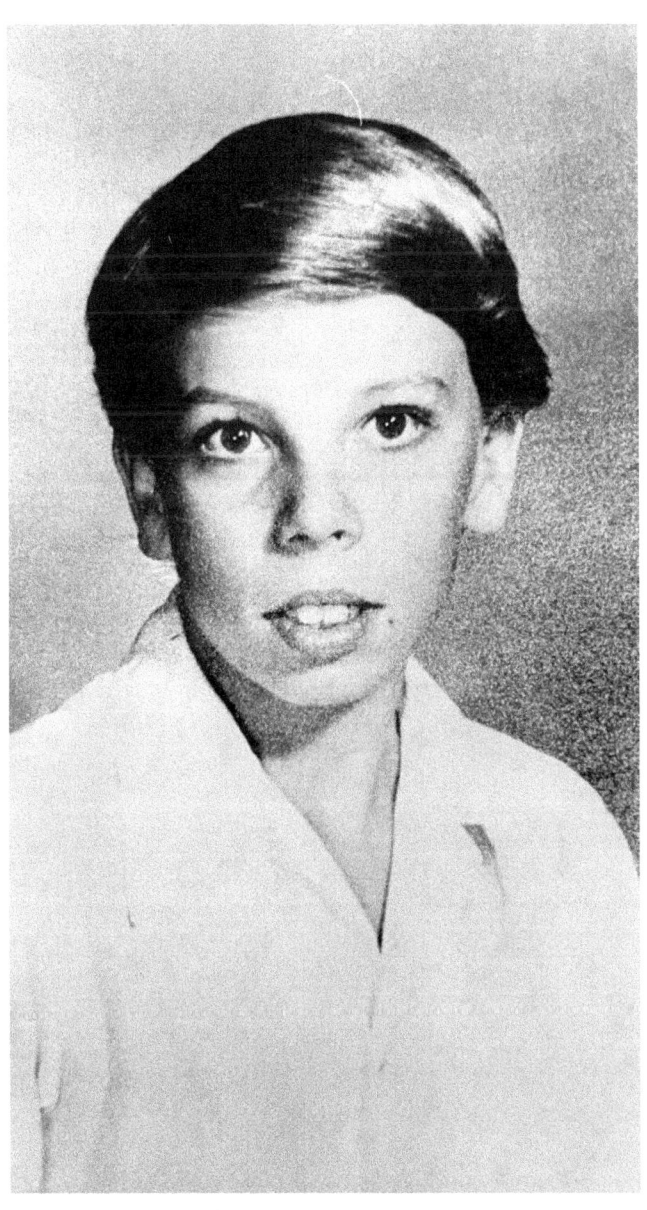

*Kenny Myers. (Courtesy Livingston
County Prosecutor's Office)*

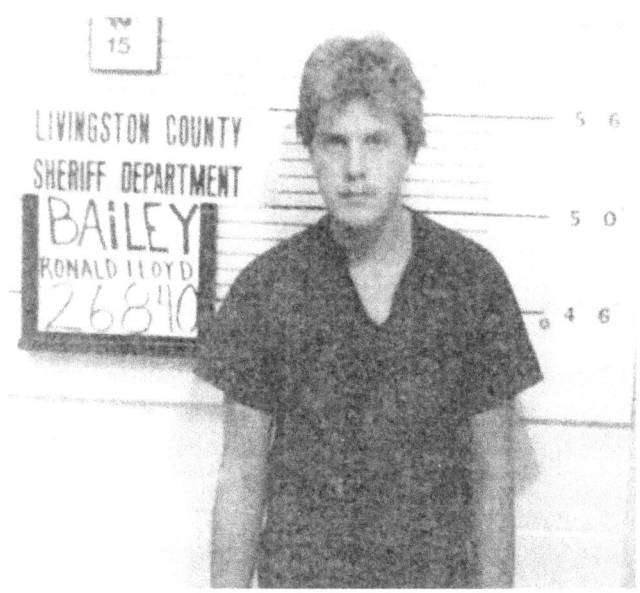

*Ronald Lloyd Bailey's mugshot from the
Livingston County Sheriff's Department. (Courtesy
Livingston County Prosecutor's Office)*

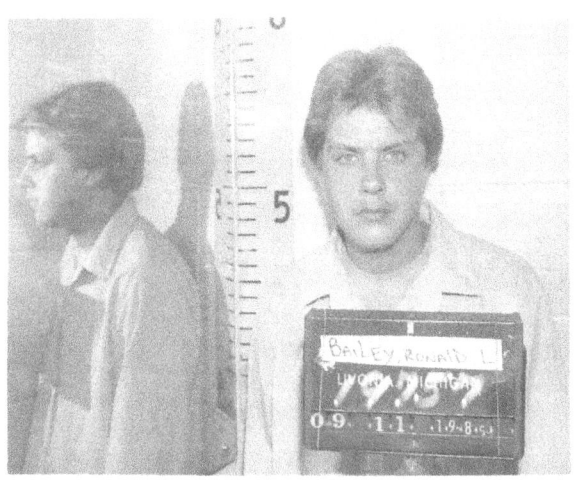

*Ronald Lloyd Bailey's mugshot from the Livonia
Police Department. (Courtesy Cory Williams)*

*The Chesney cabin along Ridge Road in Gladwin
County. (Courtesy Michigan State Police)*

*Close-up of the Chesney cabin in Gladwin
County. (Courtesy Michigan State Police)*

Interior view of Chesney cabin from front door. Bunk beds visible in photo. (Courtesy Michigan State Police)

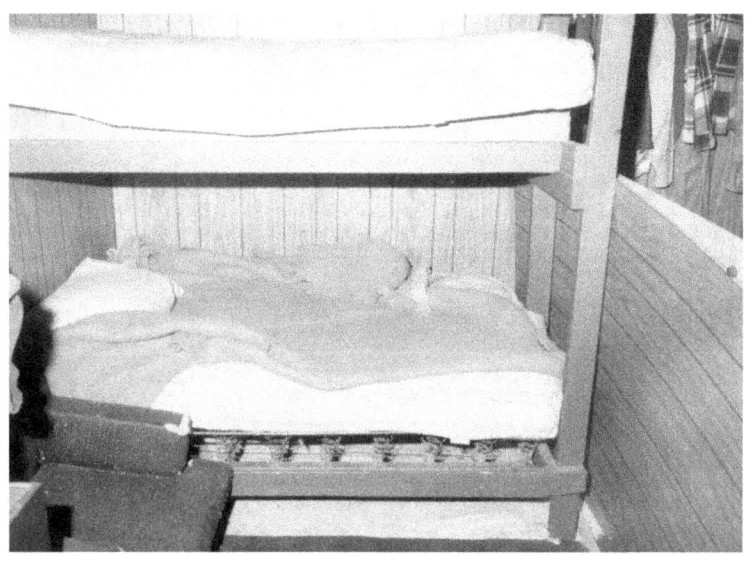

Bunk bed where Shawn Moore was murdered. (Courtesy Michigan State Police)

Wooded area where Shawn Moore's body was found. (Courtesy Michigan State Police)

13
How Safe Are the Children?

Ray Cassar was concerned, and so was his co-counsel. There was intense media pressure, and he was having doubts about whether or not he could handle the case. Everyone hated his client, and every time he turned on the television, Ron Bailey's picture and a story about the case was still there. Not only was his client charged with snatching a young teen off a bike and murdering him, but police began to suspect that Bailey could be involved in another kidnapping and murder of a teen from Ferndale.

Although Cassar and Bailey trusted one another, the attorney was concerned about other kids who might have had some contact with Bailey because the police were investigating some cases in Florida, but Bailey told him there weren't any.

Even with his client's assurance that there were no other victims, the media began reporting that Ron Bailey was tied to two more cases where teen boys had survived the sexual assaults. In one of the cases, a teen identified Bailey as the man who had tried to coax him out of a mall just thirty minutes or so before Shawn Moore was abducted. The second case involved a teen who was abducted in 1984 and taken to Hines Park just one month before Kenny Myers's murder.

Ray Cassar's concern was deepening.

Murphy and Cassar had already started building their defense. After Bailey's guilty plea to sexual assault in 1976, his treatment at the Hawthorn Center by Dr. Tombo would be a key part of their strategy.

Ten days after Bailey's capture, two reporters from the *Ann Arbor News*, Stephen Cain and Tina Lam, met with Cassar and Murphy at their office in Farmington Hills. Bailey's attorneys described the accusations their client was making against his former doctor at Northville. It was everyone's understanding that the interview was on the record but at the halfway point, Chuck Murphy said he wanted the interview to be kept off the record. Cain raised his voice at their suggestion and told both of them that it was too late for them to change their mind mid-interview; he was going to print the story anyway.

Chuck Murphy realized he had made a huge mistake.

Cain and Lam's intention was to quote Cassar and Murphy in their story about Bailey's accusations against Tombo. They dug deeper. In a request filed under Michigan's Freedom of Information Act, they received a report from MSP regarding an investigation conducted five years earlier. The investigation was based on accusations made by former patients and hospital staff from the Northville Psychiatric Hospital accusing Dr. Tombo of having sexual relations with patients.

In 1980, Tombo was accused by six former patients of having homosexual relationships with them, some dating back to as early as 1974, and those allegations were investigated by MSP. The thirty-page police report read that there had been two sex acts between Dr. Tombo and a patient at his outpatient clinic and one at Tombo's home. Charges were sought against Tombo for criminal sexual conduct in Wayne County at the time the report was completed, but the patient was an adult and there was suspicion he might have consented to the sexual acts. Dr. Tombo denied the allegations in an interview during the investigation and only admitted to lending that patient $900 to repair his car, lending his own car to the patient, and providing that patient with rides. As a result of MSP's investigation, Tombo was suspended for six days by the hospital for unauthorized financial transactions with a patient and using his position to force the patient to comply with deeds for his own benefit.

The journalists from the *Ann Arbor News* were able to track down one of the former patients, who seemed to verify the 1980 investigation into Dr. Tombo's behavior. He told Cain and Lam, "I wanted it to stop. I knew it was wrong."[97] The two reporters interviewed his family to confirm his story and were told that Tombo had showered the family with Christmas gifts that year.

With the new allegations by Ronald Bailey five years later, the Department of Public Health chose to have an independent investigation. After the accusations were made against Tombo in 1980 and the MSP investigation was complete, the hospital was provided with the report, but the Michigan Department of Public Health never saw it. Now they were seeking legal advice regarding the possibility of disciplining Dr. Tombo, and the director ordered a review of why State mental health officials hadn't requested the results of the MSP investigation in 1980. Department of Mental Health Director C. Patrick Babcock only requested a copy of the MSP report after the *Ann Arbor News* ran the story on October 6. The Department of Mental Health was going to follow up on the original investigation, and their biggest concern was the timeliness of it.

Cain and Lam dug even deeper and learned that one year before the MSP investigation in 1980, there was an ethics investigation done by the Michigan Psychiatric Society after a patient told a Dearborn doctor, Dr. George Newman, about Tombo having had oral sex with him on several occasions. When Tombo resigned from the Society

97. Cain, Stephen, *Relentless,* self-published, 2024

amid the allegations, the ethics investigation was dropped. Newman was interviewed by Cain and Lam, and he told them he didn't make a complaint to Northville about it. The patient's family hadn't asked him to, and he decided not to do it on his own because of doctor-patient confidentiality. On October 9, 1985, Dr. Tombo was suspended from Northville Regional Psychiatric Hospital pending the reopening of the original investigation and an investigation by the Michigan Attorney General's Office.

Ron Bailey's dad was bewildered. When he spoke of Dr. Tombo's sexual conduct, he said, "I don't know if this affected him or not." He continued, "You put your trust in a doctor, and you put your faith in their abilities, and we put the same trust and everything in the doctors at Northville, and ten years later to find these things out just scares me."[98]

Bailey, who had been ordered to have a psychiatric evaluation when he was arraigned, was still at the Livingston County Jail. Frank Del Vero knew it could take up to forty-five days for the evaluation to take place.

Murphy and Cassar were convinced that Dr. Tombo, whom they desperately needed to testify at Bailey's trial, was going to flee the country because of the media attention now being brought by the case. The two attorneys filed a motion in Livingston County District Court to have the doctor declared a material witness in the Ronald Bailey case and be required to post a bond to ensure his testimony during Bailey's trial. In the motion, they wrote that Tombo's treatment of Ronald Bailey was cause to have him declared as a material witness, and because he was from the Philippines and still held a valid passport, he might flee, not to mention his suspension from Northville and the accusations against him by their client. "It is crucial to the defense that this doctor remain available for testimony," the

---

98. Kresnak, Jack, "Bailey's Ex-psychiatrist is Suspended," *Detroit Free Press*, October 10, 1985

document read.[99] Judge Michael Merritt signed the motion ordering Dr. Tombo to appear in court for a hearing about the request. He would be required to produce evidence of why the motion put forth by Cassar and Murphy should be denied.

—

From the Brighton community and beyond, many believed that when Shawn Moore was kidnapped and murdered, Brighton lost its innocence. Each time a story aired in the media about Ron Bailey, there were more and more questions from the community, and they wanted answers.

With an onslaught of suggestions on how to keep the children safe, some were asking how much time would elapse before they wouldn't have to be concerned anymore. Was it three months? Five months? Three years? The fear felt within the community and beyond was still there even a month and a half after the kidnapping. Kids were afraid to be left home alone. Many were having nightmares, wondering how they would ever be able to protect themselves from being abducted and dying a horrible death. Parents who never believed it could happen in their own community were now face to face with the reality that it did, and they asked themselves if it could happen to their child. Knowing that Shawn wasn't seduced but instead, grabbed off his bike, made it that much more terrifying, and they were asking themselves what they could do to ensure their own children's safety.

Shawn's parents, along with several law enforcement representatives, were hoping the community forum they were sponsoring at Brighton High School might answer some of those questions and put parents' concerns at ease.

---

99. Kresnak, Jack, "Suspect's Lawyers Seek to Keep Doctor in State," *Detroit Free Press,* October 17, 1985

It was the first time Bruce Moore spoke publicly about what had happened since the murder of his son, and over 200 people were there to listen. Television station WDIV Channel 4 in Detroit aired portions of the forum, titled "How Safe Are the Children?" in a specially televised program hosted by Mort Crimm and Carmen Harlan. Channel 7 had already run a special segment called "Second Look."

Representing the Michigan State Police Child Abuse Unit, Det/Lt. Jack Shepherd introduced Officer Dave Ostrem to a round of thunderous applause. The Green Oak Township officer was dressed in his class A uniform and tie as he stood at the podium and described how the investigation into Shawn's kidnapping began and how it progressed with over 2,000 tips. "This assistance was priceless, and without it, this investigation could not have moved forward as it did."[100]

Ostrem had spent countless hours with the Moores, and he had witnessed how they were painfully affected by Shawn's murder, yet he described how, from the start, Bruce and Sharon Moore wanted to see something positive come out of the loss of their son. It was the hope of Shawn's parents that through the community forum, they might help prevent anything like that from ever happening again.

Bruce and Sharon Moore held hands in the audience as they watched Dave Ostrem speak about their son's murder. Bruce, dressed in a navy blue business suit, took a deep breath as Ostrem spoke and introduced them along with their two adult children, Scott and Kathy.

Marie Edenstrom sat in the audience. She had come to support the Moores. "I have a lot of Kennys out there. There's a lot of Shawns, and they're all going to have a better life... with our support," she said.[101]

---

100. Ostrem, David, "How Safe Are the Children?" WDIV, October 15, 1985

101. Edenstrom, Marie, "How Safe Are the Children?" WDIV, October 15, 1985

With a tight-lipped smile, Sharon joined the audience in applause as her husband took the stage to speak. "The thoughts of what our Shawn must have gone through—the terror, the fear, the hurt—at the hands of his abductor, have left deep emotional hurt and feelings that none…" he said, pausing to regain his emotions. "None of our family has ever experienced." He spoke for his entire family when he said those feelings that Shawn experienced must never happen again to another child and that child's family. In the Moore home, the prevention of future crimes like Shawn's kidnapping had become a major goal. "Children are very precious. All of us, by God, we must prevent this from ever happening again," he said. "By the grace of God and you, we'll do it."

Moore described how during the investigation, even before Shawn's body had been found, letters of support and money flooded in, and collectively, the Moores didn't know what to do with it. After much discussion, they decided to donate the money to the State of Michigan's Children's Trust Fund in a preventative effort.

Bruce and Sharon had taken a few days away to try to get their lives back in order. He wiped his hand across his forehead and his voice quivered as he spoke of their time away and how he tried to write down a few things to convey the Moore family's feelings, then realized it wouldn't work. He decided to simply talk about their feelings to the audience rather than use a prepared statement. He smiled at his wife from the podium. "You didn't know that, did ya, Mum?" She smiled back at him from the front row. Bruce admitted they hadn't held up all that well. They cried, dreamed of Shawn, felt bitterness, hatred, frustration, helplessness, and depression. He added love. "Believe it or not—love," he said. He admitted that with all of those feelings, it was confusing. "If we have stood up well, it has been partly the great love the family has for one another."

Bruce Moore spoke of the overwhelming community support the family had received over the previous six weeks when he spoke of the thousands of cards and letters, phone calls, and visits from people they didn't even know. Everyone was praying for Shawn and the Moores' piece of mind. The cards and letters were from people of all ages, including children, and were from all across the United States.

The support the Moore family received from law enforcement was also overwhelming. "Guys like Al Moffatt from the state police, Dave, the FBI; my goodness. They were the guardians keeping me out of trouble," he said, admitting that they thought he might try to do something to his son's killer. "I could have, believe me. As God stands there in front of me, I could have." The FBI had talked him out of it. He didn't say whom he talked to, but someone from the FBI had told him, "Suppose you go out and blow his brains out. What have we got?" The agent told him that once the killer was captured, the trial should be perfect, and after the conviction, question the killer to see why the killer thinks the way he does, and what makes him tick. Bruce admitted that it sounded more sensible to do things that way, and he gave up the idea of applying for a gun permit. He knew he wouldn't be able to get one anyway, and the audience smiled silently, some with tears welling in their eyes.

Shawn's dad smiled as he spoke of the love they felt at Shawn's memorial service. With over 600 people there, the Moore family stood to leave, and so did everyone else. Everyone at the service was lined up—parents, grandparents, great-grandparents, and children of all ages, each one waiting for the opportunity to hug each member of Shawn's family. Bruce Moore could only end his commentary with a thank you to everyone for all of the love and for keeping them sane. The applause and standing ovation for Shawn's dad was emotional as he left the stage.[102]

Charles Pickett, a representative of the National Center for Missing and Exploited Children, was a guest at the forum and was asked to speak. He read the letter sent to President Reagan from the kids at Scranton Middle School first, and then spoke of how awareness, instead of hysteria, was something positive to come out of Shawn's abduction. He commended Dave Ostrem for his quick actions when Shawn was abducted, and he hoped that the techniques, strategies, and level of support put forth by law enforcement in Shawn's abduction could be utilized around the country.

A missing child in Michigan was anyone sixteen years or younger, and the custodial parent didn't know the whereabouts of the child. That included runaways, custodial disputes, stranger abductions, and what MSP referred to as throwaways, or homeless youths. The definition was given by Lt. Richard Schoenberger as he spoke at the forum following Charles Pickett. He warned the audience to be cautious of statistics, knowing the only statistics that should be important to them were the statistics for their own communities. A study done by MSP in 1984 indicated there were approximately 1,000 missing children around the state, and that included the runaways, children involved with custody disputes, stranger abductions, and the homeless. Of those, eighty-five percent were runaways, fifteen percent were parental kidnappings or custody disputes, and less than one percent were stranger abductions. A study done in 1985 culminated with the same results. Schoenberger cautioned the audience to check with their local jurisdictions for the statistics in their areas about what was occurring with missing children and to look at prevention programs already in place within their communities.

---

102. Moore, Bruce, "How Safe Are the Children?" WDIV, October 15, 1985

Many in the audience believed there was a state law that required a person to wait twenty-four hours before reporting someone missing. It was a fallacy. Lt. Schoenberger assured the audience there was no state law requiring a waiting period, but there might be departmental policies in place by various police jurisdictions that required a twenty-four-hour waiting period. He suggested the group focus their goals into prevention, education, and after-the-fact, stressing the milk carton campaigns featuring missing children and billboards were considered after-the-fact from a law enforcement perspective. Having a child fingerprinted wouldn't protect a child from an abduction but would make the job easier for the police.

A parent in the audience asked if a kidnapper was successful in an abduction, should a child be taught to remain calm and do whatever was necessary to survive until they have a chance to escape? Pickett said the child should be an opportunist. As an example, if the child could jump out when the car stopped at a stop sign or get their body half out of the car when the car slowed down, the child should take every chance to escape or draw attention to themselves. He said he'd had kidnappers, after the fact, tell him that they abducted a child for no reason at all, and the child, out of fear, was completely cooperative.

There were more questions, and a woman asked what she might do if she saw something like an abduction happening. Lt. Schoenberger told her the best thing she could do was to be a good witness and observe what was going on. He used Shawn's case as an example when he said the most heartwarming thing that had come out of Shawn's abduction was the number of tips received by the police.

During the special WDIV program, a child psychologist suggested that being realistic with children was the best way to talk about strangers, telling them that most strangers were "fine, kind people" and "a few strangers were bad people." Since it was difficult to tell the good from the bad, it was best to keep away from all strangers. She added the best way to explain "stranger danger" to a child was to use a children's book. Many had stories explaining strangers, and then discussing it with them and talking about what "stranger" really meant. For older kids, discussing different scenarios that might happen in an abduction was the best way to approach it.

Afterward, Bruce and Sharon Moore sat in the studio with Mort Crimm, WDIV's news anchor. They felt hurt and helpless after Shawn's death and wanted to talk about what had happened. They also wanted to thank the public for all of the support they had received. There were days when they would get up in the morning and weren't sure how they were going to make it through the day but through the support and prayers of others. Bruce recognized that child abuse was a cycle, and people who were victims of abuse as children continued that cycle as adults by abusing other children. That was why the Children's Trust Fund was so important to them after Shawn's death.

There was no doubt that Bruce and Sharon had helped a lot of people by setting an example in how they handled Shawn's death. The people who attended the forum, and those who watched the special report from WDIV, had many of their questions answered that night and walked away knowing that communication with their children was one of the keys to keeping them safe. The Moores were a true inspiration to the entire community and beyond.

—

On the morning after the forum, Ronald Bailey was charged by the Wayne County Prosecutor's Office with the kidnapping and first-degree murder of Kenny Myers and the kidnapping and sexual assault of Mark Chadwick one month before that.

The Livonia Police were building their case against Bailey in the Chadwick abduction, and another search warrant was executed at the Bailey home for a gold, non-digital type wristwatch that the teen had described his kidnapper wearing. MSP Laboratory Scientist Charlotte Day had already analyzed the semen stains left on Chadwick's shorts. They were compared to known blood and hair samples from both the teen and his kidnapper. Her lab report read:

Ronald Bailey was not eliminated and is included as a possible contributor of semen identified on the jockey shorts. Mark Chadwick was eliminated as a contributor of the semen.[103]

The following day, Bailey was arraigned in Livonia and Westland while he stood quietly with his dad on one side of him and both Cassar and Murphy, his attorneys in the Moore case, on his other side. Livonia District Judge Brzezinski ordered that he be evaluated for competency at the Forensic Center, and Cassar and Murphy asked that Wayne County's Chief Circuit Court Judge Richard Dunn appoint them as counsel for Bailey in the new Livonia case because he had signed an affidavit stating he had no money to pay for an attorney.

—

Dr. Tombo was fighting back against his suspension from Northville Hospital. He filed three grievances with the hospital, and he said his suspension from Northville was due to "politically motivated pressure" created from the onslaught of media coverage.

---

103. Day, Charlotte, *Laboratory Report*, 12080-84, Michigan State Police, October 15, 1985

In the grievances, he claimed that his due process rights were violated by the Michigan Department of Public Health when he was suspended on October 9. He also wrote that the Department improperly released information in his personnel file without his permission, and his contract required the suspensions be superseded by disciplinary suspension, dismissal, or reinstatement within seven calendar days unless it was extended by the appointing authority.

Dr. Tombo's attorney, Paul Stevenson, claimed his client hadn't even been given a reason for the suspension.

—

Eight days after Bailey's arraignments in Livonia and Westland on the new charges, Frank Del Vero and David Morse had the three-page report they had been waiting for in hand. It was Ron Bailey's competency evaluation from the Forensic Center. The report stated quite clearly that Bailey was competent to stand trial. Morse spoke with the media and said, "Without going into the report, let me make one thing very clear: Ronald Bailey is quite competent to stand trial."[104]

In the report, Dr. Harley Stock and Dr. Lynn Blunt recommended that Judge Merritt find Bailey competent to stand trial. Bailey knew what he was doing at the time.

Cassar and Murphy had the report too, and they asked for an extension on the competency hearing in Livingston County until they could have an independent psychiatric evaluation done on their client.

Their hopes of keeping tabs on Dr. Tombo so he would testify in Bailey's case were starting to fade. The only reason to have him testify was their intended use of the insanity

104. UPI, "Kidnap-Murder Suspect Deemed Competent," *Petoskey News-Review*, October 24, 1985

defense. They wanted the jury to know what Tombo had done to their client, and they believed it led to him being insane at the time of Shawn's kidnapping and murder.

Witness bonds were rare in Michigan and were typically used for a witness who had already left the state, or one who was threatened.

Paul Stevenson accused both of Bailey's attorneys of harassing the doctor and misleading the judges who had scheduled show cause hearings for Tombo to appear. Murphy had been in Florida for the week, and Stevenson accused him of breaking his word. He alleged that Cassar and Murphy hadn't waited for a deal to have Tombo agree to testify before they filed the bond motions. "[My client] is a US citizen who has lived here and served his patients well for over twenty years. He's been here since this thing started, and he intends to stand and fight," Stevenson said.[105] Murphy disagreed and said he hadn't misled anyone. He and Cassar, in order to avoid any need to testify in front of the jury, had proposed an alternative but Stevenson had ignored it. In Livingston County, Judge Merritt denied the motion, even after he had scheduled a show cause hearing to have Tombo explain why he shouldn't be considered a material witness. He said he had seen nothing that might indicate Dr. Tombo would flee the country.

Stevenson told Judge Merritt, "I really doubt, down the line, that you're going to see the defense call Dr. Tombo. I think this is a smokescreen to divert the public's attention." He continued, "The defense's real fear in this case, Your Honor, is not that [Tombo] might leave, but what he might testify to." Tombo hadn't been charged with any crime, and Stevenson knew it. There was a presumption of innocence on the part of Tombo, but Stevenson felt that Cassar and Murphy wanted it both ways. "They want the full benefit of

105. Kresnak, Jack, "Psychiatrist Harassed, His Lawyers Say in Bailey Case," *Detroit Free Press*, October 16, 1985

the Bill of Rights for their client but would roll it up and use it as a torch to burn Joe Tombo at the stake."

Murphy and Cassar had filed papers with the Court stating that as Bailey's treating psychiatrist for three years (1976-1978), several irregularities regarding the treatment of their client had occurred. According to the two attorneys, it included sexual misconduct on Tombo's part. They added, "These acts are clearly outside the scope of professional conduct and involve an illicit, homosexual relationship." It was their opinion that the sexual relationship between the two men had an impact on Bailey's state of mind.[106]

Dr. Tombo sat quietly at the hearing and said nothing as Stevenson argued against the motion. Afterward, Tombo didn't speak to the media, but his attorney did. Stevenson said it was a clear win for his client.

In the aftermath, judges in Livonia and Westland followed suit. They denied the motion put forth by Bailey's attorneys. There wouldn't be a bond placed on Tombo, and he didn't have to surrender his passport. To Ray Cassar, it was a travesty of justice. His sole intention was to put Tombo on the stand and let the jury hear it for themselves. He wouldn't argue that Bailey didn't kidnap and kill Shawn. He would argue that Bailey was insane, explain why he was insane and why he did what he did. He and Murphy knew it wouldn't excuse the crime, but it would be enough for the jury to say that Ron Bailey was mentally ill. He was hoping for a verdict of guilty but mentally ill, or not guilty by reason of insanity. Cassar was certain that all of the abuse suffered by Ron Bailey at the hands of Dr. Jose Tombo, both as a teen and then as a young adult, put him in an altered state and made him the person he had become.

Cassar and Murphy still hadn't filed any notice with the courts of the insanity defense, and now that the competency

---

106. Schabath, Gene and Martindale, Mike, "Dr. Tombo Plans to Fight Accusers in Bailey Case," *Detroit News,* October 27, 1985

report from the Forensic Center was complete, Bailey's competency hearing was re-scheduled for mid-November. Livingston County's Judge Merritt would decide if Bailey was competent to stand trial. Cassar and Murphy planned to counter the competency claim from the State with their own report from an independent psychiatrist. David Morse, Livingston County's chief assistant prosecutor, objected to the delay for the competency hearing. He maintained that it should have already been done, but Judge Merritt overruled his objection and gave the defense some extra time for the independent evaluation. Murphy and Cassar argued that the large amount of publicity in the case had hampered their efforts to get their independent examination done.

14
The Exams

It was an uphill battle, and Ray Cassar and Chuck Murphy knew it. David Morse, Livingston County's Chief Assistant Prosecutor, knew the competency hearing was simply a formality, and he knew that Bailey still had to undergo two additional competency evaluations for the kidnapping and sexual assault in Livonia, as well as for the kidnapping and murder of Kenny Myers. He didn't believe the results of the other two tests would have any bearing on the Shawn Moore case. The evaluation would go toward determining if Bailey could understand the nature of the crime and whether he was mentally competent to assist his attorneys. The report said he was able to do both.

—

Oh, my God, Cassar thought to himself. The competency hearing was almost ready to start, and Dr. Harley Stock walked by him in the corridor, stopping just briefly.

"Did Bailey tell you what he did to those puppies?" Stock asked Ray Cassar.

The young defense attorney was puzzled. "Puppies? What are you talking about?"

Stock said, "So he didn't tell you what he did to those puppies?"

"No."

"You know he ground those puppies up in a garbage disposal."

Whenever Dr. Stock interviewed serial criminals, he always asked questions pertaining to what was known as the MacDonald Triad, or the triad of sociopathy. Three factors were considered to be predictive of violent tendencies and serial offenses. It was first introduced in 1963 by a psychiatrist named J. M. MacDonald in the *American Journal of Psychiatry*. Late studies by two other psychiatrists and FBI agents John Douglas and Robert Ressler, along with Ann Burgess, claimed there was substantiating evidence to associate the childhood patterns with later predatory behavior. It linked animal cruelty, obsession with setting fires, and persistent bedwetting past the age of five to violent behaviors, particularly homicidal and sexually predatory behavior.

Ray Cassar couldn't believe what he had just heard. "What?" he said, almost in a whisper.

"Yeah. That's how sick he is," Stock said.

For just a moment, Cassar wasn't sure what he should do. The hearing was almost ready to start. He knew he had to talk to his client. Back in the solitary cell at the courthouse where Bailey was being held before the hearing started, Ray Cassar said, "Look. We've got this hearing in five minutes. What about these puppies?" He explained what Dr. Stock had just said to him.

"What?" Bailey said. "That's not true. Why would I lie to you? I never told him I ground up puppies in the garbage disposal." Bailey seemed sincere, and Cassar had no choice but to trust him. "He's lying," Bailey said.[107]

---

107. Cassar, Raymond, Interview with author, February 27, 2024

Cassar left his client in the cell and cornered Bailey's dad. Their conversation was short. Cassar simply asked him if the family had ever had puppies. According to Alfred Bailey, they hadn't.

Dr. Harley Stock had a reputation as one of the top board-certified psychologists in the state. He was on the staff at the Center for Forensic Psychiatry in Ypsilanti and was the Deputy Director of Outpatient Evaluation. His specialty at the Forensic Center was murder and sex crimes, but he mostly saw murderers. He worked in conjunction with Dr. Lynn Blunt, a psychiatrist, and the two worked well together. Dr. Stock enjoyed the types of cases that were difficult diagnostically. They were a challenge. Over his tenure at the Center for Forensic Psychiatry, he saw as many as 3,000 cases and, in the mid to late seventies, had served on the task force in search of the Oakland County Child Killer.

Stock knew from his experience that it was extraordinarily rare for someone to be insane. Primarily, two things were evaluated at the Center: The first was a person's competency to proceed to trial. There were around ten percent who were found incompetent to proceed to trial. It was a pretty low threshold. There was an incredibly small number of people who were recommended to be found not guilty by reason of insanity, and that was one-tenth of one percent. Stock got paid the same regardless of his opinion. That didn't necessarily hold true for private consultants who had their own agendas.

Stock didn't spread innuendos about the patients he had evaluated, but after the exchange with Ray Cassar, Cassar believed he was simply trying to rattle him before the hearing.

Security was tight during the hearing. Scott Moore sat quietly in the courtroom taking his own notes. In the competency report authored by Dr. Stock, he wrote, "Bailey has angry thoughts toward Northville Regional Psychiatric

Hospital regarding previous treatment there." He also wrote that Bailey understood the nature of the proceedings and was able to assist in his own defense. Bailey had been interviewed for six and a half hours and, according to the report, he was "well groomed," though he had been biting his fingernails. There were times when he would cry, but at other times he would smile at appropriate things. Bailey described his mood to the doctors when he said, "I have my up days and my down days." He would read the Bible on his down days but would also watch some television.

The subject of suicidal thoughts came up, and while he had thought about it, he read the Bible, or he would talk himself out of it. Bailey described himself by saying, "I'm basically good. I don't put people down for whatever they are. I help a few people out."

At the end of the report, Dr. Stock wrote that in his opinion, and that of Dr. Blunt, Ron Bailey didn't suffer from any major mood disorder such as major depression, though he did exhibit mixed personality disorder, with antisocial narcissistic and borderline features.[108]

Chuck Murphy had suggested that the State's psychiatrists ask Bailey about his interactions with Dr. Tombo, but they didn't.

Cassar and Murphy were still trying to delay the impending preliminary exam and argued that just one interview, either by the State's psychiatrist or their own, wasn't enough to determine if their client was competent to stand trial. They hadn't presented any reports from their own psychiatrist and said the doctor they had retained to evaluate their client told them it would take several interviews to determine Bailey's competency, not just one, because Bailey had a complex personality. The judge disagreed. At the end of the hearing, relying on the testimony from

---

108. Kresnak, Jack, "Bailey Ruled Fit to Stand Trial in Slaying of Teen," *Detroit Free Press*, November 13, 1985

Dr. Harley Stock, Judge Merritt found that Ronald Bailey was competent to stand trial for the kidnapping and murder of Shawn Moore. He set the date for Bailey's preliminary examination on December 10 and 11.

After the hearing, Cassar and Murphy allowed two MSP detectives to interview Bailey about his allegations against Dr. Tombo.

—

Both of Ron Bailey's attorneys knew the only way to get Tombo into court now was to subpoena him, but that was a problem. No one knew where Tombo was. He had vanished after the motions to have him post a bond and have his passport confiscated were dismissed, and Cassar was certain they would never see Dr. Jose Tombo again. It was starting to look like he was right. Ray Cassar was going to do everything he could to find Tombo and have him served with a subpoena because he knew his client wasn't simply a predator going around abducting kids, but a man with a legitimate problem.

—

Frank Del Vero knew that the case against Bailey, at least in Livingston County, was largely based on circumstantial evidence. There was no denying it. There was no physical evidence in the case. He knew that if there was some way they could tie Shawn to the cabin in Gladwin, they would have the one piece of evidence they needed. MSP hadn't found any trace evidence in Bailey's Jeep or in his old Buick station wagon they had seized.

In late November, Del Vero got what he was hoping for. A fingerprint expert with MSP positively matched a partial palm print found on the stove inside the Gladwin cabin with Shawn Moore. *We got him,* Frank said to himself.[109]

When the media heard the news, they spoke with Det/Sgt. Beaupre, who said, "This is the first real piece of evidence that we've obtained that we can say Shawn Moore was in the cabin."[110]

Fingerprint experts generally agreed that seven points of identification in a fingerprint were needed to make a positive identification, but sometimes fewer points were accepted by the courts. Del Vero told the media he couldn't confirm or deny the report from the state police. He couldn't make any comments about it because the canons of legal ethics prevented him from talking about it.

Bailey's preliminary exam for kidnapping the Redford Township teen a month before he kidnapped and murdered Kenny Myers was fast approaching. On November 22, he appeared in front of Judge Brzezinski in Livonia. Brzezinski closed the courtroom to both the media and spectators. In their attempt to be allowed in the courtroom, the media pleaded their case, saying they should be allowed in since the identity of the victim and the details of the crime were already known. An attorney for WXYZ and the *Detroit Free Press* asked why the Court would suppress information in the public domain. He told Brzezinski it was a "futile act" because the teen would end up having to testify in circuit court anyway when the case went to trial.

The teen was very uncomfortable at the idea of repeating what had happened to him in court, and his own attorney told Brzezinski that because of the chaos in the boy's life since the kidnapping, he was asking that the judge close the courtroom for the boy's protection and support.

---

109. Del Vero, Frank, Interview with author, April 2, 2024

110. AP, "Palm Print Puts Victim at Cabin," *Petoskey News*, November 21, 1985

Both Wayne County Assistant Prosecutor Tim Kenny and Bailey's attorneys supported the request from the teen's attorney, and Judge Robert Brzezinski stood firm. He barred the press and spectators from the courtroom. By the end of the day, after hearing the testimony from the victim, he ordered Ron Bailey to stand trial in the kidnapping and sexual assault of the teen.

—

December was fast approaching, and Ron Bailey's preliminary examination for the murder of Kenny Myers was set to begin in Wayne County one week before his second preliminary exam for the murder of Shawn Moore in Livingston County.

—

Timothy Kenny had grown up in New Jersey's Bergen County about ten miles west of the George Washington Bridge, and he was one of Wayne County's best assistant prosecuting attorneys. He received his undergraduate degree from the University of Michigan as a psychology major and, after graduation, he began to wonder what he was going to do with it. Not quite convinced that he wanted to get his Ph.D., he knew other psychology majors who had taken the LSAT, so he decided to take it and see if he passed. He did, and he attended the University of Minnesota Law School. He knew they had excellent clinical programs there, yet he still didn't know what he wanted to do.

Early in the spring of his second year in law school, he received a newspaper clipping from his dad advertising for interns at the Wayne County Prosecutor's Office. His dad thought he might be interested. Tim Kenny had no idea what prosecutors even did, but he went ahead and applied for the internship anyway. It didn't take long for him to discover that prosecutors were the voice and champion for victims, and he learned that his role in the criminal justice system was much more impactful on a victim's quality of life. It was much more rewarding to him than working as a defense attorney.

After his internship, he stayed in touch with his co-workers at Wayne County, and at the right time, they invited him back as an assistant prosecutor. He gladly accepted.

For his first two years at Wayne County, he worked as a courtroom prosecutor. During that time, Wayne County was forming a career criminal prosecution team that would focus on repeat offenders who were responsible for a disproportionate amount of crime in Wayne County. They were tasked with identifying cases involving career criminals and violent crimes.

Tim Kenny was the youngest in the group of assistant prosecutors, and he liked what he had been doing. While he was working on the career criminal prosecution team, a position on Detroit Police Department's Squad Seven opened up, and he took it. To the young prosecutor, it was a little overwhelming at first because he had only tried a couple homicides, but he knew he would gain valuable experience with Squad Seven. He was the team's legal advisor, and in that position, he had the authority to grant immunity if he felt it would be of some benefit. As an assistant prosecutor, Tim Kenny knew the delicate balance between his job and that of law enforcement. He analogized it as the relationship between a parent and a teenage child. Like a parent, he had to maintain a good working relationship with law enforcement. He had to get along with them, but he also had to be the one to say, "No. We're not doing that."[111]

With the number of homicides in Detroit, it was tough work because Squad Seven only dealt with felony murder

111. Kenny, Timothy, Interview with author, May 23, 2024

and high-profile cases. Kenny also discovered that the position with Squad Seven helped him learn how to deal with the media. When Wayne County's chief trial lawyer moved into an administrative position, Tim Kenny gladly took that position.

Tim Kenny had been following the Shawn Moore kidnapping and murder, and as law enforcement began to connect Bailey with the Kenny Myers murder, he met with MSP to review the investigation. There was a legitimate concern between Livingston County and Wayne County. Neither wanted to do anything that might jeopardize the other case.

—

Wayne County's district court was packed with spectators at Ron Bailey's preliminary examination, and Frank Del Vero was one of them. Like a good football coach, he had come to scout the opposition and see what he would be up against in the upcoming exam for Shawn's murder. He already knew Tim Kenny. He had been to a school sponsored by the Prosecuting Attorneys Association of Michigan for trial lawyers, and Kenny was the instructor. He knew that the Wayne County assistant prosecutor was experienced and accomplished in the courtroom.

It was early December 1985. There was extra security everywhere, and it was the first time that Tim Kenny had met with Ray Cassar and Chuck Murphy. To Kenny, Chuck Murphy was trying to convey a persona that he was a very experienced attorney and knew the score. Tim Kenny quietly thought to himself, *Hey, this isn't my first rodeo either.*

In Wayne County, Westland District Judge Gail McKnight presided over the exam. She had been a colleague of Kenny's at the prosecutor's office before being elected as a district judge.

Ron Bailey was brought in wearing an orange jumpsuit and took a seat at the defendant's table. As Bailey sat quietly, Murphy said to Tim Kenny, "Why is it that Bailey is in here and in a bright orange jumpsuit?" Kenny looked at Bailey and came to the realization that there were some people in society whom someone might see and immediately become suspicious of. With Bailey, there was nothing that leaped out to give that sense of "creep factor." Ron Bailey could be walking through the mall, and there wouldn't be anything about him to make someone suspect him as a pedophile and child killer.

He looked at Murphy and without hesitating, said, "If he runs, they want to know which guy to go after."[112]

The courtroom was packed, and Murphy took a seat next to his client while Ray Cassar sat on the other side of Bailey. There were so many people that Cassar wondered if they were handing out spectator passes. He knew it didn't look good for his client, and although he respected Judge McKnight, he felt really uncomfortable in the courtroom. He glanced over his shoulder at the crowd and saw a man sitting in back of the jammed courtroom making gang signs and pointing at him. Cassar was certain the gang sign symbolized the devil.

What the fuck is this? he thought to himself.

He nudged his co-counsel. "Chuck, what the hell is this guy doing?" he asked Murphy. Ray Cassar was already on edge because of the media in the courtroom. He thought, *I don't need this shit.* Just before the preliminary exam started, he turned toward the back of the courtroom, and when he was certain the man in the back was looking at him, he made his own hand signal directed at the spectator. Deciding that a little discretion was in order because of the crowd, he chose not to extend his middle finger but instead

---

112. Kenny, Timothy, Interview with author, May 23, 2024

made a hand gesture to signify, "In one ear and out the other." He wasn't about to be intimidated by a spectator.[113]

As the hearing began, an unidentified woman in the back of the courtroom suddenly stood up and yelled something, but Kenny couldn't tell what she had said as she was escorted out by security. He thought of Cassar and Murphy and what they were up against. Not only was this a high-profile case, but the crowd hated their client.

When witness testimony began, the courtroom was completely silent, and some said a pin could have been heard if it were dropped.

Tim Kenny wove together key details about the kidnapping and murder of Kenny Myers he hoped would tie Ron Bailey to the crime. His key pieces of evidence were the teen's blue football jersey, his Byron wristwatch, Bailey's 1970 Buick station wagon, and the Kenny Myers autopsy report.

Three residents of the Holliday Park Cooperative townhouses testified that they had seen Kenny Myers's royal blue football jersey with the number "66" behind the townhouses between Wayne Road and Hines Park in Westland in July 1984.

An emotional Marie Edenstrom testified about Kenny and the night he disappeared as she held two framed pictures of her son. "Kenneth was my only son," she said from the witness stand.

The assistant prosecutor showed her a photo.

"That's Kenny." Mrs. Edenstrom's testimony was hard to listen to. When Tim Kenny handed her son's football jersey to her, she fought back tears. "That was Kenny's shirt."

Judge McKnight handed her a tissue.

"I'm okay," she said.

---

113. Cassar, Raymond, Interview with author, February 27, 2024

Dolly May Banks was a key witness too, because she had witnessed Kenny Myers's abduction. She described the station wagon she had seen and how Kenny had been riding his bike when the driver pulled over and backed into a driveway near him. Mrs. Banks became confused when she was asked what time it had happened. There was no doubt in anyone's mind that Kenny had left the house in the evening and never returned, but Mrs. Banks thought that she had witnessed the kidnapping at 2:00 p.m. She said she thought it was the boy's father at first, but after the bike was left behind, she realized it was something more than that.

Chuck Murphy watched closely as Mrs. Banks testified. He picked up on her confusion over the time of the kidnapping, and he was sure he could cross-examine her and confuse her even more. He leaned over to Ray Cassar and said, "Let me take her."

Cassar agreed.

Murphy was doing an admirable job as he shot question after question at Mrs. Banks. "You wear glasses, don't you? You really don't know what time it was, do you? You're making things up, aren't you?" Mrs. Banks was becoming frustrated, and Ray Cassar thought his partner was doing a pretty good job during her cross-examination.

Chuck Murphy finished his cross-examination and turned around to face the gallery in the courtroom, his co-counsel, his client, and the press. There was complete silence. Murphy was thinking, *I got her, didn't I?* as he looked at Ray Cassar for approval. Nothing. There was a split second of complete quiet, and the spectators in the gallery erupted in laughter. Murphy was puzzled, but Cassar wasn't and neither were the spectators. Ray Cassar saw everything everyone else was seeing. The zipper on Chuck Murphy's pants was wide open. It took another split second for Murphy to realize the laughter was directed at him and for both attorneys to realize that they had just lost all credibility.

Tim Kenny still had to link Bailey to Hines Park, where the teen's body was found. That testimony came from the sixteen-year-old girl, Jennifer DeChane, who had seen a man behind the apartment complex in Westland. It was the man who had asked for directions to Ann Arbor Trail on the night Kenny Myers disappeared. She pointed to Ron Bailey in the courtroom and identified him as the person she had seen. Her friend, sixteen-year-old Steve Parzuchowski, also identified Ron Bailey as the man they had seen on the night that Kenny disappeared. Gerrilynn Higgins, a fourteen-year-old who was with DeChane and Parzuchowski, also described a man asking for directions, but she wasn't asked to identify Bailey.

Two key elements in Kenny Myers's autopsy were at the forefront of Wayne County's deputy chief medical examiner's testimony at the preliminary exam. Dr. Harish Mirchandani testified that Kenny Myers had drunk two or three ounces of liquor, or he had two to three beers within an hour of his death. That analysis was based on the teen's size of being five feet tall, weighing just ninety-five pounds, and the amount of alcohol detected in his system. The alcohol level in the boy's blood was .09 percent while the level determined in a urine analysis was .08 percent. There was no significant difference between the two. He had become intoxicated within an hour before his death.

The teen had died within three hours of eating his last meal. Mirchandani also said that Kenny Myers was strangled on two separate occasions over a matter of a few minutes. There were two separate sets of marks on the teen's neck, and Kenny's cause of death was ligature strangulation. The parallel red lines were 1-3/8 inches apart and stretched across the boy's throat. One of those marks was consistent with a belt buckle. There was also evidence of internal hemorrhaging in the soft tissue of the throat.

"At some point, pressure was released and applied again," Mirchandani said. "With that kind of pressure, it would be a matter of minutes before a person became unconscious and a matter of death in five to eight minutes." He had discovered petechial hemorrhaging in Kenny's eyelids— pinpoint bleeding caused by a significant obstruction of the blood supply to the brain in cases of strangulation.

Tim Kenny wanted to ensure that the testimony about the teen's alcohol level at his autopsy was noted because he was going to argue that during the kidnapping and sexual assault of another teen one month before Kenny Myers's kidnapping and murder, there were similar circumstances when that victim was forced to drink two beers before Ron Bailey sexually assaulted him.

Police had the watch that Ron Bailey was wearing when he was arrested by Al Moffatt in Florida after the manhunt. It was Kenny Myers's Byron digital watch with a silver band, and although Mrs. Edenstrom had given it to Kenny as gift, she couldn't positively say it was the one she had actually gifted to her son, though other witnesses were able to testify that it did belong to her son. Moffatt said that Bailey had "shown an unusual interest in knowing what happened to his silver digital watch" after his arrest.[114]

By the end of the day, Judge McKnight adjourned the rest of the preliminary examination until December 13. As Frank Del Vero left, he knew Cassar and Murphy didn't have much of a defense, and they were already exploring the possibility of an insanity defense for Bailey.

In a letter dated December 16, 1985, Dr. Thomas Kaiser, a licensed clinical psychologist with Comprehensive Psychological Services in Southfield, relayed his opinion regarding the evaluation of Ron Bailey that he had done on December 6.

Kaiser had met with Ron Bailey at the Livingston County Jail, where he administered four standard psychological

---

114. Martindale, Mike, "The People vs. Ronald Lloyd Bailey," *Detroit News*, February 16, 1986

tests to him. Those were the Wechsler Adult Intelligence Scale, the Rorschach, the Thematic Apperception Test, and the Minnesota Multiphasic Personality Inventory. The testing had lasted four and a half hours, and Bailey had been very cooperative when he took the tests.

Ron Bailey's IQ was measured at 105. Kaiser felt he was of average intelligence, and the testing didn't show any abnormal features or reveal any cognitive deficits. Bailey had a fear of closeness and intimacy rising to the level where the doctor diagnosed him as having a "schizoid personality."

Bailey had also told Dr. Kaiser that there were times when he acted without being aware of what he was doing. Kaiser didn't believe him because the testing didn't show any evidence of dissociative states. If Bailey did, in fact, do things without any awareness, Kaiser attributed it to his heavy drinking and substance abuse. In the final paragraph of his diagnosis, Kaiser wrote:

There are no findings from the interview or test results to support a tendency to dissociative states or irresistible impulses and, while he appears to have basically schizoid personality disorder compounded by homosexuality, from my assessment... I conclude that Mr. Bailey is not insane in any legal sense, nor is he psychotic in [a] purely psychological sense. Chronic drug and alcohol abuse, in my opinion, may contribute to Mr. Bailey's difficulties, but voluntary use of controlled substances does not define insanity.[115]

It wasn't the opinion that Ray Cassar and Chuck Murphy had hoped for.

—

115. Dr. Thomas W. Keiser to Mr. Charles Murphy and Mr. Ray Cassar, December 16, 1985

The old courthouse in Howell, Michigan stood at the center of the town square like a large sentinel watching over the city's business district and nineteenth-century homes. The two-and-a-half-story red brick structure, with curved arches trimmed in stone over the doors and windows, was built in 1889 and had been renovated in the mid-1970s. A clock tower sat in the middle of its multi-gabled roof.

It wasn't surprising to Ray Cassar that the district court in Livingston County was extremely small. It was almost time for Ron Bailey's preliminary exam to start, but Cassar had to use the bathroom. He walked into the tiny one-stall, one-urinal, one-sink bathroom. He was surprised when he came face to face with Shawn Moore's dad, Bruce. The twenty-five-year-old attorney froze, not knowing what to say. Mr. Moore could see it in his eyes. Cassar already felt horrible that Bruce Moore had lost his son. Cassar had nowhere to go. As he looked Bruce Moore in the eye, he softly said, "I want you to know I feel horrible about the loss of your son." He added, "I hope you can understand I'm just trying to my job."

With great compassion, Shawn Moore's dad said, "It's okay, young man. I understand."

Cassar stood there in disbelief. Here was Shawn's dad easing an extremely uncomfortable and awkward situation in a very tiny bathroom when he was dealing with his own sorrow and pain over the murder of his son. As Cassar walked out, he was suddenly at ease. He knew Bruce Moore, a man of extreme character, didn't perceive him as an evil defense attorney but simply a man trying to do his job.[116]

Judge Michael Merritt presided over Ron Bailey's preliminary exam at the Livingston County Courthouse on December 10. His first order of business was to admonish Ray Cassar and Charles Murphy for being ten minutes late. He had gotten word of their tardiness but told them when

---

116. Cassar, Raymond, Interview with author, February 27, 2024

they arrived that the court date and time had been set for a month in advance. Almost light-heartedly, he said, "I think there'll be a talk later, and maybe our health fund will be enriched." Without fining the two, he suggested they be on time next time.[117]

After the controversy with Judge Gee over the delay in signing the kidnapping warrant for Ron Bailey, Gee had disqualified himself from any further involvement in the case but didn't offer an explanation. To many, it was obvious. In a request form he filled out, he simply wrote, "To avoid all impropriety and any appearance of impropriety." He told the media he had no other choice, and he felt it was the proper thing to do. Chuck Murphy had called Gee and told him he was going to request that he disqualify himself.

Frank Del Vero knew Bailey's other preliminary exam in the Myers murder had been adjourned until December 13.

Just as Tim Kenny had done a week or so before, Frank Del Vero and David Morse knew they had to weave together the evidence and link Ronald Bailey to the kidnapping and murder of Shawn Moore. In anticipation of the hearing, Morse said, "I think just about everyone knows what is going to be testified to, and we're just going to try and flesh everything out."[118] Two of the witnesses included Shawn's dad and his brother.

Ron's cousin, Thomas Bailey, was one of the first to testify at his cousin's preliminary exam. Under oath, he said Ron visited the family farm near Fowlerville on August 3, and the two of them had split a six pack of beer before Ron left at around 2:30 p.m. "I asked him what he was doing out there, and he said he was heading up north to his girlfriend's

---

117. Grantham, Daniel, "Bailey Exam Continuing Today," *Livingston County Daily Press*, December 11, 1985

118. Gallagher, Mike, "Ronald Bailey Faces Murder Exam Today," *Lansing State Journal*, December 10, 1985

cabin, and they were going to meet him there," he said.[119] Thomas Bailey's testimony put his cousin in Livingston County, and within a short distance of Brighton, just before Shawn Moore's kidnapping.

Testimony from the fourteen-year-old boy who had encountered Ron Bailey thirty minutes before Shawn's kidnapping was essential in showing that Bailey was in Brighton. Bailey had tried to lure the boy out of the mall under the pretext of helping him with something in the parking lot but the teen refused. Del Vero was able to establish the time of that encounter by having the teen's mother testify about the time stamped on the receipt she had from the mall that day. The receipt had been printed at 2:50 p.m.

One of the eighteen people set to testify was Sherry Huey. The college student sat nervously on the stand in the old courtroom and quietly identified a photo of Shawn Moore and Ron Bailey as the two people she had seen on Whitmore Lake Road on August 31. Del Vero asked her what she had seen, and she described the man "walking towards the little boy. It wasn't quite a run." When she spoke of Shawn, she said he was on his bicycle and "looking over his shoulder, and he was scared looking." Frank Del Vero knew it was difficult for her. He asked Huey if the man was in the courtroom. Huey was uncomfortable. She began swaying back and forth in her chair for several moments as she glanced at Ron Bailey. "Yes," she said as she identified him.

It was important for Del Vero to connect Ron Bailey with the Chesney cabin in Gladwin. He called Deb Chesney's brother, Fred, to the stand. Chesney owned the cabin where Shawn Moore was murdered, and he said he had given Bailey permission to use the cabin when he gave the keys to

---

119. Grantham, Daniel, "Bailey Exam Continuing Today," *Livingston County Daily Press*, December 11, 1985

him on August 28, just three days before Shawn's abduction. Bailey had been there on several occasions according to Chesney, both with and without his sister.

Frank Del Vero had shown that Bailey had access to the Chesney cabin in Gladwin, and now he was set to show that Bailey was actually there. Michael Garner was from Carleton, a small town south of Detroit, but he was at his family's cabin in Gladwin on Labor Day weekend. It was just a few doors down from the Chesney cabin, and on August 31, he had seen a Jeep resembling Ron Bailey's Renegade pull up to the Chesneys' cabin. He recalled seeing two people in the Jeep, and although he didn't pay too much attention, he told the Court that later, he only saw one person come out of the cabin.

Garner was married to Lillian Knope's daughter. Lillian had been interviewed by the investigators in Gladwin, and she testified that she had met the man at the Chesney cabin on Labor Day weekend, and he had mentioned that he was married to Deb Chesney when he had come over to their cabin and offered to shoot some bats. On Labor Day, she had watched him loading his Jeep as he walked back and forth to the cabin, then drive off to the east toward the wooded area along Ridge Road instead of toward the highway. Ten minutes or so later, he was driving back to the west and continued without stopping back at the cabin.

Del Vero asked her about her identification of Bailey in the police lineup. Mrs. Knope said that when she looked at the lineup, she chose the man in the number two position. Ron Bailey had been in the number two position. Frank Del Vero wasn't expecting what happened next when he asked her if she saw that same man in the courtroom. Mrs. Knope was confused. She looked over everyone in the courtroom and glanced toward the jury box, where a police detective was sitting. She pointed at the detective and said, "Now I recognize the man." It was embarrassing and it complicated things, but it was a minor setback for Del Vero.

Jim Gabriel's eleven-year-old son, Jeremy, took the stand and told the Court about riding his three-wheeler along a sandy trail "up north" when he and his dad saw a Jeep coming toward them. Just a few minutes later, they had turned around and were riding back in the opposite direction when they saw the driver sitting on the hood of the parked Jeep, whittling. Jeremy identified Bailey as the man they had seen whittling on the Jeep.

When Detective Harold Janiszewski testified after Jeremy, he described how he had met with Jeremy and his dad on September 17 in Gladwin County. Jeremy pointed to the spot where he had seen Bailey sitting on the Jeep, and it was within forty-five feet of where Shawn's body was later found.

All of the testimony at the preliminary exam in Livingston County was circumstantial up to that point, but Del Vero had the one piece of evidence that would tie Shawn Moore to the cabin where Ron Bailey had been staying over the Labor Day weekend. It came from the fingerprint specialist from MSP, Michael Sinke. He told Del Vero and the Court that on November 20, he was able to identify a partial palm print that had been lifted from the oven handle on the stove in the cabin. That partial palm print belonged to Shawn Moore. A week after that identification was made, lab specialists also submitted a report that said some hairs found at the Gladwin cabin shared many of the same characteristics as Shawn's hair.

Finally, Dr. Laurence Simson, the forensic pathologist from Sparrow Hospital in Lansing who had done Shawn's autopsy, testified that a cause of death was impossible to determine because of the decomposition to Shawn's body, but his death was still classified as a homicide. Shawn died "through the agency of some other individual," and his death wasn't a natural death, nor was it a suicide.

Frank Del Vero had done it. He had shown that Bailey was in Livingston County near the time of the kidnapping, and he had witnesses who identified Ron Bailey as the man who had grabbed Shawn Moore. He tied Bailey to the cabin and to the area where the body was found, and he had Shawn's palm print inside the cabin along with his hair. In his closing statement, he said, "We have shown that Shawn Moore was forcibly taken from this county, against his will, and moved to an area miles away from his home, where he was found dead of a homicide." He continued, "We have put Ron Bailey fifty feet from where the body was found. The description of the man, time and time again, fits Ronald Bailey."[120]

The defense team didn't call any witnesses. In their closing arguments, Ray Cassar and Chuck Murphy argued that there was no way the witnesses to the abduction could identify Ron Bailey when they were driving fifty-five miles per hour by the site where it happened. There were too many discrepancies in their accounts of what they had seen. Murphy said, "In their mind's eye, they are identifying that picture of Ronald Bailey that they've seen on television every night at six o'clock."

Judge Michael Merritt agreed that there were some discrepancies, but he also said, "It would be strange were there not some discrepancies in the testimony."[121] He continued, "There is certainly probable cause to believe he abducted and murdered a thirteen-year-old Brighton boy."[122]

With that, Ronald Bailey sat motionless as the judge announced his decision to bind him over to the circuit court to stand trial for the kidnapping and murder of Shawn Moore.

---

120. Grantham, Daniel, "Prosecutors Try to Solve Puzzle," *Livingston County Daily Press*, December 18, 1985

121. Kresnak, Jack, "Bailey Will Stand Trial in Shawn Moore's Death," *Detroit Free Press,* December 12, 1985

122. Galagher, Mike, "Bailey Ordered to Stand Trial," *Lansing State Journal*, December 12, 1985

Alfred Bailey fought back his emotions as Judge Merritt made the decision. He wasn't angry, but rather, distraught. Through it all, he was thankful to the deputies and other police officers for the extra courtesy they had shown to him. He said he had been watching the proceedings against his son much like a juror would watch them, and he admitted he had to take things one step at a time.

Bruce Moore was pleased with Judge Merritt's decision but said he would rather not comment on things until after the trial, and he thanked the media for their thoughts.

The media was quick to get statements from both Frank Del Vero and Bailey's attorneys.

Del Vero reminded them that Ron Bailey was still considered innocent, and there was a long road ahead before he would be judged by a jury of his peers.

Cassar and Murphy were convinced that the witnesses who identified their client believed what they had said but formed their opinions after watching the news reports and seeing Bailey's picture on the news. He also believed that because Shawn's kidnapping and murder were such high-profile crimes in the media, it "practically ensured a bind-over" by Judge Merritt, though he added that Merritt had done an exceptionally good job in handling it.

—

Tim Kenny stood before the Westland District Court on December 13 as the preliminary examination for Ron Bailey in the kidnapping and murder of Kenny Myers came to a close, and he described the circumstantial evidence against Cassar and Murphy's client. In his analogy before Judge McKnight, he said the evidence presented was like the strands of a rope. "While each one may not be individually strong, when accumulated together, they certainly make a strong rope."

Kenny offered the transcript of the preliminary examination that had been done on November 22 involving the sixteen-year-old Redford Township teen. The teen testified about how Ron Bailey had coaxed him out of the Livonia Mall one month before Kenny Myers's kidnapping, abducted him at knifepoint, and driven him to park in an old station wagon before sexually assaulting him. Ray Cassar and Chuck Murphy both objected but Judge McKnight allowed it into evidence. "The only significant difference between what happened to the Livonia Mall victim and what happened to Kenny Myers is the fact that the Livonia victim survived and lived to tell what happened to him," Tim Kenny said.[123]

In her decision, Judge McKnight described Ron Bailey's method of operation as his "signature" when she said the circumstances of the kidnapping and sexual assault of the youth in Livonia a month before Kenny Myers murder were similar. "That signature is more important to the Court than the identification of three youngsters," she said.

She considered the digital Byron wristwatch that was confiscated after Bailey's arrest in Florida, and she said there was enough testimony to conclude that it belonged to Kenny Myers.

When McKnight spoke of the Kenny Myers autopsy, she noted his blood alcohol level of .09 and the pathologist's testimony that he had likely drunk two or three beers, or liquor, about an hour before his murder. Along with that, ligature strangulation on and off for a period of three to eight minutes certainly gave ample time for the killer to "consider and reflect" on what he was doing. Ron Bailey was bound over to circuit court for the kidnapping and murder of Kenny Myers.

---

123. Kresnak, Jack, "Bailey to Face Trial in Death of Another Boy," *Detroit Free Press*, December 14, 1985

15
The Reagan Effect

There was a lot of speculation on whether Ray Cassar and Chuck Murphy were going to use the insanity defense. They were required to notify the prosecutor's office and the Court at least thirty days before Bailey's trial so they still had plenty of time. Under the insanity defense, four verdicts were possible. If Bailey was found not guilty by reason of insanity, he would be taken to a psychiatric institution and held there until it was determined by doctors that he was cured and no longer a threat to himself or to society. He would be released after that. If he was found to be guilty but mentally ill, he would be sent to prison but would supposedly receive treatment there. He wouldn't go to a forensic center. If Ron Bailey was found not guilty in the Moore case, he would still face charges in the two other pending cases, and if he were found guilty, he could be sentenced to life in prison.

Frank Del Vero said they would be watching the other two cases closely in an effort to determine what the defense might plan to do in Livingston County.

—

Word had reached Ray Cassar and Chuck Murphy that the investigation by the Michigan Attorney General's Office into allegations about Dr. Jose Tombo had substantiated claims made by a patient that he had been sexually abused and, in fact, he had been linked to sex acts with at least seven patients, including Ron Bailey. Bailey's name was the only one mentioned in the report, though, because his accusations against Tombo had already been made public. Michigan Attorney General Frank Kelley had made the recommendation that Tombo have his medical license revoked and that he be fired. Kelley said there was, "Sufficient evidence to support criminal charges." He added that since the allegations stemmed from one incident in 1979, it exceeded the statute of limitations and Tombo couldn't legally be charged. The attorney general was frustrated that the statute of limitations prevented the prosecution of Tombo. He wrote, "I believe that criminal sexual conduct is such an abhorrent and heinous crime that the time limitation on commencing a prosecution should be extended to at least ten years."

In the State's investigation, eighty-four people had been interviewed. Bailey was one of them, and he referred to Dr. Tombo as "the master." He maintained that the homosexual relationship between himself and his doctor was a forced relationship that started in 1976 when he "reciprocally performed fellatio"[124] with Tombo. He mentioned his trip to the Windsor Raceway with the doctor and having sex with him afterward. Bailey estimated that he and Tombo had sex at least fifteen times over the course of the forced relationship.

Both Ray Cassar and Chuck Murphy knew it was what they needed for their motion to have Tombo declared a material witness. They planned to appear for a third time

124. Kresnak, Jack, "Kelley Urges Firing of Northville Doctor," *Detroit Free Press*, December 12, 1985

in court in an effort to force the now-suspended doctor to surrender his passport, or to post a bond to ensure that he would be available as a hostile witness to Ron Bailey.

Tombo's attorney had already said he wouldn't be surprised if his client was fired. He was certain the State had decided to fire Tombo even before the investigation was completed. Indirectly, referring to the investigation of Tombo as a witch hunt, Stevenson said, "I just hope there's some witches left for the children next Halloween."[125] He said Cassar and Murphy were using his client to distract attention from Ron Bailey. "It is preposterous to think, as some do, that Joe Tombo made a violent, criminal sexual monster out of Bailey." He continued, "Joe Tombo is no Frankenstein. He created no monster, for the monster was already there."[126]

Ron Bailey's defense hinged on the allegations that Tombo had sexually abused him and made him into the monster who went around killing young boys. It was the only line of defense for him, but the problem was that Bailey had never complained about Tombo until after his arrest for Shawn's kidnapping and murder.

The day after Judge McKnight bound Bailey over for trial, the *Detroit Free Press* reported that on December 10, Dr. Jose Tombo had been fired by Al Sipes, the director of employee relations with the Michigan Department of Public Health. The decision to terminate Tombo was made by the State's mental health director. There was a brief news conference, and Tombo was visibly shaken.

In an interview four days later, Tombo said there would come a time when he would show Ron Bailey was lying. He mentioned speaking to several people at the hospital before he was fired, and it was clear to everyone that Bailey was

---

125. Kresnak, Jack, "Kelley Urges Firing of Northville Doctor," *Detroit Free Press*, December 12, 1985

126. Kresnak, Jack, "Psychiatrist Denies Allegations Made by Ronald Bailey," *Detroit Free Press*, November 15, 1985

lying to "save his butt." He added, "I feel sorry for Bailey's parents."[127]

The attorney general, in his letter recommending Tombo's dismissal, admitted that the information gathered from current and former mental patients is "inherently unreliable," but nine separate patients of Tombo's had given statements, and the investigation hadn't uncovered any reason for any of those people to make accusations against him.

To corroborate Bailey's statement, his old roommate and former employee at Northville Regional Psychiatric Hospital, Jack Zaccardo, told the investigator he had answered a phone call about a year after he had quit his job, and the call was from a person he believed to be Tombo because he recognized the doctor's voice. Tombo thought Zaccardo was Bailey, and for fifteen minutes, Tombo talked about masturbation and oral sex. There were two other times at the hospital when patients had told Zaccardo they had to have sex with Tombo in order to get a day pass. Zaccardo hadn't reported those to anyone because he thought another doctor was covering for Tombo.

Alfred Bailey agreed with the State's investigation and said Tombo's abuse was meant to change his son's already confused life.

Ray Cassar felt his client was being honest about the relationship he had with Tombo, and his credibility came from Bailey being able to describe the curvature in Dr. Tombo's penis.

How else could he know that? Cassar thought. The young attorney knew it wasn't a consensual situation. There was no way it could have been. It had occurred in a mental hospital.

---

127. Kresnak, Jack, "Tombo Abused Bailey, Others, Report Alleges," *Detroit Free Press*, December 15, 1985

Both Ray Cassar and Chuck Murphy felt overwhelmed at times. They knew they would have to find a psychiatrist willing to defend their client, they would likely have to find Dr. Tombo because they were sure he would flee, and they would have to overcome the Reagan Effect.

—

"Getting shot hurts," Ronald Reagan said to his wife, Nancy, after the assassination attempt on March 31, 1981.[128] Two months after his inauguration, the president had just finished speaking to 5,000 AFL-CIO members at the Washington, DC Hilton. As he walked from the hotel, six shots rang out. John Hinkley had fired his .22 caliber six-shot revolver at the president. The first shot struck Press Secretary James Brady, critically wounding him. The second shot struck police officer Thomas Delahanty. The third shot went astray, while the fourth struck Secret Service Agent Timothy McCarthy, who had intentionally stepped between the president and the shooter. The fifth shot struck the glass window on the limousine, and the sixth shot ricocheted off the presidential limousine and struck President Reagan under his left armpit. President Reagan's wound wasn't noticed until he started coughing up blood as the limousine raced toward the White House. They quickly redirected to George Washington University Hospital, where President Reagan underwent emergency surgery and survived.

John Hinkley had moved with his family to Evergreen, Colorado after he graduated from high school in 1973. He attended college at Texas Tech University but dropped out after an on-again off-again attendance. After moving to Los Angeles in 1975, he would mention a girlfriend to

---

128. "Assassination Attempt," Ronald Reagan Presidential Library, https://www.reaganlibrary.gov/permanent-exhibits/assassination-attempt

his parents when he wrote to them asking for cash while describing the various problems he was having on his own. The girlfriend was fictitious.

After he moved back to Evergreen in the mid-seventies, Hinkley began purchasing guns. He became obsessed with the movie *Taxi Driver*, a 1976 film about a man who plots to assassinate a presidential candidate. Partly based on the diaries of Arthur Bremer, who had shot presidential candidate George Wallace, the movie starred actress Jodie Foster as a twelve-year-old victim of sexual trafficking. Hinkley was so obsessed with the movie, he began to dress like the lead character.

Hinkley began to stalk Jodie Foster, and he moved to Connecticut when she began attending Yale University. He had been given money by his parents so he could attend a writing class through Yale but instead, he used the money to survive while he wrote love letters to Foster and continually stalked her. Hinkley wanted her attention so badly that he fantasized about hijacking a plane to impress her or killing himself in front of her. Instead, he plotted to assassinate the President of the United States so he would have his place in history, and he would appeal to Jodie Foster as an equal.

John Hinkley trailed President Jimmy Carter across the country in 1980 and, at one point, he got within twenty feet of him in Dayton, Ohio. In October 1980, he was arrested in Nashville, Tennessee, while trying to board a flight with three handguns and a set of handcuffs. His guns were seized by the Nashville Police Department, he was fined fifty dollars, and released later that day.

By October 13, Hinkley had flown to Dallas and purchased a .22 caliber revolver. With the money his parents had given to him now gone, he returned to Colorado broke and spent four months in psychiatric treatment for depression. During those four months, there was no improvement. When Ronald Reagan won the presidential election in 1980 and took office in 1981, Hinkley set his sights on a new target.

Hinkley arrived in Washington, DC on March 29, after taking a bus from Los Angeles. He found the president's schedule posted in the newspaper and knew he would be at the Washington, DC Hilton later that day. He penned a letter to Jodie Foster saying that he was going through with the assassination because he couldn't wait anymore to impress her. When he finished the letter, he took a cab to the Hilton, where he thought he would surely achieve his place in history.

In the aftermath of the assassination attempt on President Reagan, Hinkley, who was immediately tackled by a Secret Service agent and bystanders, was charged under federal law. At his trial, the prosecution focused on Hinkley's premeditation. Not only had he purchased the gun, but he had also stalked the president, traveled to Washington, DC, chosen very destructive ammunition for the revolver, detailed his plan in a letter, and fired every round in the gun.

John Hinkley's defense team maintained that he was insane at the time of the assassination attempt, and because he was charged in federal court, it was up to the prosecution to prove his sanity beyond a reasonable doubt. His trial turned into a battle of the mental health experts.

Hinckley was diagnosed with schizophrenia by the first defense expert who testified that he had merged several personalities from his own life and from fiction. One of those included the character from *Taxi Driver*. The expert testifying for the defense said that Hinckley didn't understand that his actions were wrong because of the delusion of his affinity with Jodie Foster.

A second expert testified that Hinckley didn't show any evidence of lying about his supposed mental illness, and his actions were the very opposite of logical. That expert said Hinckley's CAT scan showed widened grooves on his brain. That anomaly in the brain was found on one-third of people with schizophrenia but only two percent of non-schizophrenics.

The last expert to testify said that Hinckley's results from the Minnesota Multiphasic Personality Inventory were abnormal, and only one person out of one million with a score similar to his wouldn't be suffering from mental illness.

The prosecution experts disagreed. Hinckley had dysthymia, a disorder primarily of mood, and three types of personality disorders. Those included narcissism, schizoid, and a mix with borderline passive/aggressive features. None of those supported Hinckley's contention that he was insane. There wasn't any evidence that he was so impaired he couldn't appreciate the wrongfulness of his actions or conform his conduct to the law.

A second prosecution expert who had interviewed Hinckley the most simply said he planned the shooting. In fact, she emphasized the planning of it and said he was engrossed with being famous himself. His infatuation with Jodie Foster was no different than any young man's interest in a celebrity.

After twenty-four hours of deliberations over three days, Hinckley was found not guilty by reason of insanity.

The insanity defense had only been used in two percent of felony cases in America with only one half of one percent of those being successful.

Across the United States, the public was outraged at the Hinckley verdict. They couldn't believe it. Incredulous people were thinking, *I can't believe this guy is trying to get out. He shoots the president. He's declared insane. He's placed in a hospital instead of a prison?*

Several states, in addition to Congress, enacted legislation restricting the insanity defense even more than it already was, and many of the reforms that were put in place shifted the burden of proof to the defense and away from the prosecution. The majority of the reforms had started in

1978 and were still on-going when Hinckley shot President Reagan.

After the Hinckley verdict, media coverage was intense, and there was a push to get rid of the insanity defense nationwide. Locally, L. Brooks Patterson was pushing for it, and Ray Cassar was beginning to think they couldn't get an insanity verdict even if they could find Tombo and have him testify.

16

Without Kids, There Is No Tomorrow

While Ray Cassar turned to his Catholicism to get him through, Chuck Murphy confided to him that he had thought about walking away from the case at one point. Maybe they should let a Court-appointed attorney handle it. Cassar disagreed. Ron Bailey wouldn't get the same representation he was getting from the two of them, and he honestly didn't believe that Bailey was evil. He believed his client was mentally ill.

Cassar spent many hours with Bailey discussing the case and the strategies they were going to use, and Bailey trusted him.

In addition to all of the issues plaguing them and the motions they were going to file in the case, Ray Cassar knew he would have to research a very unusual topic for the trial—erotic asphyxiation. It was Ron Bailey's signature.

Cassar learned that erotic asphyxiation was a practice used during some sort of sexual activity, often masturbation, that led to cerebral hypoxia, or starving the brain of oxygen, which caused a euphoric feeling. The practice had been around for centuries.

—

Both of Bailey's attorneys knew they would have to seek a change of venue for their client's trial in Livingston County. Bailey's face was everywhere and had been since September. The pre-trial publicity would surely be mentioned in the motion to change the venue. Both he and Murphy firmly believed that the prosecution witnesses' testimony had been affected by news reports, and they had already mentioned they would be asking for the change. "I think some of the people believe what they testified to, but I think their minds have been influenced by seeing, day after day after day, the pictures of Ronald Bailey on TV," Cassar said.[129]

Following Ron Bailey's bind-over to circuit court in Wayne County, his attorneys told both Wayne County Circuit Judge William Cahalan and Tim Kenny that they were going to defend their client using the insanity defense in the case of the Redford Township teen who Bailey was accused of kidnapping one month before Kenny Myers was murdered. They said Bailey's treatment at the Northville Regional Psychiatric Hospital was partly to blame. The two attorneys were considering using the same defense in both the Myers and Moore cases. When they spoke to media, they added that Tombo was a crucial witness in their defense because of Bailey's claims against him.

"It's not a formal admission," Cassar said. "There are still problems with the facts. It's just saying that, if in fact he did commit the crime, at the time of the alleged offense he was either mentally insane and/or operating under diminished capacity."[130]

The Christmas season had already begun, and while twinkling lights decorated homes and businesses around Howell and carolers walked from door to door singing traditional Christmas songs, Shawn Moore's killer stood

129. Grantham, Daniel, "Testimony Is 'Tainted' by Media," *Livingston County Daily Press*, December 18, 1985

130. Kresnak, Jack, "Lawyers Plan Insanity Plea in Bailey Case," *Detroit Free Press*, December 19, 1985

before Livingston County Judge Stanley Latreille for his arraignment in circuit court. The charges against him were open murder and kidnapping. Latreille ordered him held without any bond being set.

—

Judge Stanley Latreille, a family man raised in Detroit who eventually moved to Howell, had been a reporter for the *Detroit News* before his legal career began. He had served in the Army Reserve and afterward, while working as a journalist, he attended night classes at the University of Detroit. After he and his wife moved to Howell, he started his law practice, and feeling as if it was his calling, he ran a successful campaign for the circuit court in Livingston County in 1983. His colleagues and the community considered Latreille calm and steady as well as fair.

Latreille wanted the Moore case to move along smoothly without any glitches. To ensure that happened, he set a schedule that included dates for all motions and arguments from both sides to be presented, as well as a trial date in March.

Frank Del Vero was surprised at the schedule. He had never seen one so complete.

Judge Latreille didn't want the Moore case tried in the media so he took an opportunity to address both the prosecution and defense when he read part of the *Code of Ethics* to them, then reminded them not to divulge certain aspects of the case to the press.

Nine days after Ron Bailey's arraignment in Livingston County Circuit Court, he stood before Wayne County Circuit Judge William Cahalan for his circuit court arraignment in the Myers case. Bailey didn't offer a plea. He was charged with first-degree murder, felony murder, and kidnapping. Judge Cahalan entered a not guilty plea for him.

Bailey's pending defense was no secret. Ray Cassar gave the Court official notice that they intended to use the insanity defense in the murder case against their client. In Livingston County, David Morse knew it wouldn't affect their case against Ron Bailey. Now that Cassar and Murphy had officially shown their hand, Morse said, "Before, we were arguing that he was the one that did it. The main thrust of our case now is that he ought to be criminally responsible."[131]

The forensic exam that Ron Bailey had gone through three months earlier was to determine if he was competent to stand trial. Now that his attorneys intended to use the insanity defense, he would have to be evaluated again at the Regional Forensic Center in Ypsilanti to see if he could have been criminally responsible for his actions. Both sides expected the trial date to be delayed.

—

With both the prosecution and defense jockeying for position, State lawmakers across Michigan were making sure taxpayers understood what the Children's Trust Fund was and how they could donate.

State Representative Debbie Stabenow, who was born in Gladwin and went to school in nearby Clare, said there was an epidemic of child abuse and neglect in Michigan with over 42,000 cases in 1985 alone. "We find ourselves in a situation where there's not enough money for prevention programs, let alone treatment programs."

Three years earlier, the Children's Trust Fund had been set up under a bill that Stabenow sponsored. To donate, a taxpayer could simply check a box on their tax return to designate part of their refund to the Trust Fund. The plan

131. Grantham, Daniel, "Insanity Defense is Reserved," *Livingston County Daily Press*, January 8, 1986

hadn't been very successful in the first three years because taxpayers thought the CTF on their tax form was an educational fund. That changed in 1986 when it was labeled CTF For Child Abuse.

The hope was that the program might be helped by the publicity surrounding Shawn Moore's abduction and murder because Bruce and Sharon Moore had asked that donations be made to the Trust Fund in Shawn's name.

—

While State Representative Stabenow was pushing for taxpayer dollar donations to the Children's Trust Fund, Kenny Myers's mom was trying to educate the public about child safety.

Marie Edenstrom spoke in Hartland, near Howell, about the organization she had formed called KENNY. She was surprised that experts were asking her opinion about child safety. The week before, she had been in South Lyon doing the same thing, and it was extremely difficult for her to talk about her son because the following day would have been his birthday. "I can't bring Kenny back," she said. "Nothing ever will, but maybe there will be just one child that can live past the age of fourteen, and then it's worthwhile."

Marie Edenstrom had over 170 members in the new organization she had formed, and their goal was to present educational programs for children and parents across the entire state. KENNY offered posters of missing children, tapes, and games related to child abductions, and their main goal was educating children as well as adults. She said when her son disappeared, there was a need for family members to go to a support group. There was one, and Edenstrom said that the group, titled My Son Is Missing, Help Me, operated with volunteers, fundraisers, and donations.

Her pleas were passionate when she said, "I'm only one person. There's a lot to do and a lot of children to protect."[132] She asked that teachers join the fight against child abuse because school boards were asking for her program. "Your children are my children. Without kids, there is no tomorrow."

As the evening moved forward, she asked that people write letters to their legislators to support a bill that would establish videotaping the testimony of children under sixteen so they wouldn't have to repeat their story again and again. As an example, she mentioned an eleven-year-old victim of sexual abuse who had to re-tell her story to eighteen different people before she ever took the witness stand in a trial.

In closing the program, she warned, "If this can happen to Kenny, it can happen to your child."

—

By mid-January, the list of crimes against Ron Bailey had grown when Frank Del Vero charged him with being a habitual offender. A habitual offender with four prior felony convictions could face a maximum penalty of life in prison. If Bailey was convicted of a charge that carried less than mandatory life without parole, the judge could increase the number of years in the sentence by half. Del Vero had been looking for a way to enhance the sentence as a precaution. He wanted to cover all of the bases.

Cassar wasn't sure why Frank Del Vero was doing it, but it didn't matter. He and Murphy were preparing a motion to present to Judge Latreille to move their client's trial out of Livingston County, and Cassar was busy collecting all the information he could from newspaper and other media

---

132. Robertson, Nicole, "KENNY Seeking Volunteers," *Livingston County Daily Press*, January 29, 1986

accounts of Shawn's kidnapping and his client's court proceedings. They would be presented to Judge Latreille because the judge wanted to know how much media coverage there actually had been.

Three weeks later, the trial date for Ron Bailey was postponed indefinitely because of delays in his evaluation at the Center for Forensic Psychiatry. At the same hearing, the defense team showed a fifty-minute video presentation from Channel 7 news reports about Shawn Moore's kidnapping and the arrest of Ron Bailey. The news accounts Cassar had collected in the papers were presented as part of the motion. Cassar and Murphy argued that the news coverage alone had inflamed the community and biased prospective jurors.

"This case has inflamed the passions of the community," Murphy said. "There's no way that a jury selected in this venue, in this county, will be able to give Mr. Bailey a fair trial."

Judge Latreille, known for his calm demeanor and fairness, responded to Murphy, saying, "Let's do this right the first time and not let it come back on appeal."

Frank Del Vero agreed there had been a lot of publicity but thought their motion was premature because he knew that, by law, there had to be an attempt to pick a jury before a motion for a change of venue could be filed. "If you change the venue now, you have no way of knowing whether this pattern of bitter prejudice that's alleged to exist, does," he said. "You're making a leap from a given set of facts to another, and why do that? Why make that leap when all you have to do is sit them down and ask them?" He continued, "We don't have people jumping up and down on the street corner saying, 'Let's hang Ronald Bailey.'"

Cassar and Murphy told Latreille that it would be too hard to screen prospective jurors when the case went to trial.

Judge Latreille denied their defense motion, saying, "The key issue is whether the jury will abide by the law." He continued, "Will they put aside any opinion and base their decision on what they hear in the courtroom?" At trial, if they were unable to seat a jury, he would reconsider their request, but for now, he wasn't going to grant their motion.

Frank Del Vero had a motion to present to Judge Latreille too. He wanted to include what he called "signature evidence" from two of Bailey's other victims who had been sexually assaulted in the same manner. Latreille denied Del Vero's motion but said it might be allowed at trial if it was necessary in the identification of Bailey and wouldn't be prejudicial to the jury.[133]

The trial probably wasn't going to occur until at least September. The psychiatric evaluation was done but the report hadn't been completed yet, and it wasn't expected until mid-June.

—

While Ron Bailey sat in jail, charged with kidnapping three teens and murdering two of them, the world was still processing the January explosion of the space shuttle Challenger and the deaths of the seven-member crew. The Statue of Liberty reopened in New York after a two-year renovation. The Chicago Bears won Super Bowl XX in New Orleans after defeating the New England Patriots. *Ferris Bueller's Day Off* and *The Karate Kid* were released in theaters, and Frank Del Vero received the report he had been waiting for.

A psychiatrist and a psychologist from the Center for Forensic Psychiatry determined that Ron Bailey was sane at the time of Shawn Moore's disappearance. According to their report, he wasn't mentally ill or legally insane.

Murphy and Cassar saw a lot of problems with the thirty-page report because there was a lot of speculation on

133. Grantham, Daniel, "Judge Refuses to Move Trial Outside County," *Livingston County Daily Press*, February 19, 1986

the part of the doctors, and Cassar said it was just an opinion of his client. They wanted the chance to show it to Bailey and ask him if the statements in it had actually been made by him. Chuck Murphy said he was surprised at the report given his client's psychiatric history. He and Cassar had said all along that they would have an independent evaluation of Ron Bailey done by their own expert.

A tentative trial date was set for September 3.

17
The Leak

Ray Cassar and Chuck Murphy had searched long and hard for a psychiatrist who could help them defend their client. No one wanted to be part of the defense. The Bailey case was taboo to many people because they feared it might hurt their practice. They didn't want to touch it, and Cassar knew why. Their client had killed two children in a heinous way, and at least one of them was sexually assaulted. Even some of Cassar's old friends from Garden City couldn't believe he was defending Bailey. It was no wonder they couldn't find a psychiatrist as part of the defense team.

—

"The cruel, needless tragedy that struck our family only a few months ago has left an emptiness in our lives that can never be filled."

The letter of thanks from the Moore family was published in the *Detroit Free Press*, and it was meant to say thank you to the thousands of people who had reached out to them. Shawn's horror and the anguish they experienced was beyond comprehension. Through the love and support of the community and from across the country and into Canada, they were able to survive. People prayed with the Moores, cried with them, and shared their feelings of frustration, helplessness, bitterness, and grief. The community and beyond raised reward funds and produced hundreds of thousands of Missing posters. They donated to the Children's Trust Fund too. All of the love and compassion shown was done for Shawn. In his letter of thanks, Bruce Moore wrote, "Each of you has our gratitude. Please know that we love you all, very dearly, for your prayers, help and support."[134]

—

Some said he was narcissistic. Others called him a charlatan, a publicity hound, a buffoon, and even an outright asshole. His rambling television commercials on Detroit's Channel 7 aired several times per day. He looked empathetically into the camera with his dark hair, chiseled good looks, and perfect teeth, asking if the audience needed someone to talk to. He asked if they needed someone who wouldn't pass judgment on them, and someone who cared. If they did, they should come talk to him. In other late night television ads, the viewer was told they had to be crazy to see him.

His name was Dr. Joel Dreyer. As a native Detroiter and corporate psychiatrist, his treatment center on the seventh floor of the Travelers Tower in Southfield employed over eighty physicians, psychologists, and therapists. Called InnerVisions, he had named the center after a Stevie Wonder record album, and it occupied two floors of the high-rise building. In addition to the treatment center, he was an expert witness in mostly defense cases, and many of those were high profile. With his clinic, private practice, and expert witness business, Dr. Dreyer had become a public figure and a wealthy man. He liked people to think he was a Neo-Freudian and a precedent-setter in forensic psychiatry

134. Moore, Bruce, "A Family's Thanks," *Detroit Free Press*, June 23, 1986

as one of the only psychiatrists to do successful television commercials. He believed he was both charismatic and flamboyant, and that was why his ads were so successful. There was no hesitation in his mind about advertising his services. "If I saved one life, it was worth all the advertising," he said.[135]

To some, it appeared he loved being the center of attention. In passing conversations, he liked to mention his associations with famed lawyer F. Lee Bailey and Melvin Belli. In the mid-seventies, Dreyer had been contacted by F. Lee Bailey during the trial of Patty Hearst. Hearst was the granddaughter of William Randolph Hearst, an American publishing magnate. She was kidnapped in 1974 by the Symbionese Liberation Army. When she was found over eighteen months later, she was considered a fugitive wanted for crimes committed with her group of kidnappers. When Dreyer concluded she wasn't insane, he was dropped from her defense team.

There were times when Dreyer would wear his Elvis Presley bedazzled costume to work. Other pieces of his wardrobe included platform shoes, sweaters in all different wild colors, cowboy hats, purple cowboy boots, and even a fox head and tail that he would wrap around his neck. His office was adorned with illustrations of himself testifying in court. He owned a red Ferrari and, on one occasion, he had a photo taken of himself in front of the car while he held an AK-47 rifle.

In spite of Dreyer's narcissism and flamboyant lifestyle, many believed he loved what he was doing—helping people, many of whom were depressed and abused. Others disagreed. One of his former employees, a forensic psychiatrist who had worked at InnerVisions, said that Dreyer was the type that "shrink lawyers wanted to buy an

135. Beer, Matt, "Dr. Joel Dreyer," *Detroit Monthly*, October 1986

opinion from."[136] Dreyer didn't see it that way. "Juries look at docs as hired guns," he said. "I'm not a hired gun. That's what's good about what I do. I like to be pedantic. I have a very high IQ."[137]

Cassar and Murphy met with Dreyer to see if he could help defend their client and show he was insane when he kidnapped the teen from Redford Township, Shawn Moore, and Kenny Myers. Neither attorney expected what they saw when they arrived at Dreyer's offices. The waiting room had two large aquariums and a standing display ad for a pain-blocking device. His office was lined with dirty shag carpeting, brown Play Pit modular furniture, abstract art with grieving faces, a stuffed vulture suspended from the ceiling, and mood lighting. To both men, it looked like a hippie pad from the seventies. Dreyer greeted them with a simple, "Hey, guys. Have a seat."[138]

After the initial meeting, Ray Cassar was convinced that the reason Dreyer had reached out to help them was for the publicity from a high-profile case. He agreed to work for the court fee only for each of the three cases. "We're gonna [sic] be able to show Bailey's crazy," he said at their first meeting. After that meeting, Cassar's impression of Dreyer was that while he was a well-known and flamboyant psychiatrist, he was also a hippie.

Cassar and Murphy told the Court that the independent evaluation on their client would be conducted by Dr. Joel Dreyer, and toward the end of July, they had Dreyer's report.

When Dreyer spoke to the media, he said, "Across the board, I feel there's pathology; across the board, I feel there's sickness." He added, "And practically, the attorneys

---

136. Hayasaki, Erika, "A Criminal Mind," *California Sunday Magazine*, October 4, 2015

137. Cain, Stephen, "Bailey Attorneys to Employ Insanity Defense," *Ann Arbor News,* August 31, 1986

138. Cassar, Raymond, Interview with author, February 27, 2024

will be able to use my information to translate to the Court the issue of insanity."[139]

—

On March 8, 1986, Joel Dreyer walked into the Livingston County Jail at 12:55 p.m. His appointment with Bailey was at 1:00 in the Outreach Office. Dreyer hadn't reviewed any of the police reports from any of the three cases, and his initial meeting with Bailey lasted just three hours. In a lengthy, single-spaced, often rambling, eighteen-page letter to Cassar and Murphy, he outlined the meeting and his opinion.

Dreyer was building Bailey's defense when, as a result of his interview, he described some of Bailey's sexual experiences. Before his experiences with Dr. Tombo, Ron Bailey had varied experiences with boys, most of whom were "brown-haired, olive skin, and had dark eyes." In Dreyer's letter, he specifically wrote, "He never went down on anyone in his whole life until Dr. Tombo taught him how to do it."

After Bailey's experiences with Tombo, according to Dr. Dreyer, he turned to drugs and alcohol over his guilt and to suppress the sexual urges he had. Dreyer wrote that suddenly, after his experiences at Northville, all of Bailey's victims looked exactly like him. He added that after Bailey's experiences with Tombo, he would use some sort of ligature around his neck when he masturbated because he would getter a better high during his sexual experience.

During their first meeting, Bailey told Dreyer of his sexual encounters with Tombo and how much he hated him. Dr. Tombo would always begin those encounters by saying, "Relax. Come on now, relax." Dreyer maintained that that

139. Kresnak, Jack, "Star Witness in Murder Trial May be Defendant Bailey," *Detroit Free Press*, August 31, 1986

was what Bailey would tell his victims before sexually assaulting them.

Bailey didn't care for his mother. "Too strict and was always complaining and playing the martyr role about how bad and terrible and rotten and poor her childhood was, and how poor she was financially." Bailey told Dreyer he liked his father better, but they didn't get along.[140]

Dreyer made sure to recount all of Ron Bailey's sexual encounters from age eleven through the murders of Kenny Myers and Shawn Moore, and he included an alleged blackmail scheme involving a computer operator in the Michigan Supreme Court System who had come across Bailey's name and contacted him. Bailey and the State employee had a brief sexual encounter as a result.

When Ron Bailey moved to Florida, Dreyer wrote that he began to stalk children again and experienced anger like never before. "Now he's driven to it, whereas before it was for pleasure and he enjoyed it, and didn't feel driven. It wasn't horribly often in his own mind, and it was usually mutually with kids that he either found or found him." He added they were all fourteen or fifteen years old, all blond, and they all looked like Bailey had when he was the same age.

Dr. Dreyer knew there was a rumor of some unsolved child murders in Florida. "I didn't kill any of them. I had sex with them. I didn't try to kill any of them. I didn't strangle or choke them, or put my cord around their neck, but was feeling some anger," Bailey said. "I could feel it well in me but I didn't kill any kids in Florida."

After his fourth run-in with Florida authorities, he fled the state. He claimed he hadn't had sex with the boy but to avoid getting in trouble again, he left. He pointed out to Dr. Dreyer, "You know, he was Mexican, dark, Spanish

---

140. Dr. Joel Dreyer to Raymond Cassar and Charles Murphy, March 8, 1986

kid. Maybe that's why I didn't have sex with him. All I did was buy him beer, and the charge against me was strictly aiding and abetting a minor in the solicitation of alcoholic beverages."

When Ron Bailey described kidnapping and murdering Kenny Myers, he told Dreyer he had put a belt around the teen's neck. He felt good when he did that to himself while masturbating, and he figured the boy would enjoy it too. He claimed he heard some motorcycles nearby, and he was afraid of getting caught. He left Kenny for a short period to make sure no one was coming. "By the time I came back from looking to see about those motorcycle kids, I forgot about the noose and the kid was dead." He added, "I had taken his shirt off just like Tombo used to do to me, and I put it in my pocket, and I was walking. When I went over a fence, I left the shirt there, I guess, or it fell out of my pocket. I can't remember."

Dr. Dreyer's report was filled with his own editorial comments that were out of place. When he described Ron Bailey's murder of Shawn Moore, he wrote:

He was with Shawn Moore from Saturday to Monday. But one of the times when he went outside, because he felt sick because he had too much to drink and too much pot to smoke and he had his noose belt around the boy's neck, this time to prove he could put it around his neck and not kill somebody, he came back and went to sleep, and when he woke up laying next to him was a dead corpse, a little boy who had affixiated from the noose belt he'd had around his neck. He took the boy into the woods and he said he placed him on a nice pair of fern beds for a little burial ground on Labor Day Weekend 1985 [sic].[141]

---

141. Dr. Joel Dreyer to Raymond Cassar and Charles Murphy, March 8, 1986

Now that he was in custody, Ron Bailey told Dreyer his main concern was L. Brooks Patterson. Bailey had seen the news reports, and he thought if Patterson had it his way, he would be executed. If capital punishment was ever reinstated in Michigan, he felt he would be Patterson's first target.

As Bailey and Dreyer talked, Bailey said he wasn't sure why he had kidnapped the kids. It was something inside him, and he was angry. No one told him to do it, and there weren't any voices. It was simply an urge, and he enjoyed sex. It was enjoyment before he was sent to Northville, but afterward, he was driven by anger. He felt the anger when he was in Florida, and his alcohol and drug use increased along with his depraved obsession with kids. Bailey knew he was different than everyone else, and he craved sex more and more with kids.

Dreyer looked at Bailey. "Did it ever occur to you that all these kids that look like you, may be you and that you are acting as if you're Dr. Tombo?" As Dreyer described Bailey's reaction to the suggestion, he wrote in his letter, "All of a sudden, he started to shake, tears, huge tears just poured out of his eyes. It wasn't a game, wasn't a put on, wasn't fake, or some Ganser syndrome to make a point. He had an insight." As Dreyer went on, he wrote:

He was like Tony Perkins in Psycho, that he's been playing a role, a role that he's obsessed to play called "the kids will be me and I'll be Dr. Tombo." I'll take off their shirt, I'll unzip their pants, I'll play with them, I'll suck them and they won't come, but I will, just like Tombo, and we'll be friends, just like me and Tombo. [sic]. You were and you did choke a few of them to death. Maybe you were trying to kill that part of you, or maybe you were killing you because you hated you so much when you were with Tombo.

To Dr. Joel Dreyer, Ron Bailey wasn't the victimizer. Ron Bailey was the victim. Dreyer was convinced that Bailey wasn't smart enough to fool him. He did opine that Bailey was competent to stand trial, but he had "urges he couldn't control," and because of that, he couldn't live with the ordinary demands of life. Bailey's mind was "filled with sexual pleasures and sexual promiscuity right from a little boy up."

"I'm certain also that if we convict him and put him in a prison, his anus will be everybody's, and he will kill himself." He continued, "At this point, can we have enough objectivity to get past what we see was awful, heinous, horrible crimes against society, long enough to set the objectivity of how he's been criminalized and victimized first?"[142]

Dreyer had a second meeting with Ron Bailey on July 3, where he allowed him to talk about whatever he wanted. Bailey told Dreyer he didn't trust Drs. Stock and Blunt from the Forensic Center. Dreyer and Bailey spoke about his auditory and visual hallucinations. He was having dreams about Dr. Tombo. He said he also heard the voice of the devil when the devil said, "You're doing wrong, you're bad." He felt he was possessed by the devil until he became a born-again Christian.

—

There was no doubt that his report contradicted the prosecution experts who said Bailey wasn't insane. At Bailey's trial, the experts from both sides were prepared to testify about their opinions on Ron Bailey's sanity and whether he was criminally responsible for the murders.

142. Dr. Joel Dreyer to Raymond Cassar and Charles Murphy, March 8, 1986

Wayne County's chief trial attorney, Tim Kenny, was familiar with Joel Dreyer. The Wayne County Prosecutor's Office had an entire notebook about Dreyer and the cases he had testified in. Kenny was of the opinion that Dreyer should have been the patient on the couch rather than a doctor listening to a patient.

David Morse had gotten copies of Dreyer's report too. They sat down with Dr. Stock and Dr. Blunt and went over their reports in addition to Dreyer's. The reports were a stark contrast to one another. Stock and Blunt provided an entire bibliography for Morse to go over so he would understand exactly where they were coming from and why Ron Bailey wasn't insane.

Chuck Murphy was certain the findings of prosecution expert Dr. Harley Stock were tainted. Murphy claimed that Dr. Stock tried to find out from Bailey if there were other crimes he had committed that hadn't been reported yet, and he had overstepped his bounds as a forensic examiner by asking Bailey about unsolved crimes in other states.

When Murphy asked that Stock's findings be thrown out because of what Stock had done, Judge Latreille denied the request. Murphy was still doubting an impartial jury could be found in Livingston County.

Cassar felt that when it went to trial, it would come down to how the interviews were conducted, and he knew Bailey had a very good rapport with Dreyer. Bailey had felt very comfortable around Dr. Dreyer, and he was uncomfortable around Dr. Stock and Dr. Blunt because they had acted like they were detectives when they started asking about unsolved crimes in Ohio. Murphy maintained that there were several unsolved crimes in Ohio, and both Stock and Blunt were interrogating Bailey to see if he had any involvement in them. Both attorneys felt that because of the way their client was questioned, he didn't get a fair and accurate evaluation.

Something was wrong, and Ray Cassar couldn't put his finger on it. He would go to the jail and discuss the case with Ron Bailey, and they would strategize about how the case was going to be handled and what they were going to do. The next day, everything that Bailey had told Cassar during their meeting would be in the news. It was obvious that there was a leak somewhere.

Ron Bailey confronted Cassar about it and accused him of leaking information to the media. "I confided in you," he said. "I trusted you."

On the defense now, Cassar said, "Ron, do you really think I'm going to tell anyone? There's no way I'd tell anyone."

As the two talked, Cassar pondered that the only person he had talked to about what was discussed in the meeting was his co-counsel, Chuck Murphy.

Bailey spoke up. "I'm going to start telling you things, but you're not going to repeat it."

Cassar knew he had to find out what was going on.

Over time, reporters had become more and more familiar with Chuck Murphy and Ray Cassar. As defense attorneys, they wanted to be friends with the media, and that's what the media wanted too. There was a professional courtesy between all of them. In his own mind, Cassar believed that Chuck Murphy was in it for the notoriety.

Nancy McCauley was a Fox Channel 2 reporter for WJBK, and she could tell that Cassar genuinely wanted to help Ron Bailey. One afternoon in court, she took the attorney aside and told him that some of the reporters covering the Bailey case, including herself, had a meeting.

"About what?" Cassar asked.

She told him they needed to talk. As the two sat down, the conversation first turned to Dr. Dreyer. Nancy McCauley had done an interview with him about the case, and he tried to psychoanalyze her. She thought Dreyer was crazy.

Still naïve in his early legal career, Ray Cassar was stunned at what she said next. "Look, Ray, we're getting a lot of information about the case, and you need to know that."

Puzzled, Cassar said softly, "How are you getting this information?"

She told him the information was coming from Chuck Murphy.

"No! No way. He wouldn't do that," Ray said.

McCauley knew Cassar was really trying to help his client but the other media people who participated in the meeting all felt bad for him. It was obvious that he didn't know, and while some of the reporters loved getting the inside information, others didn't think it was fair.

Ray Cassar was stunned as the realization began to set in. "It's Chuck?" Never in a million years would he have thought Chuck was leaking information to the media. Cassar figured it was coming from inside the jail, thinking it was a corrections officer or someone else on the inside, but not Chuck.

Ray began to process what he had just been told by Nancy McCauley. It suddenly all made sense. He was getting very specific details from Ron Bailey about the case and, as his attorney, he was the only person who knew those details. He would go back to the office and share those details and strategies that he had discussed with his co-counsel, Chuck Murphy.

As Ray Cassar sat there, his disbelief turned to anger. He would have to confront him.

When Ron Bailey's two attorneys met the next time, Cassar asked his partner about the news leak. Murphy said he had no idea how the information was getting out. Cassar told Murphy about the meeting with Nancy McCauley.

"I can explain," Murphy said.

"No. You can't explain it," Cassar told him. "You're revealing secrets that are hurting and compromising my case, and Ron knows. He knows it's coming from either you or me, and he knows it's not me."[143]

"Ray, you don't understand," his partner said. "It'll never happen again."

Cassar had to believe him because he had put him on the spot. Deep down, he believed Chuck was a good guy and, more than that, he was a good friend—but he realized that as the case progressed, Murphy was spending more and more time with the press and less time on the case.

Cassar was heartbroken to think that his partner would do that. He tried to rationalize it because he didn't know if it was intentional, or if Murphy had a few beers with some colleagues and was letting information out without considering the ramifications.

He realized he only had one choice. He still had to share information with Chuck Murphy that was given to him by Bailey. He also came to the realization that he might be doing the opening arguments, arguing the entire case, and doing the closing argument too. He knew Chuck Murphy had been around for a long time and had built up his credibility, but he also knew he might have to do it all on his own now.

—

The former *Detroit News* reporter turned judge already had a plan in place to manage the throng of media that was expected for Ron Bailey's trial in Livingston County. To prevent either side from talking to the press, Judge Latreille issued a gag order. The order prevented the attorneys, the county clerk, the medical examiner, law enforcement, and others associated with the case from talking to the media prior to the trial. His goal was to ensure that Ron Bailey got

143. Cassar, Raymond, Interview with author, February 27, 2024

a fair trial. He fully expected that once the trial approached, there would be a new onslaught of media coverage, and he didn't want it to affect jury selection. He also put together an eighteen-page press packet that included biographical information about the attorneys, key dates in the case, a history of the courthouse and Livingston County in general, and a glossary of legal terms. It was simply a way to help the media because Latreille had a newspaper background.

Ray Cassar had reservations about providing biographical information for the press. He was thinking, *No, this isn't right. This isn't a media show.* In a formal statement, he said, "We refuse to participate in providing biographical information to the Court because it's not pertinent due to the severity of the case."[144]

To many, at least on the surface, it looked like Chuck Murphy was trying to get as much information out into the public as he could, and he was upset over the gag order. He felt it was directed at both his partner and him. Both men had been warned several times by Latreille not to try the case in the media, and in Latreille's order he referred to "certain attorneys" continually speaking to the media and aggravating the situation. In a letter to Judge Latreille, Murphy wrote:

> *The situation approached absurdity when, as a means of discovery, both Mr. Cassar and myself would call the news media to find out what new evidence, if any, the task force had discovered, because we would receive more reliable and more detailed information from the news media than we could receive from the task force itself. Although Your Honor's feelings seem directed at the defense counsel, we can assure you that any comments made*

---

144. Krensak, Jack, "Star Witness in Murder Trial May be Defendant Bailey," *Detroit Free Press*, August 31, 1986

by us were subsequent to leaks or comments made by investigative authorities or the prosecution itself.[145]

Murphy was right. It seemed the FBI was another major source of information being leaked to the media, at least to the larger outlets. Frank Del Vero suspected the same thing. Those outlets had a lot of other sources the smaller papers didn't have. The local papers weren't getting the information the larger papers and television stations were getting. Dan Grantham from the *Livingston County Daily Press* was only getting information from his local sources and trying to figure out what was going on. Once Judge Latreille put the gag order in place, it evened the playing field for all of the media to a certain degree and began benefitting the local papers. Grantham's coverage, as well as coverage from the other local reporters, became just as relevant as the *Detroit Free Press*, the *Detroit News*, the *Ann Arbor News*, and the TV stations because the attorneys weren't allowed to speak to anyone.

—

Even a year after Shawn Moore's abduction and murder, the Brighton community and beyond were still in fear for their children.

What if it had been my child? Many of the people in and around Brighton would drive by the spot where Shawn was kidnapped and couldn't help but think of him. Shawn's case was every parent's nightmare. They still worried. To the community as a whole, Shawn felt like a close friend or a relative, and they wondered what they would do if someone tried to harm one of their children.

---

145. Cain, Stephen, "Bailey Defense Team a Study in Contrasts," *Ann Arbor News*, August 31, 1986

Though the immediate hysteria had died down, people were more cautious than they had been the previous year.

Locally, the Brighton Police had started the United Parent Program that centered around child safety but after a year, there seemed to be little interest in volunteering for it. Even though the initial shock had worn off, parents still kept a closer eye on their kids. Interest in the new programs that were announced following Shawn's kidnapping and murder had waned.

The community hadn't forgotten. One parent said she had become more protective while her son had become resentful. "You do the best you can," she said. "No plan is one-hundred-percent safe. If you want your children to be independent, you give them guidelines, and hopefully, they follow them even though you are not with them."

The owner of Lynn's Main Street Café, Lynn Todd, said she would never again be able to see a child on a bike without thinking of Shawn Moore. "You always feel that your girls are more vulnerable than boys, but I guess this proves that's wrong."[146]

—

With a trial date set for early September, Ray Cassar was hesitant. He felt intimidated. Much like when he initially agreed to represent his client, every time the television was turned on, Ron Bailey's face was there as the trial date approached. Every time he picked up a newspaper, there was a story about his client.

Do I have the experience to handle a case like Bailey's? Cassar wondered. The more he doubted himself, the more he came back to what his father had told him: *"Your job is*

---

146. Robertson, Nicole, "Community Still Remembers," *Livingston County Daily Press,* August 27, 1986

not to judge. Your job is to represent rights. Do what you've got to do."[147]

On the one-year anniversary of Shawn's kidnapping, an article written by Jack Krensak appeared in the *Detroit Free Press.* Kresnak had covered the case extensively and written numerous articles about it.

The article highlighted the case. No one knew for certain if Bailey would testify, but many thought it was likely. If he did, no one knew if he would admit to abducting Shawn Moore, giving him alcohol and drugs, then sexually assaulting him in Gladwin for two days before killing him. In the article, Kresnak noted that if Bailey testified, he would be questioned about his forced homosexual affair with Dr. Tombo. It was common knowledge that Cassar and Murphy were going to argue that the affair either "caused or compounded mental illness that began when Bailey was a child."[148]

Neither defense attorney could comment in the article because of the gag order in place.

—

The search was on for Dr. Jose Tombo. Cassar had tried to have him served with a subpoena for the trial, but he couldn't be found. He enlisted the help of the Livingston County Prosecutor's Office and still couldn't be found. The state police were asked to try and find him, but still no Tombo. Cassar suspected he was being hidden among Detroit's Filipino community.

—

147. Cassar, Raymond, Interview with author, February 27, 2024
148. Kresnak, Jack, "Star Witness in Murder Trial May be Defendant Bailey," *Detroit Free Press*, August 31, 1986

Frank Del Vero was prepared for the trial. He planned to call as many as seventy-six witnesses to prove Ron Bailey was guilty. Some of those would include the motorists who saw the abduction, and other witnesses who saw Bailey in Gladwin near where Shawn's body was found.

Judge Latreille was ready too. He announced it was his intention to question perspective jurors himself. He would review questions from both the prosecution and defense first, rather than allowing the attorneys to question jurors themselves. He had done it before in other cases. Both the prosecution and defense would still be able to dismiss jurors with or without cause.

Cassar and Murphy still questioned whether an impartial jury could be seated because of the pre-trial publicity.

Before the trial could even start, Latreille set a hearing for the following week to determine if another defense psychiatric expert's report held by the defense should be turned over to the prosecution. It was the first report from the psychiatrist who had opined that Bailey wasn't insane. It would certainly contradict Dr. Joel Dreyer's report that said Bailey was insane. The psychiatrist visited Bailey on his own and prepared the report, but his services were terminated prior to that over a fee dispute.

—

Fall was fast approaching, and so was Ron Bailey's day in court. Ray Cassar's father had passed away just before Bailey's preliminary exam the year before. He had gone to his father's funeral thinking, *Maybe I can't do this. Maybe I'm just not qualified,* and he was still intimidated by public interest in the Bailey case and the immensity of it all as the trial approached. He was apprehensive but would always return to the thought of his dad saying, *"You're not there to judge people, you're there to represent their rights."* Cassar was quickly learning that he had to stand by his beliefs and do what was right even when everyone else seemed to be against him.

—

On September 3, seventy-five Livingston County residents reported to the Livingston County Courthouse for jury duty. On the second floor of the red brick Richardsonian Romanesque building in downtown Howell, the gallery was packed as Frank Del Vero and David Morse sat on one side of the courtroom. Ray Cassar and Chuck Murphy sat on the other side with Ronald Bailey.

Two words on the transom window over the large oak doors read "Court Room." Thick oak trim surrounded both the doors and the transom. Inside, portraits of past circuit court judges lined the walls. Four-foot decorative wood paneling surrounded the lower part of the interior walls while ornate stenciling above the paneling encompassed the entire courtroom. The red carpet offered a sharp contrast to the salmon-pink-colored walls. The windows were arched with oak trim and intricate wooden blinds, while globe-shaped lights hung from the high ceiling. It was a beautifully preserved courtroom from yesteryear.

There was still speculation that a fair and impartial jury would be difficult to find, if not impossible. Judge Latreille was certain that with Bailey's arrest having been made over a year earlier, much of the publicity and the effects of it had passed. With over 100,000 residents in Livingston County, surely they could find fourteen qualified men and women. Some experts believed that even with some people who hadn't heard of the case, it would be impossible, in a laboratory sense, to find a "pure" jury. Livingston County residents would have to rely on the honesty and good faith of the potential jurors and the judge's abilities.

Everyone knew Frank Del Vero would be questioning the potential jurors about whether they might feel, in order for conviction, that a specific cause of death had to be determined. He would also be asking questions about circumstantial evidence and their feelings toward it. Del Vero planned to deliver the prosecution's circumstantial evidence during the trial, and David Morse would handle the defense to the insanity claims made by Cassar and Murphy.

The defense team would focus juror questions about the insanity defense, psychiatry, and mental illness. An important question they provided to Judge Latreille for him to ask the prospective jurors read:

Do you understand that is an appropriate defense for a defendant to show that he had a mental illness and because of the mental illness he lacked substantial capacity to appreciate the wrongness of his conduct or conform his conduct to the requirements of the law? In other words, that, as a result of mental illness, the person did not know what he was doing or whether it was right or wrong.

Whether or not Ron Bailey could control himself and conform his behavior were key questions.

Everyone was aware that there were reforms being sought to the insanity defense because of the Reagan assassination attempt five years earlier. Dr. Joel Dreyer said there were forty-two bills in the Senate to change provisions of the federal insanity defense. "This is Ku Klux Klan, right wing. If our great father of the country is shot, we're going to change the rules."[149] It was clear he didn't agree with the reforms.

—

149. Cain, Stephen, "Bailey Attorneys to Employ Insanity Defense," *Ann Arbor News*, August 31, 1986

One criminal justice expert said picking a jury was like going through Customs at the airport. It was a hit or miss process. They might ask what you bought or what you are bringing back, but they seldom ask a person to open their bag so they can see what is inside. He meant that the attorneys couldn't open up a juror's mind and see what they were thinking. If a person truly wanted to be chosen for jury duty, for whatever reason, they would be able to.

Security was tight as five deputies used metal detectors to screen people coming into the courthouse for jury selection. Eight women and six men sat in the jury box of the Victorian-era courtroom. The wicker-backed chairs were uncomfortable. They were the first prospective jurors to be questioned by Judge Stanley Latreille, and when he asked if any of them had heard of the case, all fourteen raised their hands. Everyone knew jury selection was going to be a long process.

With just a few spectators, there were four panels of seventy-five prospective jurists, eight sketch artists, and fifteen reporters. Bruce Moore and Alfred Bailey silently watched from the gallery. Sitting at the defense table with his hands folded, Ron Bailey quietly whispered to Cassar and Murphy as the process began. Bailey was dressed in a pale blue shirt, gray sweater vest, and gray pants. If he didn't care for a prospective juror, his expression would reflect antipathy. If he liked an answer, he would nod to his attorneys.

Most of the questions asked by Latreille had been provided by the prosecution and defense, but he had re-written them in his own words to query the jurors.

One of the first to be questioned was a disabled veteran. He had an eighth-grade education and in spite of some medical problems, he was sure he could sit through the trial. Admitting he had seen some of the news coverage surrounding the case, he said he didn't believe everything he had read.

Chuck Murphy didn't agree with the jury selection process imposed by Latreille, and he let the judge know. He would renew his motion for change of venue, and the judge told him he would reconsider the motion if they couldn't pick a jury. Latreille allowed both the prosecution and the defense to ask each potential juror one question, but each side had to let the judge know what the question was before it was asked.

The defense team also wanted to have an equal number of experts on both sides. They only had Dr. Joel Dreyer, while the prosecution had Dr. Harley Stock and Dr. Lynn Blunt. Latreille denied their motion and told them there was no legal requirement for the number of witnesses, and he would let the jury know that the number of experts on either side didn't matter.

It was a very long and slow process, but it was necessary to ensure Ron Bailey got a fair jury. One juror told Latreille he got bored easily. Another said she found it hard for any person to do something like what Bailey was accused of. Both were excused.

During jury selection, the prosecution and defense had a limited number of peremptory challenges. By law, the prosecution had fifteen and the defense had twenty. Either side could use one of those challenges to excuse a potential juror for no reason at all, and to those well-versed in jury selection, it was much like a chess game. Both sides had to sometimes use their own gut feelings and combine them with their expertise in nonverbal behavior to weed out jurors who might not be truthful in answering questions. After four days, twenty-five had been excused for cause. Some of those were unable to put aside their prejudices in the case while others were excused for health issues or other problems.

While the jury selection was taking place inside the courthouse, twenty-five people, mostly teens, were taunting Ron Bailey from outside. When Bailey was transferred from the courthouse to a waiting patrol car, some in the small crowd shouted, "Get the noose!" and "Electric chair!"[150]

On Tuesday, September 9, after five days of intense questioning, jury selection ended. Both the prosecution and the defense passed on another round of potential jurors being questioned, and while Frank Del Vero and David Morse were happy with the jury, Murphy never got out of his chair when he quietly said, "We pass. I think we have a jury." Morse was surprised.

Bailey's defense team was frustrated. They accepted the jury but still had fifteen peremptory challenges they could have used to excuse jurors whom they didn't want to decide their client's fate. "But who would we have lost if we bounced a couple we thought were too favorable?" Murphy asked.[151] Ray Cassar claimed they had to pick a jury in the "back yard" of the state's most sensational crime. Each of the fifty-two prospective jurors who were questioned had heard of the Shawn Moore case. Neither defense attorney was happy. When Judge Latreille asked if they were satisfied with the jury, Murphy said they couldn't respond because they still intended to argue for a change of venue. They also let Judge Latreille know that they had been unable to find Dr. Tombo, and they were going to put together a request for a court order to compel Paul Stevenson to produce him for the trial.

Even Del Vero and Morse still had eleven peremptory challenges remaining.

The panel of jurors who would decide if Ron Bailey was guilty of kidnapping and murdering Shawn Moore or if he was insane at the time was in place. During the process, several of them mentioned they were already leaning toward a guilty verdict, but they also felt they could put

---

150. Smith, Amy, and Cain, Stephen, "Bailey Quiet, Calm as he Watches Snail-Paced Jury Selection," *Ann Arbor News,* September 4, 1986

151. Cain, Stephen, and Smith, Amy, "Bailey Jury Seated," *Ann Arbor News,* September 10, 1986

their prejudice aside and base their decision on whatever evidence was presented at the trial.

The legal community in and around the Brighton area were scratching their heads. Cassar and Murphy had only used five of their twenty peremptory challenges. While some of those attorneys questioned Cassar and Murphy's sanity, others thought they had no idea what they were doing, and still others thought they might have some other tactic up their sleeve. Many thought the two defense attorneys would use all twenty of their peremptory challenges to remove prospective jurors and then claim they couldn't seat an unbiased jury; then they could move for a change of venue. An incredulous local attorney, after hearing about the jury selection, said, "I've tried a bunch of murder cases, and I have never, never considered appointing a jury after only four, five, or six peremptory challenges."[152]

Many thought Murphy and Cassar had ruined their chance of an appeal down the road by not using all of their challenges to unseat prospective jurors.

In a comparable Michigan case, John Norman Collins, who was convicted of murdering at least one Eastern Michigan University co-ed in 1970, was denied a change of venue prior to his trial. Because of the pre-trial publicity and a change of venue being denied, he appealed his conviction in 1972. His appeal was denied because his attorneys had agreed to a jury when they still had three peremptory challenges left.

The entire process of selecting a jury was made that much more difficult by L. Brooks Patterson because he had tried to ignite public interest in the death penalty argument for Michigan and outlaw the insanity defense.

---

152. Grantham, Daniel, "Bailey Defense Tactics 'Puzzle,'" Grantham, Daniel, *Livingston County Daily Press*, September 17, 1986

18
The First Trial

In the West Security One wing at the Livingston County Jail, Ronald Bailey had a twenty-four-inch-square window in cell number 1. The ten-foot by six-foot cell had a small bed, commode, and desk. He was in isolation, though he was considered a model prisoner, and he wasn't allowed to mix with other inmates. He had been permitted one visit from his parents when they were allowed to hug him and touch him, and he had been baptized four months earlier by a minister from his family's church. The minister, Dr. Robert Woodburn, had turned into a regular visitor for Bailey at the jail. Each week he would go to the jail for an hour to discuss the Bible with him. Other than the special visit from his parents, Bailey was still allowed two thirty-minute visits per week with up to three people but had to speak to them through a telephone.

With sixty or so inmates at the jail, he was woken each day at around 7:00 a.m. when a jail trustee brought around his breakfast. He was allowed out of his cell for up to two hours per day to walk back and forth along a thirty-foot catwalk in front of his cell and two others. He had the chance to go outside, but only for one hour per week. If he did go outside, the only thing he could see was the sky. The horizon wasn't visible because the jail's exercise yard blocked the view.

When Ron Bailey was first brought to the jail, he was watched by a camera and television monitor to prevent any suicide attempts. As time went on and the trial approached, he was checked less frequently.

In his cell, he had some Louis L'Amour paperbacks lined neatly between the bars. He kept the Bible his brother had given to him on his desk, and he had a battery-powered television with a six-inch screen.

It had all come down to one day: Ronald Bailey's first of three scheduled trials. For Frank Del Vero and David Morse, there had been hours and hours of preparation for weeks on end. They knew what was at stake, and they had spent endless days and nights beyond the end of their workday talking to experts and doing research. There was no way they could do everything that had to be done between 8:00 a.m. and 5:00 p.m. The amount of work was immense, and it seemed to consume their every waking minute.

They both knew unexpected things could happen during a trial. They were anxious, and they had tried to prepare for everything they could think of but also knew there would be things that they hadn't anticipated. The big unknown was how Bailey would react under cross-examination, and they weren't sure what they would get out of him.

On September 11, opening arguments in the trial of Ron Bailey began.

Wearing a beige-colored shirt, white sweater vest, a brown knit necktie, and brown pants, he sat at the defense table looking downward.

For Frank Del Vero and David Morse, keeping the jury focused on Ron Bailey as a calculating spinner in a web of deceit was their goal.

Without a cause and time of death, some in the legal community thought the trial could be a landmark case in showing what proofs were needed to get a conviction. If it could be shown that Ron Bailey had caused the death through circumstantial evidence presented, the prosecution didn't have to prove how it was done, only that it wasn't accidental or self-inflicted. Even without the murder, Del Vero and Morse could still convict Bailey in the kidnapping of Shawn, which could result in a life sentence without parole.

Latreille had a lot of discretion in the case. Ron Bailey's juvenile record showing sexual attacks on teens could be used to show a commonality between crimes and a similar method of operation.

Frank Del Vero was ready. In his hour-long opening statement to the jury, without ever looking at a note pad, he outlined the case against the defendant.

Bailey was a liar. He had tried to get a friend to cover for him for the weekend he kidnapped and murdered Shawn. He had used an alias when he bought a plane ticket at Detroit's Metro Airport when he fled to Florida. Del Vero outlined the witnesses who would testify not only about the kidnapping on Whitmore Lake Road on August 31, 1985, but the witnesses who saw Ron Bailey in Gladwin that same weekend. The media was impressed. They had never seen an opening statement that long where the prosecutor didn't have to look at his notes.

Chuck Murphy stood before the jury to make his opening statement after Del Vero had finished. He wanted the jury to forget the prosecution's position that it was simply a gruesome crime. "The defense shares this tragedy," he said.[153] Separate from the prosecution's position, Murphy and Cassar wanted the jury to focus on Bailey's "living nightmare" of insanity and Dr. Tombo's part in creating Bailey's madness. As he read from his notes, he said the defense wasn't going to dispute the facts presented by Frank Del Vero and David Morse. "We admit the fact that Ronald

---

153. Cain, Stephen and Smith, Amy, "Prosecution, Defense Present Different Images of Bailey in Trial," *Ann Arbor News*, September 14, 1986

Bailey killed Shawn Moore." Up to that point, the defense team hadn't admitted anything.

The impression throughout the community was a "collective sigh of sorrow" when Murphy made that statement, and they were suddenly reliving the tragedy.

As Murphy's opening progressed, he told the jury his client was insane at the time of the crime because his psychiatrist had forced him into a homosexual affair when he was a teen. "It's our contention that Dr. Jose Tombo destroyed this man's sanity for the gratification of his own deviant sexual needs." The defense witnesses would include Ron Bailey's father, who would testify about how he had trusted the State's mental health system and how he was betrayed by Dr. Tombo. Tombo still hadn't been found. Other witnesses would include a former cellmate of Bailey's who was going to testify about him watching a blank television screen in his cell and how he spoke of the devil. A church deacon was also set to testify that Bailey believed he was possessed. And finally, Murphy said Ron Bailey would testify in his own defense.

"This young man was sick—a very sick young man," Murphy said. "But if he had any hope at all of becoming sane, it was destroyed by Dr. Jose Tombo." He described Bailey's commitment to the Hawthorn Center in 1976 and how Tombo seduced him. "My client did succumb to Dr. Tombo's deviant sexual demands, but by doing so, he lost the last semblance of sanity he had."[154]

The following day, Frank Del Vero began calling witnesses. Everyone knew Ron Bailey was responsible for the murder, but Del Vero still had to produce each of his witnesses to keep the jury focused on the horror of the crime. He didn't want the same outcome as the Hinckley case. The entire trial of John Hinckley focused on his state

---

154. Kresnak, Jack, "Bailey Admits Killing but Was Insane Then, His Lawyer Contend," *Detroit Free Press*, September 12, 1986

of mind and not the horror of the attempted assassination of the president.

Del Vero and Morse would use two strategies. They would produce the evidence to prove what Bailey was going to testify to, and they would bring out aspects of Bailey's character and behavior. That would be used to tear apart the insanity defense and prove that Bailey was hardly insane. Why did he ask a friend to provide an alibi for him? Why did he meticulously clean his Jeep? Why flee to Florida?

In the opening minutes of the trial, with Shawn's dad on the stand as the State's first witness, Del Vero asked Bruce Moore for a physical description of his son.

"About four feet ten inches, eighty-five pounds, eighty to eighty-five pounds, depending on the time of year. Slender, fair complexion, blond—darkish blond—slender boy; handsome boy," Bruce Moore said as he spoke of his son.

"That's my boy, Shawn," Moore said as he looked at the photo shown to him by the prosecutor. Del Vero then passed the photo of Shawn to the jury as Bruce Moore began describing the last time he had seen his son. Shawn had helped with the lawn work but took a break when the mower broke. He asked if he could ride to the Pump and Pantry, and Bruce Moore told him to be back by 5:00 p.m. because the family was going to a movie.

Mr. Moore talked about Shawn's bike. It was too big for him, but he knew he would grow into it.

"Could you describe that bike for us, sir?" Del Vero asked.

"Silver-gray, a Huffy, probably twenty-six-inch, I think it was. Had some maroon or red lettering on it, the Huffy logo. Very proud of it, brand new, paid half of it himself." Shawn had only had the bike a few months.

"Did he like riding it?" Del Vero asked.

"Oh, yes. It was one of his favorite pastimes."

As Bruce Moore finished describing the last day he had seen his son, Frank Del Vero said, "Mr. Moore, did Shawn ever return home that day?"

"No."

"Did you ever see Shawn alive again after that day?"

"No."

The prosecutor touched on Shawn's health—and with good reason. Shawn was perfectly healthy in August 1985. In the winter, if Shawn had a cold and it wasn't caught right away, it would sometimes develop into a heavy chest cold. It had happened several times in the past, but at the time of his disappearance, he was healthy and wasn't taking any medication.

Del Vero asked, "Would Shawn, in your knowledge, have any reason to be in Gladwin, Michigan?"

"Definitely none."

"Had he ever been to any cabins in Gladwin, Michigan?"

"Never. He never had heard the word."

When Scott, Shawn's brother, testified about the afternoon, he said he had started to fix dinner when Shawn had mentioned how he would like to ride to the Pump and Pantry for a can of pop. By 5:00 p.m., he still wasn't back, and Scott got in his car to go look for him. That was when he came across what he initially thought was an accident and was told that police believed his younger brother had been abducted.

Scott identified Shawn's bike in the photos taken by the police at the scene.

"Have you ever seen Shawn alive again after that date?" Del Vero asked.

"No."[155]

After Bruce and Scott Moore testified, their neighbor in the Horizon Hills subdivision was called to the stand. Robert

---

155. People v. Ronald Bailey, 85-4447-FC and 85-4448-FC, Livingston County, 7, 12, September 12, 1986

Redford said that on the day of the kidnapping, he had seen Shawn riding his bike northbound on Whitmore Lake Road on his way to the Pump and Pantry. He described the chuckle that both he and Shawn had when he walked behind the counter inside the store after he had filled his gas tank. Redford also said that four or five weeks before, he had seen Ronald Bailey at the same Pump and Pantry where he and Shawn had been. It was around 9:30 p.m. when he and his wife stopped on their way back home, and he parked next to a Jeep. He described Ron Bailey's Jeep in detail because he had worked for American Motors for twenty years, and he was interested in their new line of Jeeps. When his wife went into the store, he saw Ron Bailey come out of the store with a woman, and they stood in front of the Jeep as they talked. When Redford's wife came out, she got in the car and they left.

"So, it's your testimony that perhaps, how long before the August 31, 1985, date that you saw Ronald Bailey at the Pump and Pantry?"

"Four or five weeks before, approximately. Maybe six, I don't know," Redford answered.[156]

Witness after witness testified, some about how they had witnessed the kidnapping and assumed it was a father and son dispute, and others about seeing Bailey in Gladwin.

Shawn Schneider was an acquaintance of Ron Bailey's, and Frank Del Vero called him as the next witness for the prosecution. Schneider had met Bailey through their mutual friend, Jack Zaccardo. Schneider would see Bailey every couple weeks, and just before Labor Day in 1985, Bailey had talked about going up north for the holiday. He was going to go fishing and four-wheeling. He had asked Schneider to go, and Schneider, then a teen, checked with his mom.

---

156. People v. Ronald Bailey, 85-4447-FC and 85-4448-FC, Livingston County, 7, 39, September 12, 1986

"I talked to my mother about it, and my mother had known him, knew him from the bar that she worked at. He came there kind of frequently," he said from the witness stand.

"So, your mother didn't want you to go, and you didn't go?"

"Right."[157]

Ron Bailey's old girlfriend, Deb Chesney, had married since she had quit seeing Ron. She had known Bailey for almost fifteen years, and after his arrest for the kidnapping and murder of Shawn Moore, she had broken off their relationship. When they were dating, they would see each other two or three times during a week. When she testified at Bailey's trial, she described his former vehicles.

Del Vero asked, "Were you dating Ronald Bailey when he purchased this Jeep?"

"Yes, I was."

"Did you have anything to do with the financial arrangements pertaining to that Jeep?"

"Well, I helped him to get the Jeep. I give him five hundred dollars towards it [sic]."

Bailey had asked her to go up north, but she declined because she had to work.

Del Vero wanted to make sure the jury understood the location she was talking about. "When you say 'up north,' where are you talking about?"

"Our cabin."

"Where is that?"

"In Gladwin," she answered. She told the jury it was owned by her brother, her two sisters, and her.

Bailey had told his girlfriend that since she couldn't go, he was going to take his boat to the cabin and winterize it with another male friend of his for the weekend. She thought

---

157. People v. Ronald Bailey, 85-4447-FC and 85-4448-FC, Livingston County, 7, 46, September 12, 1986

it was Mike Slavin. He also said he was going to mow the lawn while he was there.

Deb figured that her boyfriend would call her as soon as he got back from his weekend at the cabin but he didn't. She didn't see him until Tuesday or Wednesday, and the only thing he said about the weekend was that he only mowed half the lawn.

During the following weekend, Bailey told her he had been stopped by the police because he had a Jeep, and they were questioning everyone who owned one.

Del Vero asked her if she was comfortable with Ron Bailey taking care of her son, Eric, who was five at the time.

"There was one time when my son drank a beer down real fast, and then I got kind of upset with that but [Ron] did that occasionally."[158]

When Fred Chesney testified after Deb, he described the cabin in Gladwin as about twenty feet by twenty feet. The concrete floor was covered with linoleum. It was a single room with two sets of bunk beds. There was a stove and refrigerator, and it had electricity, but only a hand water pump that had to be primed each time it was used. There were dishes kept in the cupboards and an oil stove.

Fred Chesney had only met Bailey a dozen times. On August 28, Bailey had come over to Fred's house with Deb, and he asked Fred for the key to the cabin in Gladwin. Fred gave the keys to him, and Bailey told him he was going up with some friends but didn't mention any names. It wasn't unusual because Bailey had borrowed the keys on two or three other occasions.

Frank Del Vero made sure the jury understood that the initial search of the cabin by police was done with Fred and Deb Chesney's consent.

---

158. People v. Ronald Bailey, 85-4447-FC and 85-4448-FC, Livingston County, 7, 61, September 12, 1986

"When you were contacted by the police, did you give your consent for the police to search that cabin?"

"Yes."

"And do you know if anybody else in your family did that?"

"My sister. My sister did."[159]

When Ron Bailey worked for ARA, he had been a good employee and was always on time. His former boss, Harland Greenfield, testified that Bailey was better than most of his other employees and was detail-oriented when it came to the paperwork he had to do as warehouse manager.

A former subordinate of Bailey's at the warehouse, Doug Sysol, said Bailey had asked him on Friday to go up north with him but hadn't mentioned where he was going. Sysol already had plans. He also told the jury about Bailey driving his Jeep into the warehouse and meticulously cleaning the interior on the Tuesday after Labor Day. He couldn't remember Bailey ever having done that before.

A second colleague said Bailey, who usually kept himself looking good, looked really "cut down" on his first day back to work after the Labor Day weekend and a little more on edge. Bailey told him he had gone up north and found a nice place where he could drink and be alone.

Frank Del Vero was building his case piece by piece. He wanted to show Ron Bailey's attempt to create an alibi for the Labor Day weekend.

Del Vero called Alfred Bailey as his next witness.

Alfred had discussed Ron's plans for the weekend with him. Ron told him he was going up north to Caseville with a friend. Alfred recalled his son leaving around 11:00 a.m. after packing some clothes, beer, and a .22 caliber rifle.

The prosecutor continued to work his way through the list of witnesses, and those included Ron's aunt, uncle, and

---

159. People v. Ronald Bailey, 85-4447-FC and 85-4448-FC, Livingston County, 7, 76, September 12, 1986

cousins from Fowlerville describing how Ron had stopped by their home on Saturday, August 31, then left at around 2:30 p.m.

By the end of the first day of testimony, eighteen witnesses had taken the stand. Frank Del Vero ended the day by calling the teen who was approached by Bailey just thirty minutes before Shawn Moore was kidnapped. He had been shopping with his mom when they stopped at the Brighton Mall and she had gone into the Kmart store while he waited for her in the mall entrance. When Bailey tried to coerce him out of the mall, he refused, and they reported the attempt the next day when they saw reports of Shawn's kidnapping.

—

Ron Bailey's trial entered the second day with a motion brought by the defense.

Before the jury was brought in, Cassar and Murphy asked the judge for a court order demanding the appearance of Dr. Jose Tombo before the court. Paul Stevenson, his attorney, had assured the Court months before that Tombo would be available to testify, but no one had been able to find him and serve him with a subpoena. Judge Latreille finally gave in, not really knowing if Tombo was, in fact, a material witness or what he might testify to. Nobody knew what Tombo would say or if he would actually even testify. Cassar and Murphy weren't sure either.

Latreille said, "Let us keep in mind that Dr. Tombo has rights also, and the Court has an obligation to protect his rights."[160] He told Frank Del Vero to have the police help find Tombo if it was necessary, and he signed an order demanding Tombo appear before the Court on Friday, September 19.

---

160. People v. Ronald Bailey, 85-4447-FC and 85-4448-FC, Livingston County, 8, 13, September 12, 1986

After the motion to declare Tombo a material witness, the trial resumed with witnesses who had seen the actual abduction of the Brighton teen on August 31, 1985, and cabin owners in Gladwin County who had seen Bailey at the Chesney cabin. Those who witnessed the kidnapping described the look on Shawn's face as fear and gave slightly varying descriptions of his kidnapper. The witnesses included Mr. Moncman, the original witness who got off the highway and tried to circle back to get Bailey's license number after witnessing the kidnapping. The eighteen-year-old college student who drove by Bailey as he was kidnapping Shawn, Sherry Huey, also testified about witnessing the abduction.

Officer Dave Ostrem took the stand and talked about his encounter with Ronald Moncman, then described what he had seen when he finally got to the scene and met with Detective Ed Moore.

Detective Al Steinaway told the jury that the only substantial evidence taken from the scene was Shawn's bike and the can of A&W root beer.

When Lillian Knope testified, she talked of her entire family visiting for the weekend. On August 31, she had been at her daughter's trailer in Gladwin but headed back to her cabin on Ridge Road because she was expecting other family members to start arriving. She got back to her cabin at around 6:15 p.m. and found her granddaughter was there with her husband. She had noticed the Jeep already parked at the Chesney cabin, and it was parked on an angle right next to the corner of the cabin. On Sunday, when Ron Bailey came over from the Chesney cabin to the Allen cabin, she had put her hands on his arm to ask if he was Freddy, and he told her no.

As the police investigation heated up, Mrs. Knope was shown a police lineup and she identified Ron Bailey in the number two position.

Chuck Murphy cross-examined Mrs. Knope after her direct testimony knowing full well she had failed to identify

Ron Bailey at the preliminary exam. He asked Mrs. Knope if she recalled identifying anyone in the courtroom during the previous exam. When she answered yes, he asked, "Can you remember who you identified?"

"Yes, I do… I identified a detective, but I know who I see now."

"That's okay. You identified a detective, is that your answer?"

Murphy let it go at that point, and Frank Del Vero picked up where he had left off on direct examination. He knew she'd had had some difficulty at the preliminary exam, and he brought that out for the jury.

"Can you tell us why you thought you had the problem?" he asked her.

"Well, I had had a cataract operation shortly before that and when I get nervous, my eyes don't focus the way they should."

Del Vero asked if she had been nervous during the preliminary exam, and she said she had been.

"If I got you out of your chair and had you walk around the courtroom, do you think you could identify that person?"

"I can identify him without getting out of my chair," she said as she pointed to Ron Bailey.[161]

When Frank Del Vero had started calling the witnesses who had spoken to Bailey at the cabin in Gladwin, there was a stunning surprise for both Ray Cassar and Chuck Murphy.

Dawn Garner sat before the jury and described Bailey briefly coming over to the Allen cabin. For some reason, Cassar didn't have the police report that had her statement about what she had told the police when they interviewed her.

161. People v. Ronald Bailey, 85-4447-FC and 85-4448-FC, Livingston County, 8, 174, September 12, 1986

"Did there come a time while he was talking to your dad that you and your mother happened to be separated somewhat from your dad?" Del Vero asked.

"Yeah," Dawn replied.

"And did you have occasion to observe anything unusual at the Chesney cabin?"

"Yeah. Somebody walked out."

Dawn had grabbed Cassar and Murphy's attention as Del Vero asked her to describe what she had seen.

"They walked out, looked over at me, and I looked at them too. There was something on the line. There was a clothesline up and they took that off, and I turned to my mother, and I said something, and by the time we looked back, they were gone."

Del Vero asked her to describe the person as best she could.

"I know he had blond hair, and it was probably about to their shoulders, and that's about all."

"Can you tell us whether that was a male or female?"

She couldn't tell but told the jury the person wasn't big. Dawn described the person as being about "five feet or so."

"Did that person have to reach up to take something off the line?" Del Vero asked.

"Yeah, because when they reached it they looked over."

Ray Cassar turned toward Murphy, and they both stared at each other for just a moment. It was a bombshell revelation. Cassar couldn't believe it. He was thinking, *What the hell? I don't understand.* He thought Shawn was being held against his will. *Why didn't he try to escape? How do I cross-examine her?* The defense attorney wasn't sure what to do next. He wondered if Shawn had developed Stockholm syndrome, a theory suggesting why hostages, in some instances, bond with their captors.[162]

---

162. Cassar, Raymond, Interview with author, February 27, 2024

In his cross-examination, Ray Cassar wanted to make sure he had heard her testimony correctly when he asked, "You stated that you saw someone walk out the front door... and go to the line... and remove something?"

"Yeah."

"And you are not sure what it was that he removed?"

"It was a blanket or a quilt or something. I'm not sure. I know it was big. It had to have been a blanket or a sheet or something like that."[163]

He needed to know where the clothesline was that she mentioned. "It was right in the front next to the front door onto this tree here," she said as she pointed to the southwest corner of the house in the aerial photograph taken by MSP. The clothesline ran from the large pine tree and was attached to the front of the cabin.[164]

By the time Dawn had finished her testimony, it was almost 4:00 p.m. The trial was adjourned until the following Tuesday.

—

In comparison to cities like Grand Rapids, Lansing, and Detroit, Howell was a small town with a population of around 7,500. With a town of that size, the availability of dining establishments was limited at best.

To Ray Cassar, it seemed everyone hated both Chuck Murphy and him.

Each day during the trial, the two of them would go to the same small café in town for lunch, and they were always greeted by an overly kind waitress. "Hey, can I get you

163. People v. Ronald Bailey, 85-4447-FC and 85-4448-FC, Livingston County, 7, 184, September 12, 1986

164. People v. Ronald Bailey, 85-4447-FC and 85-4448-FC, Livingston County, 7, 192, September 12, 1986

another cup of coffee? Can I get you anything else?" she would ask.

At the end of the first week, Cassar wanted to thank her. "You know, Miss, I've got to tell you. This has been a horrific week," he said. "You've been so kind to us, and to me especially. I want to thank you for going the extra mile."

She kindly acknowledged his thoughtfulness and said, "I would do anything for guys like you, because it's guys like you who are trying to keep our streets safe and protect the public, and I admire the prosecution to no end."

Cassar looked at her and she looked at him just as they both realized what she had just said. She had assumed they were the prosecutors. "Oh, my," she said. Embarrassed, she turned and walked away.[165]

—

The trial progressed into the next week as Del Vero continued to call witness after witness and build the circumstantial evidence tying Ronald Bailey to Shawn Moore's abduction and murder. A former colleague at ARA, Michael Greenfield, told the jury that before Bailey was arrested in the case, his colleagues at ARA would tease him because he resembled the composite sketch done by police on a poster that was hung up near Bailey's desk at the warehouse, and he owned the same kind of Jeep that police said was used by the kidnapper. Greenfield admitted that he was the anonymous tipster who called Channel 7's tip line and gave them Bailey's name. Greenfield said Bailey eventually took down the poster hanging near his desk.

On Thursday, September 18, Frank Del Vero called his last witness, Dr. Lawrence Simson. There were no surprises. The media had been reporting about the autopsy, and Simson told the jury that because of decomposition, no

---

165. Cassar, Raymond, Interview with author, February 27, 2024

cause of death could be determined, but his opinion on the manner of Shawn's death was homicide. Simson had been given historical information about the case that included the body being found a considerable distance from home, the body was nude, and it was covered with branches and brush in an isolated, rural area.

Dr. Simson had sent tissue samples from Shawn's autopsy to Dr. James Garriott and received an analysis from the Texas Regional Crime Lab in San Antonio. Garriott was one of the foremost toxicologists in the country and, as a matter of routine, Simson regularly did toxicological studies on all of the people he was asked to examine, especially found bodies. He asked Dr. Garriott to look for any kind of chemical agents or psychoactive drugs that would have an effect on a person's consciousness or behavior in some way.

In the tests of Shawn Moore's liver, Dr. Garriott found a large concentration of a drug called phenyltoloxamine, an agent commonly found in antihistamines. The amount detected was higher than normal but wasn't high enough to have caused Shawn's death. It would have an effect on allergies and would decrease the level of consciousness by causing drowsiness and sleepiness. To Simson, it shouldn't have been in Shawn's system. It was a drug usually given by a physician and, according to Dr. Garriott, the level in the tissue was more than an amount that would have been prescribed for a simple cold. Those findings further corroborated Dr. Simson's opinion that Shawn Moore's manner of death was a homicide.

On cross-examination, Ray Cassar asked Dr. Simson if he had based his opinion regarding the manner of Shawn's death on the historical facts rather than the autopsy alone. Simson said it was a combination of both. "The absence of certain things was important too. That is, the absence of certain kinds of natural disease that might have been apparent or certain types of injury."[166] With the limited number of possibilities that could have caused Shawn's death, Simson used a combination of the things he did find and those he didn't to come to his opinion.

—

While Del Vero and Morse were wrapping up the State's case against Ronald Bailey, a defense fund had been set up for Jose Tombo by his friends to "reverse the effects of one of the most vicious, ugly witch hunts in the history of Michigan." Dr. Demetrio Timban, past president of the Philippine Medical Association of Michigan, said the fund had been set up because he and others felt Dr. Tombo should be considered innocent until it was proven otherwise. Tombo should have been treated like any other citizen in the United States. A pamphlet put out about Tombo's defense fund accused the media of being complicit in "waging a one-sided war using weapons consisting solely of hearsay, inuendo, and gossip to distort, exaggerate, and tell outright lies about Joe Tombo."[167]

—

Still no Tombo, and no sign of his attorney either. The defense was starting on Friday without their witness. A private investigator hired by Cassar and Murphy was trying to find him. Detectives from the state police had gone to Paul Stevenson's office, and they weren't allowed in.

Paul Stevenson and his client didn't appear at the show cause hearing before the defense started to present their

166. People v. Ronald Lloyd Bailey, 85-4447-FC and 85-4448-FC, 10, 26, September 18, 1986

167. Kresnak, Jack, "Prosecution Finishes Case in Bailey Trial," *Detroit Free Press*, September 19, 1986

case. Cassar and Murphy filed an emergency appeal with the Michigan Court of Appeals because Judge Latreille had denied their motion to have Tombo declared a material witness. The Court of Appeals declined to hear the case.

One of the first defense witnesses was fifty-two-year-old Alfred Bailey. His testimony was often emotional. He admitted he had begun wondering if his son was involved in the disappearance of Shawn Moore almost immediately after hearing about the kidnapping. He was fighting his emotions, his voice cracking, as he described how he had asked Ron if he knew anything about the boy's kidnapping. He said his son told him no and said there were a lot of Jeeps out there that looked like the one he drove. For ninety minutes, Mr. Bailey testified about the family's efforts to get help for Ron. By the age of fifteen, his son had molested two teen boys and had been at Hawthorn for a year, and when he was released, he did it again.

Mr. Bailey spoke of his son's arrests at thirteen and fifteen for kidnapping and sexually assaulting boys who were younger and smaller than him. He had choked the fifteen-year-old and left him unconscious in a field. "We worked with juvenile authorities there in Livonia, and we had my son admitted to Hawthorn Hospital which is a… for juveniles, to take care of mental problems," Mr. Bailey told the jury.[168] He said that case was eventually moved into the adult courts.

Ron Bailey's dad said it was when his son was eventually admitted to Northville as part of his probation that he was treated by Dr. Jose Tombo. Alfred was certain they were giving his son some sort of medication at Northville because when he would visit the ward, Ron was never very active. He was always quiet. Tombo would tell Mr. Bailey

---

168. People v. Ronald Lloyd Bailey, 85-4447-FC and 85-4448-FC, 11, 10, September 19, 1986

that the staff at Northville couldn't cure his son without the cooperation of him and the family.

"Did Ronald cooperate, to your knowledge?" Cassar asked.

"To my knowledge, he always cooperated. I don't know what… what that meant at that time. Later, we found out that it meant things that it shouldn't have meant."[169]

Alfred took the blame for many of Ron's problems, saying he had been more concerned for his career than he was for Ron. He worked in data processing at an automotive plant, and his wife had her own troubles handling all of the kids. When he got home from work, would often have to dole out the discipline.

Mr. Bailey said he later found out, after Ron had moved to Florida, that his son had had problems while he lived down there, but all he heard were rumors. When he hadn't heard from his son for a while, he phoned his son's employer in Florida, and Ron's boss told Mr. Bailey that he had a very sick young man on his hands. It was shortly after that when Ron moved back to Michigan.

Alfred Bailey described the meeting with Dr. Tombo, Ray Cassar, and Chuck Murphy to the jury. "I brought up the [Windsor] trip, and he said he would not be able to help me if that trip was made public."

Cassar asked, "Did he give you a reason why?"

"He said it would jeopardize his ability to be considered a valid witness on the stand and also that he could lose his job."[170]

During Alfred Bailey's cross-examination by David Morse, Morse highlighted Bailey's pattern of sexual assaults on teen boys long before he had ever been sent to Northville

---

169. People v. Ronald Lloyd Bailey, 85-4447-FC and 85-4448-FC, 11, 22, September 19, 1986

170. People v. Ronald Lloyd Bailey, 84-4447-FC and 85-4448-FC, 11, 42, September 19, 1986

Psychiatric Hospital and long before he had ever met Dr. Tombo.

Morse questioned Mr. Bailey about Ron's trip to the Windsor Raceway with Tombo after the senior Bailey said Ron had asked him permission to go to Windsor with Dr. Tombo. "Did Ron complain to you in any manner about events that had taken place during that day?"

"No, he did not," Mr. Bailey said.

"As far as you know, did he ever express any dissatisfaction about that trip or anything about it to anyone else?"

"Not that I know of."

David Morse was dismantling the defense when he questioned Alfred Bailey about Ron's behavior during his time at Northville. "He wasn't doing anything bizarre that you observed?" he asked Mr. Bailey.

"I think he drank too much, but that's about all."

"Okay, he wasn't talking to television sets during that time?"

"Yeah, like I do, yell at football players."

Morse pressed Mr. Bailey. "All right. Like we all do, I guess. But in terms of, as if someone were in there talking back to him?"

"Not that I know of."

"Okay. And there was nothing in his behavior that would indicate to you that he was hearing demons or hearing voices or talking to anybody during that time?"

"Not that I know of," Mr. Bailey said.[171]

Alfred Bailey admitted under cross-examination that after Ron returned from Florida, then moved back home, he was manipulative. Ron knew how to get people to do things.

Two others testified in Bailey's defense, and one of those was a prison inmate who was serving time for

---

171. People v. Ronald Lloyd Bailey, 85-4447-FC and 85-4448-FC, 11, 53, September 19, 1986

sexually assaulting a teen boy. He was in the cell next to Bailey's at the Livingston County Jail. He claimed he had seen Bailey staring at a blank television, and one night he took the television to bed with him and covered it as if it were a child. According to the inmate, Bailey also talked of demons every day.

Ron Bailey wondered if he might be controlled by demons because of the things he had done.

The press continued to follow the trial and the testimony of the defense witnesses, but according to Bailey's attorney Ray Cassar, it was about to shift into a "battle of the experts."

Opinions would be offered by psychiatrists and forensic examiners about Bailey's mental state when he kidnapped and murdered Shawn. The jury would be charged with weighing those opinions and deciding if Bailey was guilty, guilty but mentally ill, or not guilty by reason of insanity.

Tuesday was the day everyone had been waiting for. Ronald Bailey was set to take the stand in his own defense. Cassar had been preparing his client for the trial. He explained to Bailey how important it was that he convince the jury what was going through his mind when he kidnapped and killed Shawn, and that it wasn't his intent to take his life. He had to convince them it was a case of erotic asphyxiation gone wrong. Ron Bailey had to convince the jury that his intention was to release Shawn, but the sex went too far. There was a fine line between an incredible high a person experiences when they are deprived of oxygen and when they ejaculate.

David Morse was prepping for Bailey's testimony too. Every time he saw the Moore family or a picture of Shawn, he would think, *This is their one shot.* He knew he was responsible for whatever the outcome ended up being, and even with a conviction, the only just results for the Moores was to have Shawn back.

Ray Cassar took Ron Bailey through the crimes he had committed since he had been thirteen years old.

"I remember taking a young boy," Bailey said.

"Okay. Do you recall keeping him against his will?"

"Yes."

When Cassar pressed him about why, Bailey simply said, "I don't know how to explain it. It was just something, like, popped into my head and, you know, I just took him."

Bailey spoke of Dr. Wright, the doctor who treated him at Hawthorn when he was thirteen. "He wanted to know, you know, why I took that boy and, you know, did I want to have sex or didn't I want to have sex with him, and I wasn't sure."

Cassar moved to when Ron had reached the age of fifteen.

"Well, I don't know if… how to describe it; the same feeling or that same, you know, I don't know, impulsive thing jumped in my head, and I went out and kidnapped a boy."

"Was it an urge? Describe it," Cassar said.

"I'm not sure, you know. To kidnap a boy and take him. I'm not sure if it was having sex with him or what."

Bailey went on to describe his third sexual assault where he had choked his victim and dragged him into the bushes.

"Was it the same impulsive feeling that came over you when you grabbed the boy at thirteen years old?" Cassar asked.

"Yes."[172]

Ron Bailey's testimony moved to the graphic details of his sexual encounters with Dr. Tombo after he was admitted to Northville Psychiatric Hospital. "He told me not to talk about it, tell me what, you know, goes on in his office." Bailey told the jury he just assumed it was part of his treatment.[173]

---

172. People v. Ronald Lloyd Bailey, 85-4447-FC and 85-4448-FC, 12, 42, September 20, 1986

173. People v. Ronald Lloyd Bailey, 85-4447-FC and 85-4448-FC, 12, 58, September 20, 1986

The lurid details continued throughout his direct examination by his attorney. Tombo had told him that if he didn't do the things he wanted, he wouldn't be able to go home on weekends, or he would take away Bailey's privilege card. Ron Bailey said the sex continued throughout his stay at Northville.

When Bailey was in Tombo's office at the hospital, Tombo would "call demons and spirits out and put hexes on people." Tombo would talk about voodoo and the black cross that hung in his office. Bailey wanted nothing to do with it.

"Did he ever tell you what the chants were for, what they did?"

"It was to bring the demons and spirits out because he could command them to do certain things."

"Did Dr. Tombo try to bring the demons out?"

"Yes. He told me while we were doing it that I had to call him 'Master.'"[174]

Cassar led Bailey into describing the trip to Windsor and the sexual activity that happened afterward.

When Ron Bailey was eventually released from Northville, he had out-patient visits with Tombo where the sex continued three or four more times, but he maintained that he would try to avoid it.

When he moved to Florida, he had dragged his problems from Michigan along with him when he got into more trouble with young boys down there.

"Did you hurt any of those boys, Ron?"

"No," he said.

"Did you try and have sex with them?"

"Yes."[175]

---

174. People v. Ronald Lloyd Bailey, 85-4447-FC and 85-4448-FC, 12, 73, September 20, 1986

175. People v. Ronald Lloyd Bailey, 85-4447-FC and 85-4448-FC, 12, 99, September 20, 1986

When Ron Bailey spoke of fleeing Florida, he said he wasn't sure if he was coming back to Michigan or not. "I really wasn't sure where I was going. I stayed in Ohio a few days trying to decide."[176] He thought about California or Arizona but ended up back in Michigan.

Ron Bailey's testimony moved to how he had kidnapped Shawn Moore and murdered him at a Gladwin cabin the year before. He had followed Shawn. "Something in my head said, 'Do it.'"

Cassar asked him if he was afraid to kidnap the teen in the middle of the day, and Bailey said, "I wasn't afraid. I did it." Continuing the horrific testimony, he said, "I had the same impulse I had before. A feeling, 'Take him.' I did."[177]

After snatching Shawn from his bike on Whitmore Lake Road, Bailey drove the frightened teen to the Chesney cabin in Gladwin County. Shawn spoke with Bailey along the way, but it was clear he was scared. Bailey told him he wasn't going to hurt him and they were going to have a good time for the weekend. He fixed macaroni and cheese at the cabin. "Later that night, I was feeling weird, strange as I was running around the cabin. It really reminded me of what Dr. Tombo did to me."[178]

Tears streamed down his cheeks as the child killer testified, but he would regain his composure as he continued describing what he had done. To the media, he wasn't crying for what he had done; he was crying for himself. He admitted he had watched Shawn leave a party store on Labor Day weekend in 1985 and followed him.

Bailey maintained he was driven insane by Dr. Tombo's sexual demands while he was at Hawthorn and Northville,

176. People v. Ronald Lloyd Bailey, 85-4447-FC and 85-4448-FC, 12, 100, September 20, 1986

177. Martindale, Mike, "Bailey Says 'Impulse' Led Him to Kill Boy," *Detroit News*, September 24, 1986

178. People v. Ronald Lloyd Bailey, 85-4447-FC and 85-4448-FC, 12, 113, September 20, 1986

and he admitted he had a history of kidnapping and molesting young boys before he ever met Tombo.

Bailey wasn't asked about the other two cases he was charged in, but Morse made note for the jury of Bailey's other encounters with boys long before meeting Dr. Tombo. Bailey admitted that since 1973, anger and sex were the impulses that drove him to kidnap boys but he didn't know why. When he was in the third grade, he'd had his first homosexual experience. In the seventh grade, he was molested by a man who picked him up at a store, and he talked about having sex in rest areas with truck drivers as he got older. He had learned about erotic asphyxiation from those sexual encounters. Cassar was trying to build their insanity defense, and to many it was a believable story.

The first night at the cabin with Shawn Moore, Bailey made the teen drink some beer but they slept in separate beds. The next day, he forced Shawn to have sex with him.

"Did you kill that boy, Ron?" Cassar asked.

"Yeah," he said, almost in a whisper.

"How?"

Bailey said, "I strangled him."

"Why?"

"Because I thought he was me. Because he looked like me," he said. "It was a mistake… It was supposed to be me."[179]

When Ron Bailey talked about the possibility of taking his own life, Ray Cassar asked why he wanted to kill himself. "Because I can't stand it anymore… what everybody did to me."

Ray Cassar had gotten his client to admit to the killing of thirteen-year-old Shawn Moore. It was no surprise because Chuck Murphy admitted in his opening that their client had

---

179. Martindale, Mike, "Bailey Says 'Impulse' Led Him to Kill Boy," *Detroit News*, September 24, 1986

kidnapped and murdered Shawn. As Ray Cassar finished his direct examination, David Morse was waiting.

During cross-examination, Bailey's tears had disappeared, and he sat emotionless on the stand.

David Morse went through Bailey's direct examination and picked apart his testimony. Morse referred to the voices and demons Bailey said he had heard. "Now, you never heard any of these voices tell you to kidnap these kids that you told us about."

"No."

"And so, the voices really didn't have anything to do with whatever urge that you are claiming to have," Morse said.

"That's correct."[180]

Morse seized on Bailey's testimony about how he claimed he thought he was killing himself. "Where did that idea of… you weren't thinking that at the time, were you?"

"Yes, I was."

"You remember now, thinking at the time, 'He looks like me so I am going to kill him.'"

Bailey told him it just happened that way.

"In fact, wasn't it March 8 of 1986, during your first session with Dr. Dreyer?" Morse asked him. He had picked up on something. "In fact, you didn't tell him that's what you thought. He told you or asked you, 'Isn't this what you are doing, Ron Bailey? Isn't it true that you're killing yourself?' That's where the thought came from, isn't it?"

Bailey was confused.

"In fact, it was suggested to you by Dr. Dreyer in saying, 'Ron, isn't it true, don't you see that you are really killing yourself?' That's where the thought came from, isn't it?"

Ron Bailey said, "No."

"Isn't it?" Morse demanded.

---

180. People v. Ronald Lloyd Bailey, 85-4447-FC and 85-4448-FC, 12, 145, September 20, 1986

"I would say part of it did, yeah. Part of it was mine," Bailey answered.[181]

Morse brought out another revelation that during the same meeting with Dr. Dreyer in March 1986, Ron Bailey was acting as if he were Dr. Tombo and acting out the things that had been done to him by Tombo. Bailey acknowledged that in a sense, he did that.

"Dr. Tombo never kidnapped you, did he?" Morse said.

"No."

"Dr. Tombo never forced you to drink alcohol, did he?"

"No."

"Never drugged you, did he?"

"No."

"And he never choked you, did he?"

"No."[182]

Bailey acknowledged to Morse and the jury that even though he was at Tombo's beck and call, he still refused to do certain things with him. He refused to go to Tombo's home. He refused to have anal sex with Tombo. He refused money from Tombo. He refused to do voodoo chants with Tombo.

The assistant prosecutor had Bailey describe how he would make his victims hyperventilate. "And you learned this technique from the man who took your picture and performed oral sex when you were in about the seventh grade, isn't that true?"

"Right."[183]

Morse went through each of Bailey's first two assaults on the young teens and described how in each case, Bailey had used his hyperventilation technique to arouse them even

---

181. People v. Ronald Lloyd Bailey, 85-4447-FC and 85-4448-FC, 12, 147, September 20, 1986

182. People v. Ronald Lloyd Bailey, 85-4447-FC and 85-4448-FC, 12, 148, September 20, 1986

183. People v. Ronald Lloyd Bailey, 85-4447-FC and 85-4448-FC, 12, 157, September 20, 1986

more. He moved the testimony to a point when Bailey was picked up near a truck stop and had sex with an older man, and that man had taught him a new technique; a technique Bailey referred to as the elastic technique. Bailey described it to the jury as putting a piece of elastic around his own neck to cause lightheadedness. It was more effective than hyperventilation. This was before Bailey had ever met Tombo.

Morse pointed out a patient at Northville who had taught Bailey to use his palms around someone's neck. It had the same effect as using elastic. Bailey said he had used the elastic technique on another patient at the Northville too, but he never used it on Dr. Tombo. "You didn't learn that from Dr. Tombo?" Morse asked.

"No."

"And you never practiced it with him."

"No."[184]

Morse asked about Bailey's Florida stay and the boys he had gotten in trouble over while he lived there. Bailey admitted that he had shown the elastic technique to a fourteen-year-old and a sixteen-year-old boy while he was living here.

"The elastic was around their neck, true?" Morse said.[185]

"Mm-hmm."

"And there was a sexual incident, true?"

"I might have showed them that," Bailey said.

"And showed them how it would enhance the sexual experience, right?"

"Right."

When Morse pressed Bailey about there being a sexual nature to that incident, Bailey claimed he couldn't recall if there was or wasn't.

184. People v. Ronald Lloyd Bailey, 85-4447-FC and 85-4448-FC, 12, 165, September 20, 1986

185. People v. Ronald Lloyd Bailey, 85-4447-FC and 85-4448-FC, 12, 171, September 20, 1986

"You remember they were young boys; you remember there was elastic around their necks, but you can't remember if there was any sex involved. Is that what you're telling us?"

"There may have been, but I can't say for sure."

Morse pointed out to Bailey that he hadn't killed those two boys. He got Bailey to admit the problems he had in Florida were the same problems he had had in Michigan. "Young boys, sexual nature, abduction, that sort of thing?"

"Yeah."

"You didn't kill those boys either, did you?" Morse said. "No."[186]

David Morse went through a list of other sexual encounters that Bailey had had for the next two years after returning from Florida. In 1983, there was a sixteen- or seventeen-year-old boy, then in the summer of '83, another boy he had picked up hitchhiking. Someone else had picked the boy up before Bailey could get to him so Bailey followed him. After the boy was dropped off, Bailey picked him up, they partied, and Bailey used the elastic technique on him. Again, in the summer of '83, Bailey met a fifteen-year-old and had sex with him using elastic. In the fall of that same year, Bailey picked up a boy in a Dearborn park and had a sexual encounter using the elastic.

As Morse detailed Ron Bailey's sexual exploitations, he brought up another boy Bailey had had a relationship with who had similar features, fair skin, and reddish-blond hair. Then there was another boy who was seventeen years old with whom Bailey had had sex. Morse's point was that in spite of all those younger boys he had picked up over the previous two years, Ron Bailey hadn't killed any of them.

As the assistant prosecutor highlighted the fact that Bailey hadn't killed one of those kids, yet the defendant

---

186. People v. Ronald Lloyd Bailey, 85-4447-FC and 85-4448-FC, 12, 172, September 20, 1986

was claiming he had the impulse to kill before he went to Northville, then Dr. Tombo didn't give Bailey that impulse. He couldn't have. It was already there.

"That's true," Bailey said.[187]

Bailey said he could sometimes overcome the impulse by going out on his boat until the urge left him. He could, in essence, remove himself from the danger and nothing would happen. He admitted he didn't kill someone every time the urge came over him. He would take Valium because it helped to control the urge by slowing him down.

"Sometimes you would take enough Valium so that you would go to sleep and nothing would happen, true?"

"Right."[188]

By the end of the day, everyone seemed to be mentally exhausted. The jury was excused for the day, and Ron Bailey would be back on the stand in the morning.

When David Morse resumed his cross-examination the following day, he had Bailey describe the sexual practices he had used that led to Shawn's death. His testimony was frightening. In a now monotone voice, Ron Bailey described how he would use either elastic or a belt and put it around his victims' necks. He would tighten it to try to enhance their sexual arousal. When asked about Shawn, he said he put his belt around the teen's neck. Bailey had sexually assaulted Shawn twice. He wrapped his belt around Shawn's neck the second time, and he tightened it while holding Shawn's hands down.

"You put that belt around Shawn Moore's neck, didn't you, Mr. Bailey?"

"Yes."

"He complained about it being too tight, didn't he?" Morse demanded.

---

187. People v. Ronald Lloyd Bailey, 85-4447-FC and 85-4448-FC, 12, 180, September 20, 1986

188. People v. Ronald Lloyd Bailey, 85-4447-FC and 85-4448-FC, 12, 184, September 20, 1986

Bailey hesitated answering for several seconds. He stared at the floor. "I'm not sure," he finally said. The assistant prosecutor's tunnel vision, focusing solely on Bailey, suddenly shifted, and he was intensely aware of Bruce Moore in the courtroom.

"But you tightened the belt, didn't you, Mr. Bailey?"

"Yes."

"You tightened that belt, and Shawn Moore started to squirm, didn't he, Mr. Bailey?"

"No," Bailey answered.

Morse wasn't letting up. He pressed Bailey again until he said, "He might have squirmed a little."

"How long did that take, Mr. Bailey, until Shawn Moore stopped squirming and you didn't have to hold his hands down anymore? How long did it take?" Morse realized he was practically shouting at Bailey. He wasn't holding back because the Moore family deserved that. It was the very least he could do for them given the immense loss they had endured.

"You knew his name, didn't you, Mr. Bailey? You knew his name was Shawn Moore."[189]

"I wasn't killing him. I was killing me."[190]

"Mr. Bailey, the next day, you took Shawn Moore out and left him in the woods, didn't you?" Morse continued, "You covered him up with sticks and ferns, didn't you?"

"Yes."

"You did that because you didn't want anyone to find the body, correct?"

"Yes."

Bailey admitted to drinking large amounts of alcohol, taking pills, and smoking grass to "disarm" himself from an "uncontrollable urge" to kidnap young boys. He had given

189. People v. Ronald Lloyd Bailey, 85-4447-FC and 85-4448-FC, 13, 23, September 24, 1986

190. Kresnak, Jack, "Bailey Says He Knew Killing Boy Was Wrong," *Detroit Free Press*, September 25, 1986

Shawn two sedatives, made him smoke marijuana, and had him drink both beer and schnapps.

After killing Shawn, he said he had thought about killing himself in the cabin but since he didn't own it, he decided not to do it.

Three separate times during his testimony, under cross-examination by Morse, Bailey admitted that he knew killing Shawn Moore was wrong. That point alone was crucial because his insanity defense could have hinged on whether he could appreciate the wrongfulness of his actions.

David Morse had made his point. While Bailey had had more than a dozen encounters with young boys in the previous thirteen years, none of those had ended in death. "While you've had the impulse to take somebody, the decision to kill has always been your own," Morse said.[191]

Ray Cassar watched the jury as Bailey testified. He noticed that none of the jurors would look at his client. It was painful for them to hear about the teen's murder. *If they could only hear from Tombo,* he thought to himself.

Dr. Joel Dreyer, the flamboyant psychiatrist from Southfield, was the star witness for the defense. He took the stand after Ron Bailey.

Chuck Murphy questioned Dreyer about Bailey, and Dreyer said Bailey had a sexual relationship with his sister while living at home in addition to a young neighbor boy. He characterized Ron Bailey as looking like a psychopath, but that appearance was incorrect. "He has a split mind, between thoughts and feelings, a thought disturbance, and he has one... a severe one."

During the interview with Bailey, he was asked where he fit in among his siblings, and Bailey described himself as "the beginning." Dreyer equated his response as God and the devil.

---

191. Martindale, Mike, "Bailey Says 'Impulse' Led Him to Kill Boy," *Detroit News*, September 24, 1986

"Like the devil is going to take over the earth and make it the beginning." He continued, "I see Mr. Bailey as feeling, in a pathological way, as being possessed by demons, his feeling that he is a demon and feeling that from birth, he was sick; from birth, he was the demon and he is the beginning." Dreyer had never heard anyone refer to themselves as "the beginning" except in the movie *The Omen*.[192]

Dreyer saw Ron Bailey as a homosexual pedophile, but his condition worsened after seeing Dr. Tombo and he became quite crazy and psychotic. He saw the same type of sexual activity that Bailey had done from his early childhood through the abduction and murder of Shawn Moore.

Murphy asked Dr. Dreyer to distinguish between his impulse prior to being admitted to Northville and afterward. By the time Bailey was out of Northville, he was his own "pharmacopeia." He was his own drugstore. To Dreyer, the use of drugs was to draw his guilt and murderous impulses toward Dr. Tombo.

While Dreyer spoke of Bailey's abuse by Tombo, he said Ron Bailey often heard the voices of both Tombo and demons in his head. "Bailey has been in contact with Tombo or the devil, and nobody I know has been able to contact Tombo or the devil."[193] It was one of the worst cases of insanity he had ever seen, and each time Dreyer spoke, he would look directly at the jury. They turned away.

Dr. Dreyer believed Bailey had a mental illness and couldn't conform his behavior to the requirements of the law. Those were two of the three requirements for legal insanity. He didn't believe Bailey met the third requirement, which was having the inability to distinguish right from wrong.

---

192. People v. Ronald Lloyd Bailey, 85-4447-FC and 85-4448-FC, 13, 63, September 24, 1986

193. Kresnak, Jack, "Bailey Defense Ends Without Tombo Testimony," *Detroit Free Press,* September 26, 1986

The jury wasn't impressed with Dr. Dreyer's use of graphic street terms in much of his testimony. "So, you realize when he masturbated, he put a rope or cord or elastic band around his neck to get his own penis hard?" he said to the jury. The rambling testimony about autoerotic asphyxiation and the supposed origins in the Old West were filled with detailed descriptions that were offensive to many of the jurors.

Dreyer equated Bailey's submission to Dr. Tombo with Catholics and Jews submitting to the Gestapo in concentration camps during World War II. Much like the survivors from the concentration camps, Bailey felt guilty and was reenacting his guilt on others. Bailey could look completely composed but inside, he could be a raging, demon-like inferno.

According to Dreyer's evaluation, Ron Bailey believed, in his own mind, Shawn was a sex offender because the two of them had sex a few times. He believed the teen had given in to his wishes under duress, and because he did, he was doomed to guilt and homosexuality. When he had sex with Shawn the second time, Bailey was going to show him how to be a better homosexual, and he wrapped the belt around Shawn's neck.

Dreyer compared Bailey's mental condition to that of Tony Perkins's character in the movie *Psycho*. He stepped outside himself and believed it. As Bailey was strangling Shawn and claiming he was killing himself, it was because "that little boy is having sex with a stranger." Bailey's final stage of schizophrenia forced him to disassociate "and allowed him to act out as if he were Tombo and seek out young boys."[194]

Murphy asked if Bailey was schizophrenic.

"There is no doubt in my own professional opinion that Ronald Lloyd Bailey is a schizophrenic, and along with his

194. Cain, Stephen, *Relentless*, self-published, 2024

voices, his visions, his thought disorder, and his emotional disturbance, we have demon possession, devil possession, devil voices, and we have a very, very sick, disturbed man who has urges he can't control and passes boundaries for himself to others."[195] Dreyer made it clear he believed the demonic possession was a symptom rather than a reality, but to Bailey, it was his reality.

The entire jury was confused, and so were the spectators. Dreyer's long-winded and disjointed testimony was too much for Shawn's sister. She bolted from the courtroom in anger.

Bailey's relationship with Tombo made him "quite crazy, quite psychotic," Dreyer said.

His official diagnosis was "pseudo-psychopath schizophrenia." Dreyer's diagnosis wasn't anything accepted by any known forensic psychiatric associations. It meant that although Bailey was schizophrenic, he might also sometimes appear to be psychotic. The psychiatrist believed that Bailey's treatment at Northville harmed him and propagated his drives in a severe pathological direction, and the treatment was directly responsible for his behavior.

When David Morse began his cross-examination of Dr. Dreyer, he wanted the jury to know why Dreyer had named his company InnerVisions. Dreyer had heard it on a Stevie Wonder album. He thought the name was perfect for a psychiatric clinic. "A blind man who sees in, because all of us tend to be blind to our own faults and to our own skeletons, and I thought what a great, catchy name."[196]

Morse led Dr. Dreyer into questions regarding the requirement of being a board-certified psychiatrist, and Dreyer admitted he wasn't certified. He had never tested for it.

---

195. People v. Ronald Lloyd Bailey, 85-4447-FC and 85-4448-FC, 13, 113, September 24, 1986
196. People v. Ronald Lloyd Bailey, 85-4447-FC and 85-4448-FC, 13, 142, September 24, 1986

Dr. Dreyer was asked how he had become involved in the case, and he said he had received a phone call from Cassar and Murphy about it and told them they would have to be willing to hear what he had to say after he evaluated Ron Bailey.

"Doctor, isn't it true before you received that phone call, that you made some contact with them to indicate that you would be interested in taking the case?" Morse asked.

Dreyer admitted it was true, and Morse asked him why.

"Well, I have an interest in all forensic cases. As a matter of fact, it's my love. I am fond of it."

Morse wanted to know if it was typical that he would solicit his services, and Dreyer said he had done it a number of times.

Dreyer had only met with Ron Bailey for a total of five and a half hours to come to his opinion, and his last visit had come after he had already submitted his report to Cassar and Murphy. He hadn't read any police reports about Shawn's kidnapping and murder or any of the reports dealing with accusations against Dr. Tombo. He didn't believe in doing that. He didn't review any of the other doctors' reports about their interactions with Bailey either. He wanted to see Ron Bailey "clean and free of prejudice."[197] He hadn't even spoken to Bailey's parents.

He hadn't made any new findings between his second meeting with Bailey and his third in terms of his diagnosis but he had in terms of dynamic understanding. He knew he had to present his findings to a jury after his second visit, and he wasn't sure how to present them. He didn't completely understand Ron Bailey even though he knew Bailey was schizophrenic. After seeing the movie *Manhunter* and realizing he'd had a number of death threats made against him because he had taken Bailey's case, maybe he didn't

---

197. People v. Ronald Lloyd Bailey, 85-4447-FC and 85-4448-FC, 13, 154, September 24, 1986

want to find the truth. When Dreyer finally met Bailey for the third time, he understood what was going through Bailey's mind and hadn't really understood it before the last visit.

The InnerVisions doctor was asked if he had given Bailey an I.Q. test after he told David Morse that he didn't believe Bailey had the I.Q. to manufacture a false statement or accusation.

"No, I didn't give him an I.Q. test. I gave him some questions that allowed me some basic feel for what his I.Q. is." In fact, Dreyer hadn't given Bailey any tests and admitted he had just "gotten a feel" for what his I.Q. was.[198]

As David Morse's cross-examination went on, there was some contention between the two over Bailey's ability to refuse certain demands from Tombo. Dreyer said, "Sir, you are free to surmise Tombo any way you want. It's interesting we can't even find him so you can surmise, I guess, what you want. The reality is that it's just interesting he is not around."

Morse shot back, "But that's not really our province, is it, doctor? You want to get that in to support your theory of Dr. Tombo and his abuse of the defendant, would that not be true?"

Dreyer gave a long-winded response, saying, "I am not here to support a theory other than the truth, and I hate the idea that one of my colleagues, a man who represents my profession in a field that I love like psychiatry, may even be implicated in that kind of way because it only increases the stigma towards mental illness and the stigma to the idea [that] if you are [a] shrink, you must be a kook, which you have probably heard."

Morse wasn't letting up. "I think I have heard that many times from you, yourself, in the newspapers just this week."

---

198. People v. Ronald Lloyd Bailey, 85-4447-FC and 85-4448-FC, 13, 158, September 24, 1986

"You bet."

Judge Latreille stepped in and told Morse and Dreyer they were bickering. He told Dreyer to simply listen to the question.

Dr. Dreyer was accused of not verifying anything Ron Bailey had told him. "Again, sir, I am not a cop. I am not an interrogator. It is not my job to weigh the facts. The fact-finder is to my left, not you or me."[199]

Dreyer seemed antagonistic throughout much of his cross-examination. Morse asked the doctor if he could point out in his report where Bailey had said Shawn Moore was a sex offender. Dr. Dreyer began by giving a rambling explanation before saying, "From the very first report, you don't hear it. As a matter of fact, what you hear in the first report is that he made the point, and you can read it on page sixteen, first line, 'I am running away from myself.'" Dreyer moved on to an explanation about the threats made against him before Morse asked him once again to read from his report where he had written that Ron Bailey viewed Shawn Moore as a sex offender, and Dreyer said it was in his third report. The doctor's recitation from parts of his third report seemed to wander, and Morse reminded him again, "I want the words where it said the defendant felt Shawn Moore—"

"You won't understand it out of context," Dreyer snapped back.

Morse asked him to simply listen to his question, and Judge Latreille intervened again. "Would you fall silent for a moment, please, and answer the specific question, please?"

Dreyer read what Bailey had told him, verbatim, and Morse asked if he was at the point where Bailey said Shawn was the sex offender.

"Well, he said, 'He is me. He is even me,' and he told me that. I may not... It's somewhere in here, I'm sure."

---

199. People v. Ronald Lloyd Bailey, 85-4447-FC and 85-4448-FC, 13, 174, September 24, 1986

Morse knew Dreyer couldn't find it because it wasn't there.[200]

It was almost 4:00 p.m., and the jury was both tired and confused by Dreyer's ramblings.

The following morning when the Court reconvened, Dr. Joel Dreyer was still on the stand under cross-examination. David Morse had Dreyer recall his first meeting with Bailey, then confronted him with the fact that the idea of Ron Bailey killing himself hadn't, in fact, come from Bailey.

Dreyer was adamant that it was Bailey who had brought it up. It allowed Dreyer to help him understand it. "He saw it intelligently but he didn't feel it," Dreyer told the jury.

Morse knew it hadn't originated with Ron Bailey. "In other words, he didn't say to you, 'Dr. Dreyer, I saw that boy as myself, and I was killing myself.'"

Dreyer admitted those weren't Bailey's exact words.

The assistant prosecuting attorney had him, and he read from Dreyer's report as he asked him to follow along. "At the top of the page, 'All of a sudden, it hit me, and I understood him and looked at him and said, 'Did it ever occur to you that all these kids that looked like you, may be you?'" He reminded Dr. Dreyer that he had written that Bailey then had insight and understood it for the first time.

There was no doubt in David Morse's mind that Dreyer had planted the idea of Bailey killing himself by killing Shawn Moore. "He had been telling you the facts as they occurred, and you interpreted that for him and told him the meaning of them."[201]

Dreyer agreed.

Dreyer's testimony was questionable at best, and by the end he had lost whatever credibility the defense claimed he

---

200. People v. Ronald Lloyd Bailey, 85-4447-FC and 85-4448-FC, 13, 272, September 24, 1986

201. People v. Ronald Lloyd Bailey, 85-4447-FC and 85-4448-FC, 14, 4, September 25, 1986

had. Chuck Murphy told Judge Latreille that the defense was resting their case.

—

The prosecution provided rebuttal witnesses to refute what the witnesses for the defense had provided.

The first rebuttal witness was Det./Sgt. Al Moffatt. Moffatt had tailed Bailey to Florida as part of the surveillance team. He had picked up Bailey's trail at the Days Inn off the Beeline Expressway near Orlando International Airport. Ron Bailey had stayed there for one night after arriving late in Orlando. When Bailey boarded a bus, so did Moffatt, and he sat on the opposite side of the aisle, just two rows behind Bailey. Bailey sat down on the bus and looked around to see who else was on board. Moffatt watched him as Bailey stared out the window for the two-hour bus ride. Moffatt never saw him talking to himself, talking to the window, or to anyone else. Bailey acted like everyone else on the bus.

When the bus carrying Ron Bailey arrived in Belleview, it stopped at a convenience store/bar/liquor store, and Bailey got off. Moffatt said Bailey stayed inside for two hours before coming out and heading to a trailer park. By that time, the surveillance team was following.

After two hours, the team was replaced by another surveillance crew, and Moffatt told the jury that the next day was when he learned Bailey was missing.

After Bailey was captured, Moffatt sat in an interrogation room at the Marion County Sheriff's Department with him. David Morse asked Moffatt if Bailey spoke of demons or devils, or if he mentioned anything about being possessed. Bailey hadn't.

Moffatt had spent about two hours with Bailey at the jail, and both he and Jess Lopez from the FBI spoke with him the next morning. Bailey didn't mention anything about demons or devils. In fact, he hadn't complained about anything unusual. Moffatt told the jury that even on the flight back to Michigan, which took seven hours aboard an FBI plane, there was nothing unusual in the limited conversations he had with Ron Bailey, nor had he ever mentioned killing himself the entire time from his arrest to the point where he was locked up at the Livingston County Jail.

The prosecution was showing Ron Bailey wasn't insane, and they called correctional staff from the jail in addition to recalling Deb Chesney to the stand. None of them had heard Ron Bailey ever speak of demons, the devil, or of being possessed. Even Bailey's former colleagues at ARA were recalled to the stand to testify they had never heard Bailey mention demons or the devil, whether at work or outside of work, nor had he ever mentioned suicide around them.

There were two key witnesses left for the prosecution. David Morse called Dr. Harley Stock first as a rebuttal witness to counter Dr. Joel Dreyer's claims of Bailey's insanity.

Dr. Stock was the Assistant Director of Outpatient Evaluation at the Forensic Center, and his job was to evaluate people who were sent there by court order. In addition to an impressive array of education and training, Dr. Stock had also been an instructor for the Behavioral Science Unit at the FBI Academy in Quantico, Virginia. He had been at the Forensic Center for the previous eight years.

"For every expert opinion, there's an equal and opposite expert opinion," Dr. Stock once said.[202] Along with Dr. Lynn Blunt, Stock had six separate interviews with Ron Bailey, and after spending sixteen hours with him, they knew he was feigning insanity. To the doctor, Bailey looked like a choirboy with his blond hair and blue eyes. He came from a very nice family, and no one had expected anything sinister about him until he had gotten caught.

---

202. Stock, Dr. Harley, Interview with author, April 9, 2024

David Morse asked him if he always found people he was evaluating to be competent and legally sane. Stock said no and, as an example, he told the jury of a man who had assaulted an Ann Arbor police officer. When Stock interviewed him at the jail, it was clear the man was delusional. Stock recommended the man be adjudicated not guilty by reason of insanity, and he was.

In Ron Bailey's case, Stock made it clear to the jury that Bailey knew he wasn't at the Forensic Center for treatment. He was there to be evaluated. In preparation for the evaluation, Stock and Blunt had reviewed Bailey's hospital records, Forensic Center records, and police reports. It was standard practice to gather historical information for a forensic examination. "You need to have some historical data with which to compare and contrast what the defendant is telling you."[203] Bailey was also given several psychological tests by a psychometrician under the direction of Dr. Stock. Stock interpreted the tests afterward.

"Would [Dr. Dreyer] be able to do this testing?" Morse asked.

"I would think so."

Ron Bailey was given the Minnesota Multiphasic Personality Inventory (MMPI) three separate times while at the Forensic Center. The MMPI was the most widely used testing for personality assessment, and anyone who was sent to the Forensic Center was given the test. It included ten clinical scales to give a person's profile of personality functioning and three statistical scales that allowed the doctors to determine whether, at the time a person was taking the test, they were trying to be deceptive or malingering, or whether they were giving a clear picture of how they were functioning at that time. It wasn't standard practice to administer the MMPI three times. Of the three

---

203. People v. Ronald Lloyd Bailey, 85-4447-FC and 85-4448-FC, 15, 29, September 26, 1986

psychological personality tests given, the first two indicated Bailey was trying to fake being mentally ill but, in fact, was someone who was not. Stock added that some sections of the personality tests indicated he was so psychotic and out of touch with reality that he would require immediate hospitalization, yet his outward behavior didn't seem to show it, and Stock suspected he was deliberately trying to answer questions in a way he believed an insane person would answer. During that second test, the profile was essentially the same as the first, but on Scale Number Eight it was off the graph.

Stock said, "He is endorsing so many bizarre items that it can't even be plotted anymore. It's beyond the range of the test to even plot that particular score." If he was as disturbed as the test indicated, Dr. Stock wouldn't be able to continue interviewing him, but there were safeguards, or controls, built into the test, and they would indicate if the person being evaluated was lying or was so disturbed that their answers came randomly. Those built-in controls proved to Dr. Stock that Ron Bailey had tried to fake the answers to show he was mentally ill when he really wasn't. Stock could tell Bailey was lying just by his body movements and facial expressions.

By April, Stock and Blunt felt they had enough information to offer an opinion regarding Ron Bailey. Dr. Stock called Ray Cassar to let him know, and he relayed the concerns he had about Bailey trying to be deceptive. Cassar said he would talk to Bailey personally, and he asked Stock if he would interview him one more time after the visit. When Dr. Stock met with Bailey again, he told him that he felt he was malingering on the MMPI. In order for Stock and Blunt to continue and offer a fair opinion, Bailey would have to give them a legitimate profile on the MMPI. The third test was noticeably different, and all of the scales were within the statistical ranges.

Morse asked, "Did this last MMPI score more accurately reflect the person that you were observing?"

"It was more reflective of the individual that I had come to know as Ronald Bailey, yes."[204]

Bailey was an immature person with a history of drug use. He took little responsibility for his own behavior, blamed others for his problems, and had little insight into their environment. He was a homosexual pedophile with a borderline personality. His pedophilia was complicated by sexual sadism.

It was a difficult case for both Stock and Blunt. During the interviews with Dr. Stock, Bailey gave a complete description of how he had killed Shawn Moore, and why. Their purpose was to see what Ron Bailey told them about his behavior at the time, then try to explain discrepancies that appeared in the police reports compared to what he was telling them.

Dr. Stock was indicating to the jury the importance of the factual allegations in the case, yet Dr. Joel Dreyer had told the jury the factual allegations weren't significant in his evaluation.

Stock disagreed. "Well, I think as I mentioned to you before, one cannot conduct a forensic examination without knowing what happened. I mean, to me, that would be ludicrous to do that."[205]

In his description of Shawn Moore to Dr. Stock, Bailey said he thought to himself, *Why can't I look as good as he does?* He knew he had to kill Shawn.

When Dr. Stock asked Bailey why he killed the teen, Bailey answered, "Because I wanted to have sex with him." He had tried to get Shawn high by showing him how to smoke marijuana. He also made him drink beer and gave

204. People v. Ronald Lloyd Bailey, 85-4447-FC and 85-4448-FC, 15, 37, September 26, 1986

205. People v. Ronald Lloyd Bailey, 85-4447-FC and 85-4448-FC, 15, 41, September 26, 1986

him three Xanax. Xanax would provide a better high than Valium, and he wanted to get Shawn as high as he could. He was seducing the teen from the moment he kidnapped him until the time he murdered him. Bailey was providing Shawn with alcohol and drugs in the Chesney cabin and playing cards with him, all in an attempt to win him over as a friend. After more marijuana and beer, he asked Shawn if he wanted to try something fun, and he brought out a belt. He put the belt around Shawn's neck but had to go outside and urinate, so he left the cabin. When he came back in, he said he had forgotten about Shawn because of the alcohol and drugs he had taken and went to bed. The next morning, he discovered Shawn was dead.

Dr. Stock confronted him with the fact that they didn't believe his story. Stock had watched Bailey's body language during the interview, and when he spoke of "nonincriminatory" things like his past life, he looked straight at Stock and Blunt with no hesitation in his voice and no shift in his focus. His body posture remained the same. When Bailey spoke of things that might incriminate him, his voice changed along with his ability to look directly at the doctors. His body movements and body shifting changed, and his facial muscle reflexes changed. To Stock, it was a sign that Bailey was being deceptive.

Dr. Stock confronted Ron Bailey with the belief that he was lying. Bailey changed his story. Instead of going to bed when he came back in the cabin, he had become more aroused, and he tightened the belt up even tighter on Shawn's neck.

David Morse wanted some clarification for the jury. "He didn't indicate that Shawn Moore was getting more excited and that he tightened the belt for him, did he?"

"That's correct." Stock continued, "Shawn indicated that it was a little too tight on him, and Mr. Bailey told him it works better that way."

With the belt so tight around his neck, Shawn had lost his erection, and Bailey figured he would have Monday to have sex with him, so he fell asleep. The next morning, Shawn's body was cold.

After realizing Shawn was dead, Bailey was hungry and ate at least part of some breakfast before deciding he had to hide the teen's body.

Dr. Stock still had doubts about Bailey's version of events. At their next evaluation meeting, after Stock had already talked to Ray Cassar, Bailey offered a third version of events.

After he had kidnapped Shawn Moore, he was driving to the cabin and thinking about having a good time, partying, and the fact that Shawn was the "best looking of them all."[206]

Along the way, Bailey wondered why he couldn't look as good as Shawn did. He knew he would have to kill him.

"So, Mr. Bailey was telling you, at this point, that he was thinking of killing Shawn during the trip up to Gladwin," Morse asked.

"Yes."

When the two got to the cabin, Bailey didn't kill Shawn right away because he wanted to have sex with him. Dr. Stock said Bailey's seduction of the teen wasn't complete.

The next day, after Bailey had masturbated Shawn, the teen took a nap, and Bailey took some speed along with some amphetamines to stay awake.

Ron Bailey told Dr. Stock, "I kept thinking about what it would be like to have sex with him one more time, and then I would kill him."

While Shawn was asleep, Bailey left the cabin and went out to talk with the neighbors about their bat problem. When he came back in, he woke up Shawn, and they drank more beer and some schnapps before Bailey decided to have sex

---

206. People v. Ronald Lloyd Bailey, 85-4447-FC and 85-4448-FC, 15, 58, September 26, 1986

with the teen again. As he rubbed his penis on the teen's stomach, he ejaculated, and at the same time, he tightened the belt down on Shawn's neck.

Morse didn't want the jury to be confused so he asked Stock, "When Mr. Bailey ejaculated?"

"Yes."

"Does that indicate to you that this tightening of the belt, based on your opinion and your experience, whose gratification was this for in tightening that belt?"

"Mr. Bailey's."

When Bailey tightened the belt around Shawn Moore's neck, the teen began to squirm around, and Bailey held the teen's hands down until he passed out and quit breathing and his chest wasn't moving.

When Dr. Stock asked Bailey again why he had killed Shawn, he said he didn't want him to have sex with girls. He admitted he couldn't have sex with girls either.

After he knew Shawn was dead, he became aroused again, and he rubbed his hands over the boy's body, yet he was angry because Shawn looked so good. He left Shawn in the bed until the next morning. He had forgotten about the body until he woke up and reached over.

The interview between Stock, Blunt, and Baily went on, and Bailey told both of them that he had jumped out of bed, and he thought about burning the cabin down but didn't do it because he didn't own it. Instead, Bailey got in his Jeep, drove around Gladwin for a while before returning to the cabin, loaded Shawn's body into the Jeep, and concealed his body in the forest.

"During those discussions of the events, did the defendant ever indicate to you that in killing Shawn Moore, he was trying to kill himself?" Morse asked.

"No."

"Did he ever say anything about the fact that he felt he was acting as Dr. Tombo, and he was acting as if Shawn Moore were Ronald Bailey."

"No."[207]

Dr. Stock had traced Ron Bailey's sexual history all throughout the interviews that he had conducted with him, and he was aware of the allegations made by Bailey against Tombo.

Ron Bailey had a long history of sexual encounters with teenage boys. Those victims who were punched, choked, or forced to take drugs were the ones who had resisted. "The ones who were more resistant got hurt. Those who were compliant were released and sometimes recontacted," Dr. Stock said.[208]

Dr. Stock said that Bailey's "irresistible impulse" to kidnap and sexually assault young boys was an "unresisted" impulse that he chose not to resist when he abducted Shawn Moore and killed him.[209]

Ron Bailey, a serial sadistic pedophile killer, would travel in concentric circles when he would go hunting for kids. He would start the hunt close to home, and if he couldn't find someone, he would go farther and farther from home until he did. His victims were easy targets and susceptible. Until his need was met, he would build up his fantasies for long periods of time. Eventually, he would have to release his fantasies, and he would go hunting for his next victim. He became skilled at it over time. Stock equated it to shaking up a champagne bottle. The bottle is thick but when it's shaken up and the cork is released, it hits the ceiling. The crimes Bailey was accused of were goal-oriented and logical actions on his part. He knew what he wanted to do; he was out there hunting kids. He had a set way of doing it, and afterward, he was back to being a choirboy. To Dr.

207. People v. Ronald Lloyd Bailey, 85-4447-FC and 85-4448-FC, 15, 63, September 26, 1986

208. Kresnak, Jack, "Lawyers Find Going Tough in Bailey's Defense," *Detroit Free Press,* September 29, 1986

209. Kresnak, Jack, "Lawyers Find Going Tough in Bailey's Defense," *Detroit Free Press,* September 29, 1986

Stock, Ron Bailey was one of the most sadistic killers he had ever seen, who didn't care about the impact of his behavior on anybody other than himself to get what he wanted. He liked to see his victims suffer by choking them, then letting them breathe again, and seeing how the sheer presence of his hands could control life and death. Stock suspected there were a lot of other victims who would never be located.

Bailey's method of operation remained virtually the same from his first kidnapping and assault in 1973 through the abduction and murder of Shawn Moore in 1985. He stated again and again that he wanted to teach his victims techniques he had learned.

Dr. Stock said, "It's the same thing we saw back in 1973 and '74, the same thing. 'I want to teach him about sex.'"[210]

As time went on, Bailey said he had to use the belt on himself. He would go into the woods, put the belt around his neck, tighten it down, and masturbate. It was the same belt he used on Shawn Moore.

Morse asked Dr. Stock about Dr. Dreyer's diagnosis of Ron Bailey so the jury could understand. "I'm not real versed in the terminology. Would you be able to find that?"

"Pseudo psychopathic schizophrenia?"

"Yes."

"No," Stock said.

Dr. Stock knew it wasn't an American Psychiatric Association diagnosis, and it wasn't recognized in the psychiatric profession.

Stock also touched on schizophrenia and the deterioration of certain areas in a person's life. In most cases, a person's hygiene would deteriorate, they might have problems in their personal interactions, and they could have problems at work or home and with their personal relationships. Some of the signs would always be present in a schizophrenic

---

210. People v. Ronald Lloyd Bailey, 85-4447-FC and 85-4448-FC, 15, 96, September 26, 1986

diagnosis. By problems at work, he said that a person might not be able to handle complex tasks, they might have difficulty concentrating, and follow-up work could become problematic. Bailey had never been diagnosed as schizophrenic despite his prior hospitalizations.

In the sixteen hours that Dr. Stock spent with Ron Bailey, Bailey never mentioned he was trying to kill himself, and he never mentioned having an out-of-body experience while he was killing Shawn.

As the explanation of Bailey's evaluation went on, Dr. Stock explained there was a term called an "irresistible impulse." In order for that to occur, the person experiencing it had to be mentally ill. The person would also be responding to what Dr. Stock referred to as "command hallucination." It was most often an auditory command. Simply hearing voices wouldn't be classified as an irresistible impulse. The voices would have to be commanding a person to do something.

During their interview in April, Stock had asked Bailey what the impulses he claimed to have had were like, and if they were so irresistible, why weren't there more victims? Stock expected to see someone with an irresistible impulse act on it every time he experienced it. In Ron Bailey's case, he saw it as an unresisted impulse. Bailey said that there had been several times when he was able to stop himself, not just from killing kids but from having sex with them or keep from choking them. When Dr. Stock spoke of Bailey, he said, "He had the capacity to choose to resist it. It was his choice not to."[211]

Ron Bailey's judgment was impaired, but it wasn't because of a mental illness. His capacity to recognize reality wasn't significantly impaired because of a mental illness. In all of the cases where Bailey had used a knife,

---

211. People v. Ronald Lloyd Bailey, 85-4447-FC and 85-4448-FC, 15, 115, September 26, 1986

even at a young age, and in the Shawn Moore case, there were indications that Bailey recognized reality and the consequences of what he was doing. Ron Bailey had no substantial disorder of thought or mood that significantly impaired his ability to cope with the ordinary demands of life because of a mental illness.

Dr. Stock clarified that Bailey did, in fact, have problems coping with the demands of ordinary life but it wasn't because of a mental illness. It was simply because he believed he was entitled to things.

Morse had led up to the next question. "Then since we have covered all of the elements of mental illness, is it your opinion that the defendant, as a legal matter, as it relates to criminal responsibility, is he mentally ill?"

"In my opinion, the defendant does not meet the statutory criteria for being considered mentally ill."

From the time when Ron Bailey was a young teen, he recognized what he had done was wrong by denying any involvement, then telling a therapist that he was responsible. The pattern didn't change as he grew into adulthood. When he kidnapped Shawn Moore, he denied any involvement, he asked a friend to make an alibi for him, and he fled to Florida. Those actions spoke to Bailey's mental state at the time.

The second part of David Morse's question was whether, as a result of a mental illness, Bailey lacked the capacity to conform his conduct to the law he was charged with violating. Morse asked if that was an irresistible impulse situation.

Based on the fact that Bailey had sexually assaulted numerous other children, sometimes using elastic with sexual feelings involved, and some of those incidents didn't involve the murder of the child, although at the time he had the ability to stop himself from committing those crimes, the behavior was consciously within his control.

Dr. Stock didn't see any effect Dr. Tombo might have had on Ron Bailey, assuming Bailey's accusations about Tombo's sexual activity at Northville were true. Ron Bailey had already been kidnapping and sexually assaulting kids since he was thirteen years old. He had a borderline personality, and he was a homosexual pedophile with sexual sadism.

David Morse was pleased with Dr. Stock's testimony, and in sharp contrast to Dr. Dreyer's testimony, Stock's was very professional and believable.

During his cross-examination of Dr. Stock, Chuck Murphy centered the first part of his questions about how each psychiatrist or psychologist might have differing opinions about one person. He moved his questions to Stock combining his psychology skills with police investigative techniques. Murphy knew Stock had asked Bailey about an unsolved murder in Sylvania, Ohio. The defense attorney asked if Stock had any thoughts about Bailey becoming defensive when asked about murders in Ohio.

Dr. Stock was looking for Bailey's impulsivity and driven behavior to see if there were other bodies left somewhere because Bailey couldn't control himself. Stock told the defense attorney he hadn't brought the subject up to Bailey until their last interview. Stock had been contacted by the police in Sylvania, Ohio because there was an unsolved murder involving a teen whose nude body was found by a river. The teen had been strangled and had alcohol in his system.

Chuck Murphy was certain that by Stock questioning Bailey about that murder, it caused an adversarial relationship between the two. Stock reminded the attorney again that it was the last thing they talked about in their final meeting together, and Dr. Dreyer had done the same thing with Bailey.

Morse called Dr. Lynn Blunt as his next rebuttal witness. Dr. Blunt was the clinical director for the Forensic Center and had done at least 2,000 evaluations for defendants who had been referred in criminal cases since 1971. There were only 180 board-certified forensic psychiatrists in the world, and Dr. Blunt was number six. In Michigan, there were only three others.

Dr. Blunt had reviewed all of Ron Bailey's records with Dr. Stock before they ever interviewed him. They weren't accepting anything in those records as truth but would use it as a guide to see what others had said and evaluate Ron Bailey. Pre-judgment of Bailey wasn't an issue because the reports were for informational purposes only. He and Dr. Stock had tried to contact Dr. Tombo as part of their preparation for the interview, but Tombo never returned their calls.

Blunt told the jury that Ron Bailey wasn't approached by Dr. Tombo in any sort of sexual manner until he had turned eighteen. It was only after he had signed himself into Northville voluntarily. His parents couldn't sign him in anymore because of his age. Tombo thought that if Bailey were eighteen "it wouldn't look so bad to have sex with him."[212] While Tombo's actions were still inappropriate, Bailey would be a consenting adult. Bailey told Dr. Blunt that he and Tombo had approximately twenty sexual encounters while he was at Northville. When Tombo asked him about anal sex, Bailey had told him he didn't like it, and Tombo never forced the issue with him.

David Morse asked Dr. Blunt, given what Bailey had said about his relationship with Dr. Tombo, if it had any significant impact on Ron Bailey's condition when Blunt was evaluating him.

"No. I don't think it had any significant impact at all. Mr. Bailey had been involved in homosexual behavior long, long before that." Dr. Blunt continued, "In fact, since age

---

212. People v. Ronald Lloyd Bailey, 85-4447-FC and 85-4448-FC, 16, 107, September 29, 1986

fourteen—well, even as a child, he had some." He was referring to Ron Bailey's early adolescent homosexual experiences because Bailey had been forcing other children into homosexuality for so many years. He had difficulty in deciding his own sexuality and what to do.

If Bailey had, in fact, been abused by Dr. Tombo, it would have driven him away from molesting children. "If Dr. Tombo had any effect on him, it would have been a positive one in helping to promote an adult homosexual relationship."[213] Ron Bailey could have made the transition into an adult homosexual relationship rather than continue with homosexual pedophilia and sexual sadism.[214]

Dr. Blunt emphasized to the jury that, if true, Tombo's relationship with Ron Bailey was wrong and unethical, but it wouldn't have made Bailey's problem worse. It simply would have helped him clarify his sexuality. There was nothing pointing to Bailey suffering from the legal definition of mental illness under Michigan law.

As the State's psychiatry expert, Dr. Blunt explained the different types of personality disorders and told the jury that Ron Bailey had a destructive type of personality disorder. Two additional diagnoses were made. The second part was homosexual pedophilia, which meant "loving or having a tendency to have sexual desires for children of the same sex," and sexual sadism, which Dr. Blunt described as "gaining sexual pleasure by either inflicting pain or putting people in psychological distress, sometimes to the point of killing them."[215] All of those diagnoses fit Ronald Bailey's personality disorder and weren't classified as mental illnesses in the medical or psychiatric sense.

213. Kresnak, Jack, "Doctor Suggests Tombo's Impact Helpful," *Detroit Free Press,* September 20, 1986
214. AP, "Sex-Slaying Trial Near Conclusion," *Herald-Palladium*, September 30, 1986
215. People v. Ronald Lloyd Bailey, 85-4447-FC and 85-4448-FC, 16, 122, September 29, 1986

To be sure, David Morse asked Dr. Blunt if the diagnoses were a close call to being classified as mental illnesses. They weren't, and he didn't see any evidence that indicated classic schizophrenia of a psychotic nature.

During the evaluations with Stock and Blunt, Ron Bailey never made any indication that as he was killing Shawn Moore, he thought he was killing himself. It was after he had tightened the belt around Shawn's neck and discovered he had killed him when he felt like killing himself. That statement made Dr. Blunt suspicious, but Bailey explained it differently. Shawn Moore was so good looking that Bailey knew he would mature and eventually have sex with girls, but Bailey couldn't have sex with girls. He had to stop that. To Dr. Blunt, it meant that Bailey was essentially jealous of Shawn.

"So, when the defendant told you that after killing Shawn Moore, he wanted to commit suicide, that was inconsistent with any assertion he might have that he was killing himself when he killed Shawn Moore?" Morse asked.

"That would seem inconsistent to me."

The assistant prosecutor asked if Ronald Bailey fit the legal definition of insanity. "No, he does not. I believe that he is not mentally ill in the legal sense and therefore, does not meet the legal criteria for insanity."

In Dr. Blunt's cross-examination, he told Chuck Murphy he had come to the conclusion that Bailey's experiences with Dr. Tombo had been a positive experience just ten days prior to the trial starting. It was after he and Dr. Stock had already submitted their written report. When Murphy characterized Blunt's opinion of Tombo's relationship with Bailey as "positive because it would draw him away from young boys and have him go to older men," Dr. Blunt told him that it was out of context. He corrected Murphy. The experiences with Tombo would have been "more positive than negative." By using the term "positive," he meant it would "help him try to form an adult homosexual relationship… rather than going on into this sexual deviancy of homosexual pedophiliac behavior and sexual sadism."[216]

Dr. Blunt reiterated that any sexual relationship between Dr. Tombo and Ron Bailey was not appropriate, and there was no way he could approve of that type of treatment between a doctor and patient, but in relation to the effect it might have had on Bailey, it was "more likely positive than negative." He added, "It certainly didn't make him into some type of homosexual pedophiliac. He was already that. It did not make him into a sexual sadist. He was already that."[217]

The testimonies of Dr. Stock and Dr. Blunt were the final pieces to the puzzle. The defense had no witnesses for surrebuttal, and witness testimony was complete.

With closing arguments forthcoming, there was a sudden change for the prosecution. Frank Del Vero had planned on making the closing for the prosecution but the defense's entire case was based on the insanity defense, and that is what David Morse had tackled for the prosecution. The day before closing arguments, Del Vero let Morse know he should do the closing. It wasn't something Morse had planned, and there was a sudden onset of butterflies in his stomach as he tried to prepare for the next day.

As he stood before the jury, David Morse, who had done a brutal cross-examination of Ron Bailey, spoke to the fourteen-member panel seated before him in the stately courtroom. "The false issue in this case is the issue of Dr. Tombo: 'Dr. Tombo made me do it.'" He reminded the jury that Bailey had kidnapped, sexually molested, and choked at least one other victim before he ever met Dr. Tombo. Morse attacked the testimony of Dr. Joel Dreyer, saying Dreyer's theory that Bailey was killing Shawn because he thought he

---

216. People v. Ronald Lloyd Bailey, 85 4447-FC and 85-4448-FC, 16, 132, September 19, 1986

217. People v. Ronald Lloyd Bailey, 85-4447-FC and 85-4448-FC, 16, 133, September 19, 1986

was killing himself was a bunch of "psycho-babble."[218] It was only after Dreyer's first visit with Bailey that the idea of him killing himself came up, along with being possessed by demons. Morse said that idea was planted by Dr. Dreyer. "Ron Bailey knows, when there's a good excuse, to latch onto it," he said.

In closing arguments for the defense, Ray Cassar asked the jury if what Dr. Tombo did to Ron Bailey was an excuse for what his client had done to Shawn Moore. "No," Cassar answered for himself. "Dr. Tombo did not kill Shawn Moore. Ronald Bailey committed the act, not Dr. Tombo."

Cassar was passionate to the jury. "Ron Bailey was sick; he was messed up mentally, and Dr. Tombo used Ron."

Local reporter Dan Grantham had watched the trial from the gallery. Like all of the journalists covering the trial, he had approached it in a professional manner so as not to get emotionally involved. It was a journalist's unwritten rule. Even though he and the other journalists had sympathy for both the Moore family and Alfred Bailey, they were certain they could remain detached. They never realized how difficult that would be. There were horrific descriptions of how Bailey had killed Shawn, and it was difficult even for the press to hear those. Grantham was shocked at the details and incredulous as to what Bailey had done. Grantham wrote, "When I saw the trial that way, and not as a story I was covering, it astonished me—it was almost unbelievable that such a thing could happen."[219]

218. Kresnak, Jack, "Jury Deliberates Bailey's Sanity in Kidnap-Slaying," *Detroit Free Press*, October 1, 1986
219. Grantham, Daniel, "Trial Breaks Traditional Barriers," *The Brighton Argus*, October 8, 1986

19

I Was Killing Me

It was a cool evening as the sun began to set around 7:00 p.m. on the last day of September. The trial of Ronald Bailey was the last criminal trial ever to be tried in that courtroom. Everyone was going to stay at the courthouse until the jury came back. Ray Cassar went outside for a breath of fresh air, and he noticed people walking around the courthouse waiting for the verdict. For a split second, he thought they were carrying lanterns around and waiting for some ominous thing to happen. It was surreal. He snapped back to reality as he realized they were carrying flashlights.

That same day, Bruce and Sharon Moore filed a lawsuit against the Baileys in Wayne County Circuit Court. The Moores' suit alleged that Ron Bailey's parents knew of his past assaults on teen boys, and they had the opportunity to conclude their son was involved in Shawn's kidnapping. With all of the publicity about it, it should have put them "on notice" that there was a strong possibility their son was involved.

Bailey waited in the holding cell behind closed doors at the courthouse. The small cell, with one wooden bench and a combination stainless steel sink and commode, matched the courtroom color with a beige-colored wall and a salmon-pink contrasting wall. The large door with horizontal squared bars secured the killer. He seemed more interested in the premier episode of the TV show *Dallas* than his own fate during his trial.

Of the fourteen jurors who listened to the evidence, two were drawn at random and excused before deliberations began. On Tuesday, September 30, at 3:26 p.m., the jury began deliberations. By 6:00 p.m., they agreed that Bailey was guilty of kidnapping and felony murder. There was a nine to three split for premeditated murder by 8:30 p.m. Their deliberations continued the following day and by lunchtime, there was only one hold-out. That was resolved by the afternoon, and after nine hours over the two-day period, they reached their verdict. They had been given the option of convicting Bailey for second-degree murder also but felt the premeditation had been proven for first-degree. The verdict was returned at 2:10 p.m. Ronald Bailey was convicted for the kidnapping and murder of Shawn Moore. He sat at the defense table, emotionless, as the verdict was announced.

Scott Moore's fiancée quietly sobbed at the verdict while Shawn's aunt gently caressed Sharon Moore's hands.

After Judge Latreille left the courtroom, Bailey stood up and, with his hands in his pockets, he walked with his police escort to the temporary holding cell in the courthouse. He broke down and wept in his cell afterward.

Ron Bailey had been his own worst witness, and Dr. Joel Dreyer's testimony was inconsistent with the facts. The most convincing testimony came from Dr. Harley Stock and Dr. Lynn Blunt. Knowing that Bailey had used his belt to kill Shawn was what led the jury to convict him of first-degree murder. The jurors cited his own testimony of using elastic bands and belts wrapped around his victims' necks, or his own, to enhance the pleasure. At the onset of the trial, none of the jurors knew how Shawn had been killed. "But when he admitted that he choked him, it was awful. I felt so bad for Shawn's parents. I would have gone right after him," juror John Barrett said.

A lack of remorse on Ron Bailey's part was another factor for some of the jurors, and so was Dr. Joel Dreyer. "We weren't there to be entertained. We were there to sort out the facts; not for the Joel Dreyer Show," said Shawn Rowlette. "Dreyer was not near the professional that the other doctors were. I expected to hear testimony in clinical terms but he didn't even read the other reports on Bailey."[220] Some of the jurors were laughing at Dreyer's testimony behind closed doors and considered him to be a quack. Even Shawn's dad felt that Dreyer had helped the prosecution's case.

Much of the defense case had been prepared by Ray Cassar. Chuck Murphy had become distracted. At trial's end, David Morse spoke briefly with Cassar. "Ray, we talked to the jury after the trial was over with, and they thought you were the elder statesman, and Chuck was the young one."[221]

—

It was bittersweet. After the verdict was announced and the courtroom was empty, Bruce and Sharon Moore met with Frank Del Vero and David Morse. Sharon asked Frank if she could hug him. The Moore family was so grateful for what everyone had done to ensure Ron Bailey was convicted. In the back of Frank Del Vero's mind, he thought, *Yeah, we did it. He's going away for life.* But he also thought of Shawn. *Shawn's no longer with us, and there's nothing we can do about it.* "When I was at Shawn Moore's funeral, I vowed I would do everything in my ability to reach this [verdict]," Del Vero said.

Frank Del Vero's son was just five, and after Shawn's kidnapping and murder, he realized things had changed

---

220. George, Maryanne, "Jurors Say Use of Belt Led to Murder Verdict," *Detroit Free Press*, October 2, 1986
221. Cassar, Raymond, Interview with author, February 27, 2024

since he was a kid. As a child of ten, Del Vero could jump on a bus a few blocks from home and end up at Tiger Stadium at Michigan and Trumbull, watch a game for seventy-five cents, and never have to worry about anything. Indeed, times had changed.

When the Moores spoke to the media, Sharon said they could now grieve like normal people.

Ray Cassar and Chuck Murphy apologized to the Moores for putting Bailey on the stand. They realized how difficult it must have been for them to listen to details about their son's death.

"It helped to hear Ron," Sharon said.

Her husband said he felt sorry for the Bailey family for having to put up with it for so long. Bruce Moore was also angry with the system. "I feel like he was coddled, let's put it bluntly, by the system," he said. "I'm angry at the system. They turned him loose to kill Shawn."

Alfred Bailey was noticeably absent from the courtroom on Wednesday when the jury returned their verdict. "I'm a little upset, which would be expected," he said. "I was hoping for a guilty but mentally ill [verdict]."[222] Much like Bruce Moore, Alfred Bailey felt betrayed by the mental health system and Northville Regional Psychiatric Hospital. He took it very hard. The entire ordeal had taken a large toll on the Bailey family, and Alfred's wife wasn't well. He protected his wife and other two kids throughout the trial by keeping their identities anonymous.

It wasn't long after the verdict was returned when Tombo's attorney made a statement to the media. "[Tombo] was under no obligation to participate in a circus," Paul Stevenson said. His comments were guarded when he was asked where Tombo was now. "I have no comment on

---

222. Kresnak, Jack, "Slain Boy's Family Calls Guilty Verdict a Painful Relief," *Detroit Free Press,* October 2, 1986

that. If he had been served [with a subpoena] he would've showed."[223]

—

With over twenty reporters from daily and community papers, along with TV and radio stations from around the state, they predicted Bailey's conviction. Chris Hansen recognized the difference in the experts' testimonies. "Dreyer has not spent as much time with Bailey as Stock has. Dreyer was hired by the defense to help Bailey, not the prosecutors," he said. Hansen had recommendations for up-and-coming journalists too. "Stick with the facts. Try to present it fairly." As difficult as it was to listen to the sexual details describing Shawn's assault, Hansen said journalists needed to keep their opinions to themselves.[224]

Dan Grantham felt some empathy in the courtroom for Ron Bailey as he testified about the relationship with Dr. Tombo. Bailey knew he had a problem, and he was disturbed about it. Cassar and Murphy had done a good job of painting Bailey as sympathetically as they could, but when David Morse cross-examined him, it was the end. Morse destroyed Ron Bailey on the stand. To the local reporter, it was a big case, and knowing there was a strong chain of evidence against Bailey, he had looked forward to covering it. After the trial in Livingston County, he couldn't help but wonder what really went on at Northville.

—

223. Kresnak, Jack, "Tombo's Lawyer Breaks Silence," *Detroit Free Press*, October 2, 1986

224. Lints, Kelly, "Media Personalities Share Views on Bailey," *Livingston County Daily Press*, October 8, 1986

Ray Cassar and Chuck Murphy, having suffered defeat at the hands of the Livingston County Prosecutor's Office, knew it wasn't over. Their client was facing another trial for the kidnapping and murder of Kenny Myers in Wayne County.

—

Cassar and Murphy stood before Judge Latreille at the Livingston County Courthouse with their client. Cassar spoke briefly to Latreille before the sentencing. "One thing that has been clear from the start is that Ron Bailey is sick and has been abused by the system." He added that Bailey said to him, "Ray, all I ever wanted to be was normal."

"I'd like to say, Your Honor, that I'm sorry for the families involved, the Moores, and you know, his family, brothers and sisters, and, like, Mrs. Moore," Ron Bailey said to Judge Latreille. It was Halloween, and there was a cool fall wind in the air as the leaves would soon be at their peak color. "I'd like to say I'm sorry to my parents for going through this," he added. "I am sorry. I never intended to kill Shawn Moore."[225]

There was no way any sentence, no matter how long, could make up for the community's sense of loss, and nothing could ever make up for the fact that Shawn Moore was gone. Frank Del Vero stood before Judge Latreille and asked for the maximum possible penalty. "What we can ensure is that the loss never happens again in any county. We can ensure that no other child is ever missing, no other child is ever murdered by Ron Bailey," he said.

Both Bruce Moore and his son, Scott, spoke before Bailey was sentenced. Shawn's abduction and murder had been the "most horrible crime that a child could ever be subjected to," Bruce said. He added that the terror, fear,

225. AP, "Bailey Gets Life Sentence," *Battle Creek Enquirer,* October 31, 1986

and torture at the hands of Ronald Bailey had devastated the Moore family and left them with scars that would never heal. The prevention of future abductions and murders was now Bruce Moore's primary concern.

Scott Moore said, "There cannot be justice for Shawn, only tragedy." When he spoke of his little brother's killer, he said there couldn't be justice for Bailey because there is no just punishment, only law.[226]

Latreille looked at Bailey as he spoke:

The Court, of course, must consider the traditional factors in sentencing: rehabilitation, deterrents, protection of the public, and the Court does, in fact, consider those. However, the Court must first say that in viewing such a case, this Court cannot help but conclude that it embodies the worst fears of all families—the victim's family and the family of the murderer. Such a crime, indeed, does tear the fabric of society, tears the fabric that holds society together.

As the prosecutor indicated, there was a terrible sense of outrage in this community, but with the passage of time, calm returned to the community, and we were able to conduct a trial in a calm, deliberate atmosphere. Indeed, the response to such an outrageous crime was that of a civilized society, a calm, measured response.

In speaking of rehabilitation, one is tempted to say that such a murderer cannot be human—that is, like the rest of us. We demand answers. We look to psychology for answers, and indeed at times, that field seems to provide comforting solutions— unfortunately, often simplistic solutions.

226. Grantham, Daniel, "Bailey Receives Life Sentence," *Livingston County Daily Press*, November 5, 1986

We in the law at times—it appears to me—are too dependent on psychiatry and psychology. The fact is that psychiatry does not have all of the answers to human behavior. It provides some answers and some theories but has no final answers. It promises so much and delivers so little in terms of explaining and predicting human behavior.

I say this in the context of believing that the exploration of the human mind is the last great frontier. However, psychology is in its infancy, and we need to be reminded of that.

As I have indicated, the temptation is to not consider you, Mr. Bailey, like the rest of us. However, the fact is, Mr. Bailey, that what you did involves one of the profound mysteries of human experience. I am referring to the existence of evil, a mystery which has plagued mankind for all of its history.

In this case the question is: How could a society which is rich in a tradition of law and fairness, kindness and mercy, spawn such a person?

The easy answer would be to say that you are not truly human—but merely a lump of flesh pushed this way and that by impulses. Some psychiatrist would say that—and indeed some did say it—that you are not responsible for your actions.

Such cases certainly do exist—and the insanity defense correctly applies to them. However, this is not such a case, as a jury of your peers had decided.

The fact is, Mr. Bailey, that you are responsible for what you have done. You may be subject to impulses not common among other citizens, but you embraced and cultivated such impulses.

Mr. Bailey, you chose to do evil. You cultivated evil as a habit, until indeed you could rape and kill almost as a reflexive action—without much thought or concern. You have become a cold-calculating predator.

Mr. Bailey, I am telling you that you are responsible for these heinous crimes. In telling you that, I am affording you the greatest dignity that can be granted another human being. I am saying that you are not an animal and not a mere lump of flesh guided by wild impulses.

It is my intention in sentencing you, Mr. Bailey, that you never walk the streets again. There should be no parole or pardon or commutation of sentence in your case.

Only then can the public be protected, you and others deterred from such crimes and a sense of proportion created—a balance between the crime and the punishment.[227]

When Cassar and Murphy asked that Bailey be segregated from the rest of the prison population for his own safety, Latreille agreed to make the request to the Michigan Department of Corrections out of a sense of "fairness, mercy, and a little compassion." He added, "In short, elementary civilized behavior which was not afforded to Shawn Moore."[228]

Ronald Bailey was sentenced to sixty-five to one hundred years in prison for Shawn's kidnapping, and he was sentenced to life in prison without parole for his murder.

---

227. Grantham, Daniel, "Judge's Sentencing Comments," *Livingston County Daily Press,* November 5, 1986

228. Kresnak, Jack, "Bailey Apologizes for Killing," *Detroit Free Press,* October 31, 1986

Latreille also ordered that he undergo clinical studies as part of an effort to find out why those types of crimes were committed and how to prevent them from happening in the future.

—

Ron Bailey's redemption in the kidnapping and murder of Shawn Moore came in the form of an interview with the Michigan State Police and the FBI after the conviction in Livingston County. The FBI's Behavioral Science Unit was still in its infancy, and both agencies were hoping an interview with the convicted killer could be used in future child abduction cases. The psychological profile developed could be used to determine how child abductors operate. Not knowing why he did the things he had done, Bailey agreed to help them out, and both Murphy and Cassar agreed to allow the interview. There were guidelines agreed to beforehand, and the questioning would be limited to the Shawn Moore abduction and murder and have nothing to do with the Kenny Myers case. "There's not many true stranger abductions. It's quite a [feat] to get an arrest and get a conviction. When you do get an arrest and conviction, you critique it to pieces just to get a line on how these people operate and think," Det/Sgt. Beaupre said.[229]

When Shawn's body was discovered, he was nude. Investigators still wanted to know what Ron Bailey had done with his clothing. They also wanted to know how Shawn was controlled by his killer. "The control we're talking about occurred from Saturday night until at least Sunday night—about a twenty-four-hour period," Beaupre said. There was a host of unanswered questions they were hoping Bailey might be able to answer.

229. Robertson, Nicole, "Police Work Helped Key Baily Conviction," *Livingston County Daily Press*, October 8, 1986

Ron Bailey had been able to control Shawn Moore by telling him he wouldn't hurt him, and he even promised to drive Shawn home. Shawn had asked his abductor, "You're not going to hurt me; you're going to take me back, right?" Bailey told him he wouldn't take him to his front door, but he would drop him off so he could walk home. He reassured Shawn he wouldn't be hurt. It was those promises and some implied threats that kept Shawn from fleeing, even when Bailey allowed him to leave the cabin to use the outhouse.

After killing Shawn, he had put the teen's clothing in his Jeep, and as he neared Detroit, he stopped to get gas and saw them in the back. He ended up throwing them out along Eight Mile Road.

The two-and-a-half-hour interview with Bailey was taped and was going to be sent to the MSP Sex Crimes Unit in Lansing, where veteran investigators would view it behind closed doors. Beaupre was satisfied with the interview because it revealed how Ron Bailey was able to control Shawn Moore. Beaupre admitted that he wasn't sure how much the taped interview would help in profiling a child molester. He said he would let the experts determine that. Still, it would be a very valuable future reference for investigators.

—

Around Brighton, there was relief that Ron Bailey had been taken off the streets, but there were even those who felt he shouldn't have been charged criminally. Students who attended school with Shawn were thankful, and some felt capital punishment was in order. At The Doughnut Shop in Brighton, one customer said, "…Shoot him. When you take somcone's life, take theirs too. An eye for eye." At the Pump and Pantry on Whitmore Lake Road where Shawn had bought his root beer, which had since been re-named the Hop-In store, the manager said of Bailey, "I think they'd have to be a little off to do something like that." Others had slight notes of sympathy for Bailey, including an employee at the Hop-In, who said, "My opinion is, I think he's guilty but I think he's awful sick. I don't think he should be tried as a criminal." Still others said that Bailey was a man looking for help, and he still needed it.[230]

—

There was no way Tim Kenny was going to plea bargain the Wayne County case against Ron Bailey in the kidnapping and murder of Kenny Myers. Like the Moore case, Kenny had key witnesses who had seen Ron Bailey at key points during Kenny Myers's disappearance. There were twenty-five in all, and the case was expected to move quickly. More than that, Kenny believed that in a criminal trial, there were three elements to a criminal case: the facts of the case, the law, and the equities. By equities, he referred to a victim whom someone's heart goes out to. In the Myers case, Tim Kenny believed he had all three, and he wasn't afraid to go to trial.

Cassar and Murphy knew it. If they agreed to another jury trial and their client testified, they could face the same verdict. They considered the possibility of a bench trial. They could waive a trial by jury and simply have the presiding judge hear the case and render a verdict based on the evidence presented.

The case would be presented in front of Judge Patrick Duggan, an intelligent, no-nonsense, traditional judge who was well respected and who had been in the circuit court since 1976. He had an excellent reputation with both the prosecution and defense in criminal matters.

---

230. Case, Caroline, "Community Glad to see Bailey Taken Off Streets," *Livingston County Daily Press*, October 8, 1986

Three months earlier, just as Ron Bailey's trial for Shawn Moore's murder was getting started in Livingston County, Duggan sat at his desk in the City-County Building in downtown Detroit when his phone rang. It was President Ronald Reagan, and he was nominating Duggan for the United States District Court in eastern Michigan. The fifty-two-year-old judge had been appointed to the Wayne County Circuit Court by Governor Milliken in 1976, then was elected twice for six-year terms as a circuit judge. Duggan felt the courts should move slowly and deliberately when they were dealing with people's problems.

The testimony that convinced the jury in Livingston County that Bailey was guilty of first-degree murder was his testimony that he had strangled Shawn with a belt, and while they didn't buy the insanity defense, Cassar and Murphy planned to use it again. From Cassar's perspective, he had to worry that if a jury heard the case, they might simply conclude it didn't matter who Bailey was, and he was too dangerous to be walking around. They would never even consider the insanity defense. Judge Duggan knew the law, he knew what the statute said, and he knew what constituted legal insanity. Tim Kenny felt he stood a better chance with Duggan rather than a jury because the average juror didn't understand legalities and the insanity defense. He had every confidence in Judge Duggan.

The Kenny Myers case had become a high-profile case because it was tied to the Shawn Moore case and Ron Bailey. Picking a jury could be a problem because some prospective jurors might see the media involved and want to be chosen for the jury. During the selection process, they could have simply said what they thought the Court wanted to hear to be selected.

Eight days after Bailey was sentenced in the Moore case, his trial began in Wayne County Circuit Court. Ray Cassar gave the opening statement this time and told Judge Duggan they would be using the insanity defense. They wouldn't contest the kidnapping and murder, but they would contest the intent to commit the murder.

In the opening day of Bailey's second trial, Marie Edenstrom took the stand and described the last night she had seen her son. She quietly told the Court what he was wearing and was shown the football jersey Kenny had been wearing.

The deputy chief medical examiner testified about Kenny's autopsy and described how he had died from ligature strangulation that took between five and eight minutes. Tim Kenny showed the medical examiner a belt that was taken from the Bailey home by police. Dr. Mirchandani told the Court that the belt width and the buckle were consistent with the marks found on Kenny's neck.

Tim Kenny had to tie the belt to Bailey. Deb Chesney took the stand and testified that her once-boyfriend, Ron Bailey, used to wear a belt like the one shown to the medical examiner.

—

While Tim Kenny, Ray Cassar, and Chuck Murphy were preparing for the second day of trial, in Brighton it was a different story. What some referred to as the final chapter in the Shawn Moore case was about to begin.

The Moore family, Frank Del Vero, and others who were involved gathered to pay tribute to the police officers who had conducted the investigation into Shawn's abduction and murder. They also gathered to reward eight people who were key players in the investigation.

Timothy White was the publisher of the *Ann Arbor News*, and Joyce Rogers was Executive Director of the Brighton Chamber of Commerce. Together, they worked to set up the reward for information about Shawn's disappearance and murder. There was no doubt that without the help of these eight people, the case wouldn't have come to a conclusion like it had just a week earlier with Ron Bailey's conviction. To many, it was something good that came out of a tragic and horrible event.

Bruce Moore told the crowd he and his family were there to simply show appreciation for what the community had done during the family's tragedy. "It's not our purpose to give you thanks. We know you don't want that. Instead, we offer you our family's heartfelt appreciation." Shawn's dad said that beyond rewarding the eight people who got involved and helped solve the case, he hoped it would encourage others to get involved.

With the reward money totaling $52,259.00, Frank Del Vero, Lt. Pertner, and Det./Sgt. Beaupre chose the eight recipients.

Ronald Moncman had given the first bits of information to police after witnessing Shawn's abduction. Sherry Huey had given MSP an accurate description of the Jeep Ron Bailey was driving when she witnessed the kidnapping. Ron Bailey's former colleague, Michael Greenfield, had called the tip line with information about Bailey that led police to him. Jeremy Greenfield and his father had given police information about where they had seen Bailey along Ridge Road, and it was within forty-five feet of where Shawn's body was found. Two more witnesses to the kidnapping, Donald Parent and John Langmore, also received a portion of the reward for reporting the abduction. Lastly, the teen whom Ron Bailey had tried to entice to the parking at the Brighton Mall just thirty minutes before Shawn was abducted received a portion of the reward. His testimony at the trial put Bailey in Brighton just before the kidnapping.

Bruce Moore was especially thankful to the teen for what he had endured on the stand as he testified. He had been put through a grueling cross-examination by Bailey's defense team. When Bruce Moore spoke of him, he said, "We're very proud of you."[231]

—

On the second day of Bailey's trial in Wayne County, Det/ Sgt. Al Moffatt, who had brought Bailey back to Michigan after his arrest in Florida, testified that when Bailey was taken into custody, his property was seized at the Marion County Jail. He had been wearing a Byron digital wristwatch with a chrome-colored band. Tim Kenny believed it belonged to the murdered teen, and to show that it was Kenny Myers's watch, the prosecutor called friends of the teen as witnesses.

"He wore it all the time," Gloria Klinefelter told the Court, adding that she had actually loaned Kenny Myers the money to buy the watch from a flea market in Warren.[232] The cost was six to eight dollars, and it was too big for the teen so he wore it on his arm over a wrist sweatband. Mrs. Klinefelter's son, Michael, who was now sixteen years old, testified that he teased Kenny Myers with a play on the watch's brand name, Byron, and his friend's last name. He called Kenny "Myron."

Two of Bailey's former co-workers at ARA, along with his former boss, described Bailey's 1970 Buick station wagon that he drove in the summer of 1984.

When crime lab analysts testified, they said balls of fiber that were found on the Velcro straps of Kenny Myers's sneakers could have come from a yellowish-beige blanket that was taken from the Bailey home in September 1985.

Tim Kenny believed the insanity defense was a defense of last resort. It wasn't used very much in the courts. He

231. Grantham, Daniel, "Seven Share in Moore Reward," *Livingston County Daily Press*, November 12, 1986

232. Kresnak, Jack, "Prosecution Tries to Use Watch to Link Bailey to Teen's Kidnap-Slaying," *Detroit Free Press,* November 14, 1986

knew Dr. Harley Stock from other cases he had worked on, and he liked Dr. Stock. Most of his previous dealings had to do with a suspect's competency to stand trial rather than the use of the insanity defense. Dr. Stock gave the same testimony he had given in the Moore case.

It had only taken two days for Tim Kenny to present his witnesses. By Thursday, November 13, he rested the State's case against Ron Bailey.

After a weekend of preparation on both sides, it was time for the defense to present their case. Dr. Joel Dreyer was their star witness, and after his testimony in Livingston County, Cassar and Murphy were beginning to have their doubts. Tim Kenny was surprised when Cassar came to him and said that Dreyer wanted to do a demonstration of his interview technique and how he was able to elicit information from Bailey. Kenny asked the defense attorney if it was in terms of the questions he asked of Bailey. Dreyer wanted to actually re-enact his interview with Bailey. Kenny thought it was nonsense but knew he could use it to his advantage. He told Cassar he would allow it, but Ronald Bailey had to stay on the stand afterward so he could be cross-examined. Cassar agreed. At that moment, Tim Kenny knew he was going to win the case.

Under direct examination by his own attorney, Bailey told Ray Cassar that he had kidnapped upward of fifteen boys over the years to make friends.

"You assumed they were your friends?" Cassar asked him.

Bailey said he had given his victims alcohol and drugs, then sexually molested them because he thought they would enjoy it. He said he would get impulses to kidnap young boys to be their friend and have sex with them.

When Tim Kenny questioned him, Bailey admitted he had threatened Kenny Myers by saying he had a knife when he had kidnapped him before driving him to the secluded area in Hines Park. Tim Kenny asked him if he knew what he was doing was wrong. "I'd say, sixty percent of it; yes, I did." He later told Kenny that he knew it was wrong to a degree.[233]

The defense strategy was unprecedented in Michigan's criminal history. It had never been done before. Neither Tim Kenny, nor Cassar and Murphy had ever heard of Dreyer's method of examination being used in a criminal case. Michigan Supreme Court Justices G. Mennen Williams and Patricia Boyle had never heard of it being used in Michigan either.

The assistant prosecutor had experience in the insanity defense, and it didn't matter if it was Joel Dreyer on the stand or someone else. Psychiatrists always wanted to battle on their field by using psychoanalytic terms and phrases. Tim Kenny knew it was far better to attack them on the facts of the case. It was the essence of the trial. He would get an acknowledgement from Dreyer that he agreed a particular fact occurred, and that Ron Bailey had, in fact, done whatever it was Kenny was pointing out. Kenny wouldn't argue on the psychological playing field. He would argue the facts, and he would make sure Judge Duggan was following along.

When Dreyer took the stand, he repeated his story of Ron Bailey being a victim, and how Bailey thought he was killing himself. Tim Kenny thought to himself, *If you're trying to kill yourself and live in Livonia, why are you driving to Ferndale, abducting someone, then driving to Hines Park? How is that killing yourself?* Kenny knew Dreyer was fabricating a theory that wasn't believable when the facts of the case were presented. Dreyer's demonstration with Ron Bailey was pure theatrics and more than what anyone expected to see in a trial.

---

233. Kresnak, Jack, "Bailey Calls Kidnapped Youngsters His 'Friends,'" *Detroit Free Press*, November 19, 1986

Bailey told Dreyer in the courtroom examination that he and Kenny Myers were "partying" in Hines Park. He was giving Myers beer to drink and talking with him. Bailey admitted to putting a belt around Kenny Myers's neck in an attempt to sexually arouse him. He said he stopped when he heard someone nearby, then came back and choked him again, only this time into unconsciousness. On the stand, Bailey was near tears and Dreyer said, "Go and cry, man, just let it out. It's a bummer."[234]

Alfred Bailey was a man of respect to Cassar and Murphy. He loved his son, and he had sat through the trial in Livingston County. Now he watched from the gallery in Wayne County as his son was tried for a second murder. He listened as a host of witnesses described his son's past. It included his son's own claim that he was forced into a homosexual relationship with Dr. Tombo. The senior Bailey had seen the sadness and the horror on the faces of the victims' families, and he desperately wanted to reach out to them. But he knew he couldn't.

Alfred Bailey was thankful to Joel Dreyer because he was the only psychiatrist who had stepped up to take his son's case. As Dreyer testified about his one-time, two-and-a-half-hour interview with his son, he used graphic sexual terms and said that Bailey saw his victims as "sexual perverts" who were having sex with him because they were bad people. When Kenny Myers's mom got up and fled the courtroom during Dreyer's testimony, Al Bailey's heart went out to her. He wanted to leave the courtroom too, but he couldn't figure out how to do it quietly without making a scene. He bowed his head, closed his eyes, and shut out everything that Dreyer was saying. He prayed to God to help him get through it.

---

234. Kresnak, Jack, "Psychiatrist Questions Bailey in Myers Trial," *Detroit Free Press*, November 18, 1986

The more Dreyer went on, the more Tim Kenny thought that Dreyer wasn't hurting the prosecution's case, and now he would get to cross-examine Ron Bailey.

Ron Bailey's hesitation in answering questions from the prosecutor was evident. Kenny knew he had been coached, and each pause allowed him to think of an answer that would fit his defense. He told the packed courtroom the same thing he had said in the Moore case: he thought he was killing himself. Bailey had changed his story from his pre-trial interviews with Dr. Stock and Dr. Blunt. His first rendition of the Kenny Myers murder was that it was an accident. He had wrapped his belt around Kenny's neck to heighten his sexual arousal. In a second description of the murder, he said he had killed Kenny, so "I'd be the last person he'd have sex with. I wanted to kill him because he was so good looking."[235]

Both Tim Kenny and Bailey's defense lawyers pointed out that he was a loner obsessed with young boys. He was captivated with having sex with them, and his depraved obsession often involved hyperventilation and choking his victims.

Tim Kenny gave his closing arguments just eight days after the trial started. He spoke of Joel Dreyer's testimony. Dreyer had turned his lack of thoroughness into what the prosecutor described as a "slipshod job and tried to make it virtuous." When Tim Kenny spoke of the defendant, he told Judge Duggan that Bailey was a predator whose only interest was in self-gratification. Bailey had urges to satisfy, and those urges were fulfilled with young victims.

Ray Cassar also addressed the judge in his closing arguments, saying that he truly believed his client was sick, and it was evident simply by looking at Bailey's past history. He lived in a different world with different rules, and each

---

235. Henderson, Tom, "Bailey Convicted of Myers Murder," *Livingston County Daily Press*, November 26, 1986

time he abducted a boy, he believed the boy was his friend. Bailey was so sick that he believed Kenny Myers was going to give him his home address.

Cassar stood facing the judge as he spoke of Dr. Tombo and how his client had suffered at the hands of Tombo, causing him to become insane. Behind Cassar in the front row of the gallery sat Robert Edenstrom, Kenny's stepfather, and he couldn't take it anymore. He had listened to the testimony for the previous week, and his rage had continued to build. In the heat of the moment, he shot up from his chair and lunged for Cassar. Nearby deputies from the Wayne County Sheriff's Department grabbed the man just before he made it to the defense attorney.

—

It took seventeen minutes. Tim Kenny stood along with everyone else when the judge entered the courtroom. To Kenny, there was nothing more anxiety-inducing than a first-degree murder case when waiting for the verdict. Judge Duggan read his handwritten verdict in front of the packed courtroom. Ron Bailey was guilty of the kidnapping, felony murder, and premeditated first-degree murder of Kenny Myers. He was legally sane and wasn't mentally ill when he strangled the young teen. "Any impulse he had to kill Kenny Myers was an impulse he chose not to resist," he said. He added that Kenny Myers's murder was committed by a criminally sane person who simply didn't want to be punished for the crime he had committed.

Judge Duggan pointed out some of the convincing factors that led to his decision. One of those was Bailey's excellent work history from his job at ARA Services in Livonia, the planning that he had done in the kidnapping of Kenny Myers, and the psychiatric testing done by Dr. Harley Stock and Dr. Lynn Blunt. "I reject Dr. Dreyer's conclusion and am unswayed by his opinion." Convinced that Dreyer became involved in the case with a predisposition to find Ron Bailey insane, he added, "I find his testimony more theater than substance."

Before he was led from the courtroom by deputies, Ron Bailey stood as his father walked up to him. He quietly shook his son's hand, wrapped his arm around him, and spoke something into his ear before kissing him goodbye. Alfred Bailey knew his son was a man, and he couldn't be responsible for Ron's actions.

In the hallway outside the courtroom, Kenny's mother fought back tears. Her statement to the media was sobering when she said, "It's taken me more than two years to learn not to hate him. I don't hate him. I'm just grateful he can't touch any more children again."[236]

Tim Kenny was relieved. He knew the case was a weight carried by many people for a very long time, but he also knew the prosecution had all the evidence and the case was clearly defined. Still, Ray Cassar and Chuck Murphy couldn't understand why Kenny wouldn't accept an offer for a plea agreement wherein Bailey would plead to a charge of guilty but mentally ill to first-degree murder because he was already going to serve life for the murder of Shawn Moore.

Tim Kenny said that the plea offer wasn't accepted because of Bailey's claim that Kenny was his friend and his death was accidental. Tim Kenny said those claims had to be exposed.

As an assistant prosecutor and chief trial attorney, Tim Kenny wanted to keep a professional relationship with Mr. and Mrs. Edenstrom, and he knew there had to be some boundaries, yet he still wanted to give them the confidence that the prosecutor was their champion. The verdict had been a huge release for Kenny Myers's mom.

---

236. Henderson, Tom, "Bailey Convicted of Myers Murder," *Livingston County Daily Press*, November 26, 1986

When she hugged Tim Kenny after the trial was over, it was a confirmation that at least a small portion of her heartache had been lifted. Her son's killer had been held accountable and would never walk the streets again. Rather than closure for the Edenstroms, it was more certainty. Some families of victims never had closure.

Ray Cassar and Chuck Murphy were both disappointed with the verdict but respected the judge's decision. They had known it was going to be a tough case, and they had tried some unique strategies.

Now convicted for two kidnappings and murders, Ron Bailey faced a third upcoming trial for the kidnapping and sexual assault of another teen who had survived the ordeal just one month before Kenny Myers's murder. There was already talk of some sort of plea deal in that case.

The next day, the decision had been made. Tim Kenny knew that pursuing the case against Bailey for the kidnapping and sexual assault of the Redford Township teen from the Livonia Mall wouldn't serve any practical purpose because Ron Bailey would already be serving two life sentences without any chance for parole. On Monday, November 24, Kenny filed a motion with Judge Duggan to dismiss the matter against Bailey in the third case.

Duggan granted the motion.

—

It was early December and the temperatures had changed from a slight fall chill to a winter cold. It was judgment day for Ron Bailey, and he already knew what to expect. With his conviction in the Myers case, he was facing a second life term without parole.

The sentencing was emotional.

Marie Edenstrom was there with her husband as Ron Bailey was given the opportunity to speak. "I'd just like to say that I'm sorry to Mr. and Mrs. Edenstrom. My way of thinking at the time, if I wasn't thinking that way, it probably never would have happened, and I wouldn't be here before the court."

"You're full of shit!" screamed Kenny's stepfather. He stormed out of the courtroom.

Kenny's mom asked if she could make a statement before Bailey's sentence was imposed. He stared at Marie Edenstrom, and his face flushed when she said, "Ronald, the only person you should have ever said 'I'm sorry' to is Kenny before you murdered him. You don't owe me an 'I'm sorry,' and I will not accept it." She added, "For justice to prevail, and to protect our innocent children, Ronald Bailey must never be allowed to be a part of society again to continue his sadistic pleasures that cost the lives of our children."[237]

From the bench, Judge Duggan noticed Alfred Bailey in the courtroom. Duggan knew it was just as difficult for Bailey's dad as it was for the Edenstroms. He sentenced Ron Bailey to sixty to one hundred years for the kidnapping of Kenny Myers, and life without parole for his murder.

237. Kresnak, Jack, "Judge Sets 2nd Term of Life in Jail for Bailey," *Detroit Free Press*, December 5, 1986

20
Leavenworth

Ron Bailey was taken from the courtroom as soon as he was sentenced, and that same day he was transferred to the State Prison of Southern Michigan near Jackson. For the first ninety days, all new inmates were sent to the Reception and Guidance Center at the prison, and Bailey was in protective custody because of his convictions, but he wasn't there for very long.

In the prison hierarchy, a child killer gets no remorse and no benefit of the doubt from anyone. He is considered pure evil. Child molesters and child killers, considered the lowest form of life in prison, are often attacked because many of the other inmates have wives, and many are fathers with children of their own. They don't want their own children to be the victim of a child molester or killer.

Each day became a challenge for Ron Bailey.

By the end of his ninety days in the RGC, he had already received numerous death threats. He was getting several daily. Likely feeling that Bailey's safety couldn't be guaranteed, the Michigan Department of Corrections took no chances. By March 1987, Bailey was transferred to the United States Medical Center for Federal Prisons in Springfield, Missouri. That particular federal penitentiary had a psychiatric unit. In the federal system, Bailey had a better chance of remaining anonymous, while if he had stayed in the state system there was a greater likelihood that other inmates would know who he was and what his crimes were.

Each time Bailey would settle into a new federal institution, word would circulate about why he was there, and he would suddenly have to be transferred again for his own safety.

Within two years of his conviction, Bailey had been transferred to a different federal prison, this time in Kansas. It was called Leavenworth. Like the RGC at Jackson, Bailey, with his youthful appearance and blond hair, became an immediate attraction to the other inmates who had been serving years at the prison. Carl Bowles took an immediate interest in Bailey, and the guards at the prison knew why. Bowles, a convicted cop killer and triple murderer, was labeled as a predator by the Leavenworth staff. A predator was an inmate who forced weaker inmates to satisfy his sexual desires, but that wasn't Bowles's interest. He thought Bailey had been placed at Leavenworth because he was a snitch.

At the prison, inmates were released from their cells at 6:00 a.m. and allowed to roam the prison grounds until 10:00 p.m. Bowles found Bailey one afternoon and struck up a conversation.

When Bowles asked him what he had been convicted of, Bailey told him, "I can't say. I got an appeal, you know, still in court."[238]

The one thing Bowles did know about Bailey was that he was a state prisoner from Michigan, and there were only two reasons that Leavenworth took in state prisoners: the prisoner was too violent and they couldn't control him, or they had to get rid of him for his own safety.

It was evident to Bowles that Bailey wasn't a badass. Therefore, he had to be a snitch.

---

238. Earley, Pete, *The Hot House*, 1992, Bantam Books, New York, NY

In the first two weeks that it took prison officials time to process Bailey into Leavenworth, another predator had set his eyes on Bailey and invited him to move into his cell. Everyone, including inmates and guards, assumed that Bailey had moved in for protection in exchange for sexual favors. Just two months later, Bailey and his cellmate were accused of planning a daring escape from the prison. Bailey's cellmate had tried to hire a helicopter pilot to fly into the prison and pick up both of them. Oddly enough, that same escape had occurred in Michigan in 1975 at Jackson Prison, where Bailey had been transferred from.

When prison officials found out about the elaborate escape plan, Bailey was moved to an isolation cell in the prison's Hole while his cellmate was transferred to another federal prison in Marion, Illinois. His cellmate would be locked in his cell for twenty-three hours of the day at his new home.

It was common knowledge that the only way prison officials found out anything about anybody was when an inmate snitched. Bowles was certain that the snitch in the helicopter escape plan wasn't Bailey's cellmate who got shipped to Marion, Illinois.

When Bailey was finally removed from the Hole, he took up residence with another inmate, and it was assumed it was for the same reason he had taken up his residence with his previous cellmate. Bowles was friends with Bailey's new cellmate, and he was worried that Bailey would get him into trouble, much like he suspected Bailey had with his previous cellmate.

Bowles knew there was a rather peculiar inmate who sort of stood out. He was a counterfeiter and subscribed to magazines like *Architectural Digest.* He had several other magazines and newspapers that one wouldn't expect an inmate to have. Among them were *The New York Times,* *The New Yorker,* *The Atlantic,* and *Harpers,* as well as some seedy detective magazines.

Bowles asked if he had any true crime. The counterfeiter gave him some of the pulp magazines he had and Bowles scanned them, hoping to find anything he could about Bailey but came up with nothing. He walked back to the counterfeiter's cell and handed them back. The counterfeiter handed him a copy of *Inside Detective* and suggested he take a look at it. On page 36, Bowles found what he was looking for. Titled "Stop the Sexual Sadist from Abducting Boys," it detailed a Michigan man who had kidnapped a teen boy from his bicycle, murdered him in northern Michigan, and left his body in a forest. He had strangled the youth with his belt. As Bowles turned the page, he saw Ron Bailey's face. Under Bailey's picture, the caption read, "Bailey has a Long History of Molesting Children Sexually."

Now Bowles knew why Bailey had been sent to Leavenworth. State officials in Michigan had arranged for him to be transferred because his crimes were so despicable in Michigan and so highly publicized that he would be instantly recognized in a state institution. If he was in a federal prison, he would be anonymous.

Bowles planned on making copies of the article and distributing them around the prison, but instead, he went to Bailey's cell. Bailey wasn't there, but Bowles tossed the magazine to his cellmate.

Bailey's cellmate became enraged when he saw the article. "Why, that little fucker!"

Bowles took the magazine back and headed back to his own cell. As he walked along the catwalk, he saw Bailey walking toward him with a stack of laundry. When they passed each other, Bowles held up the magazine with Bailey's picture.

Behind him, Bowles heard, "You little bastard!"

Bailey knew he was in trouble. He dropped the laundry, turned, and fled toward two guards who quickly removed him from the cellblock.[239]

Bowles still suspected that Ron Bailey had been put in Leavenworth as a snitch, but prison officials denied it.

In the aftermath, Ron Bailey was transferred to another federal prison. By 1995, the tenth anniversary of Shawn's abduction and murder, Ron Bailey had spent virtually his entire prison life within six separate federal prisons.

—

After Bailey's conviction for the murder of Kenny Myers, he knew he would likely be testifying at some point against Dr. Tombo. Tombo was facing a hearing before the Michigan Department of Licensing and Regulation, appealing a recommendation by the attorney general's office that his medical license should be revoked.

Bailey was scared for his own safety. In a call to Ray Cassar, he refused to return to Michigan and testify against his former doctor. He told his attorney that he would love to "put Tombo down,"[240] but he didn't feel safe in Michigan. After some discussion, Bailey agreed that if he could be flown nonstop to Detroit and not lodged at the Wayne County Jail or Jackson Prison, he would agree to the hearing.

On April 14, Bailey was flown from a federal prison in Missouri back to Michigan.

Tombo's attorney, Paul Stevenson, announced in his opening statement that two of the four original accusers had rescinded their original claims and the others were simply lying. That included Ron Bailey.

239. Earley, Pete, *The Hot House*, 1992, Bantam Books, New York, NY

240. Kresnak, Jack, "Bailey Asks Protection to Testify on Tombo," *Detroit Free Press*, April 7, 1987

The attorney representing the State's case against Tombo said the doctor had "engaged in a course of reprehensible and unprofessional misconduct involving sexual abuse of his patients" at Northville Hospital.[241] He added that during Bailey's trial, Tombo's disappearance should be an inference of guilt, and his silence was a tacit admission of guilt.

Stevenson called Bailey a pathological liar. Bailey had denied that Tombo had sexually abused him when he was questioned by MSP in 1980, but after his arrest in 1985 for the murders of Shawn Moore and Kenny Myers, he made the accusations.

During the hearing, Tombo admitted to taking Bailey to the Windsor Raceway but denied any sexual acts with him.

Ron Bailey felt empowered at the hearing for Tombo. He sat in leg shackles and made occasional sardonic remarks as he castigated one of the defense attorneys. He was one of the State's witnesses against Tombo, and when he was asked why he hadn't mentioned the sexual activity prior to his arrest in 1985, he said, "It was embarrassing to say something like that was going on for two and a half years."

When Bailey was asked about how he felt when Tombo was making the demands for sex, one of Tombo's union attorneys objected, and before the judge could make a ruling, Bailey chimed in and scolded the State's attorney, saying, "Counselor, that was a little out of line."

Bailey was set to continue his testimony on Friday, but beforehand, he saw a television camera in the courtroom. There had already been a ruling that Bailey could have the media barred from the hearing. He was smug when he looked at the State's assistant attorney general handling the case against Tombo and said, "Alan, shall we take care of

---

241. Kresnak, Jack, "Tombo's Attorney Tells Judge 2 Abuse Claims Were Recanted," *Detroit Free Press*, April 16, 1987

[the camera] or I'll close this. I'll take the media out of here right now."[242]

Because of the length of the hearing and scheduling conflicts, the hearing was being spread out over several months. Just as Tombo's two lawyers began to cross-examine Bailey, the hearing was adjourned until July.

On July 6, Bailey was flown back to Michigan.

Ron Bailey's credibility was on the line. Tombo's attorneys were able to get Bailey to admit that he had lied about his criminal history on job applications in the past, and he had lied to police during the murder investigations he was serving time for. To Tombo's attorneys, it was a huge issue.

Over the previous two years, Dr. Tombo had continually refused to comment on Ron Bailey's psychiatric history at Northville because of patient confidentiality. During the July hearing, reports written by Tombo in 1975, when Bailey was first at Hawthorn, were brought out. One of the reports read that Ron Bailey was "manipulative and tried to blame his relationship with his father for three sexual attacks on young boys." Additional notes read, "Bailey's talk of anger at his father was 'an excuse so as to reduce the burden of responsibility on his part for the offense he had done.'"[243]

Ray Cassar testified at Tombo's hearing. Cassar had established himself as a legitimate attorney, yet as he prepared to testify against the doctor, he was nervous.

He took the stand. *Why am I so nervous?* he thought to himself. He knew he didn't have anything to be nervous about.

Ray Cassar's testimony was damning. In detail, he described the clandestine meeting between himself, Murphy, Alfred Bailey, and Tombo. He described what Tombo wore

---

242. Kresnak, Jack, "Bailey Makes Presence Felt at Tombo Hearing," *Detroit Free Press*, April 18, 1987

243. AP, "Fired Psychiatrist's Reports Discussed," *Lansing State Journal,* July 10, 1987

at the meeting, why it was set at 8:00 p.m., what was said, Alfred Bailey's reaction to Tombo's offer, and how he wanted to pummel the Filipino doctor. Cassar's testimony also included what Ron Bailey had told him about the curvature of Tombo's penis. It wasn't as if he needed to do it, but Ray Cassar was building his own credibility. He was honest, he was a man of integrity, and he was believable. There was no doubt in anyone's mind afterward. Ray Cassar had the most credibility of all the witnesses who testified.

With another adjournment because of scheduling conflicts, Dr. Jose Tombo was set to give his version of the events he had adamantly refused to talk about for the previous two years.

Only two people testified against Dr. Tombo in the licensing regulatory hearing overseen by an arbitrator and an administrative law judge: one former patient, who was identified by his initials only, and Ron Bailey. One of the other accusers' allegations had been dismissed because they were proven false, and the other patients weren't medically capable of testifying. All of their previous allegations were dismissed.

In his testimony, Dr. Tombo denied all of the allegations made against him but did admit that he had taken Bailey to Windsor. He knew it was a technical violation of the hospital policy but his plan was to socialize Bailey. When he had first seen Bailey at Hawthorn, Bailey wasn't just angry at his father. He was angry at his mom, too, and he resented her because she was preaching too much to him.

When Tombo was cross-examined about his notes, it was noted he hadn't written anything about the trip to Windsor. He told the attorney the trip wasn't important enough to put in Bailey's progress notes. When the attorney said it wasn't important enough to put in the progress notes but important enough to take him across an international border,

Tombo shot back, "That is your statement, Mr. Hoffman, not mine."[244]

The administrative hearing to determine if Dr. Tombo's medical license should be revoked had lasted for almost two years because of scheduling conflicts between attorneys, judges, and arbitrators. On January 11, 1989, the *Detroit Free Press* reported that Administrative Law Judge Gregory Holiday had found that Dr. Tombo had engaged in "immoral conduct with two former patients at Northville Regional Psychiatric Hospital." Those findings were forwarded to the state Board of Medicine to determine if the doctor's license should be revoked. Two months later, in a seven to five decision among board members, Dr. Jose Tombo's medical license was revoked.

---

244. Kresnak, Jack, "Tombo Disputes Sexual Allegations," *Detroit Free Press*, December 29, 1987

21
The Existence of Evil

It was the pinnacle of his career as a prosecuting attorney, and it was something he would never forget. Though Frank Del Vero had other high-profile cases in his career before the case against Ron Bailey, Shawn Moore's murder was the high point just before winning the election as a judge in Livingston County. He was impressed by the community involvement during a very difficult time because nothing like that had ever happened before. Sadly, Del Vero believed the age of innocence was over for the community and Livingston County as a whole. Shawn Moore's abduction and murder at the hands of Ronald Bailey changed the way of life in Livingston County.

As Del Vero looked back on the case, he wasn't sure if anyone would ever know if Ron Bailey was being truthful when he said he thought he was killing himself as he murdered Shawn Moore.

The bittersweet meeting he had with Bruce and Sharon Moore will always be remembered by Frank Del Vero. Like anyone else who ever had an encounter with the Moore family during that most difficult time, the former prosecutor felt they were so graceful during one of the hardest times of their lives, and after Bailey's conviction they were so grateful.

"Evil incarnate" is the term Frank Del Vero used to describe Ron Bailey and what he had done not only to Shawn Moore and Kenny Myers, but to so many other kids. Once a pedophile, always a pedophile. Ron Bailey had to be in prison for the rest of life. Looking back at Bailey's sorrow after the trial, Del Vero felt it wasn't because of what he had done; it was because he had gotten caught. "They don't see the light. They feel the heat," he said.[245]

Del Vero told the media, "I wish it had never happened. I wish Shawn Moore was still here." He continued, "It happened. It has its place in the history of this county and the history of my life. What I'm sorry about is that Ronald Bailey is still here, and Shawn Moore isn't."[246]

—

"I think Ron Bailey was evil," David Morse said. After the trial, Morse realized his job had limitations.

It was a very stressful time for everyone. Just like his former boss, David Morse felt the Shawn Moore murder had affected the entire Livingston County community in a very traumatic way. His every thought leading up to the trial was of the case. He knew he had to be successful. Every night he would lie awake. In his own words, "I felt like the standard bearer of the community."[247]

Livingston County had been relatively free of violent crime up to that point. There was a murder every few years, but the crime rate in the county was nothing like the crime rates in Flint or Detroit. Many of the county residents had moved there to get away from crime, so there were high expectations of him. He felt first-degree murder was the

245. Del Vero, Frank, Interview with author, April 2, 2024
246. Menko, Fred, "Del Vero Still Thinks About Shawn Moore," *The Brighton Argus*, August 30, 1995
247. Morse, David, Interview with author, March 31, 2024

only acceptable verdict. Morse felt that the Bailey case was a defining moment not just for the Moore and Myers families, but for the community and the careers of everyone involved in the case. It had a very deep impact and remained vivid in Morse's mind.

Shawn Moore was the all-American boy and, after his kidnapping and murder, parents were suddenly faced with the question, "What can I do to protect my child?" It was something they shouldn't have to think about.

When Morse recalled the Ron Bailey case, he felt Bailey's manipulation was part of his act, and there was no doubt Bailey had psychological problems in his life and likely had some trauma thrown into the mix. He felt that the killer, though he was troubled, was also intelligent, and he channeled his troubled past into doing the terrible crimes he committed.

When Morse thought of the Moore family, he remembered they were the prime example of good people. It proved to him that there were, in fact, really good people in the world. Morse was quoted in the media saying, "Some cases come and go, but this case… there was a tremendous sense of community here, and it struck at the heart and nerve of the community—our children and our children's safety."[248]

—

"You can't say the last evil person in this world was Hitler."[249]

Those were Tim Kenny's words as he recalled the case of The People v. Ronald Bailey. One outrage was that someone who was sent to Hawthorn to get better, or to change, had

248. Stuart, Maria, "I Had to Give Something to the Moore Family," *The Brighton Argus*, August 30, 1995

249. Kenny, Timothy, Interview with author, May 23, 2024

been victimized by the very people who were there to care for him. It was another element of tragedy in the whole matter. Still, Ron Bailey was a very dangerous person, and whatever had happened at Hawthorn and Northville didn't take away from what he had done.

Looking back on the team of Cassar and Murphy, Tim Kenny thought the longer the case went on, the less Chuck Murphy played a role in it. Murphy had other things going on that posed a distraction for him. He thought it was odd that with a high-profile case like the Kenny Myers abduction and murder, something could distract Murphy.

Tim Kenny had done his public service by getting Ron Bailey off the streets but wondered about other victims. Bailey had left an evil trail of what he had done. Kenny had been told by someone that Bailey might be responsible for as many as a dozen murders along I-75 to Florida. Yes, he couldn't help but wonder.

—

Ray Cassar reflected back on the Bailey case long after it had concluded. He knew, as tragic as the Kenny Myers and Shawn Moore cases had been, there was, in a small way, redemption on Bailey's part. He was sure of that. Abuse is a circular pattern; those who have been abused are prone to abusing others in their life. Like the state police, the FBI had come to Ron Bailey shortly after his conviction in the Moore homicide. Their Behavioral Sciences Unit was new, and they wanted to know what made Bailey tick. Had he been abused in some way as a child? Cassar knew he had come from a loving family, and his dad had displayed that love during the trial. But according to reports written by Tombo, Ron Bailey hated his father because the two never spent time together, and his mom preached to him about staying away from girls.

Bailey consented to the interview in the hope that it might help prevent the abuse of children in the future. Cassar told Bailey that it was a step in the right direction for his client because it might help save a life down the road.

For Cassar, as he thought back on it, as unpopular as he was with other attorneys and judges when he defended Bailey, he still felt he was doing what his dad had wanted. There was no divine intervention. He became a defense attorney because he liked to help people. As a very young and novice attorney at the time, he didn't make a lot of money from the case, but it had been an incredible journey. His friend and co-counsel, Chuck Murphy, had passed away. Unfortunately, as the tide turned during the trials, Murphy had spent more time with the press than on the cases themselves. While Ray shared office space in Murphy's firm, they weren't law partners. Ultimately, Chuck Murphy had been more interested in what the case could do for his firm.

Not condoning what Ron Bailey had done, Cassar believes to this day that Ron Bailey wasn't evil. He was mentally ill, and he still believes that at the time of the murders he was insane. The things that Bailey had told him convinced him of that. Sex was a part of those murders, and it all circled back to Dr. Tombo. During Tombo's arbitration hearing, several people testified about how Tombo would inject them with Thorazine. Cassar recalled visiting Northville Regional Psychiatric Hospital and seeing patients walking around like zombies. Like many others, he called it the "Thorazine Shuffle." He considered Northville a cesspool.

Tombo had perpetrated so much on so many, and he had gotten away with it for a very long time. Cassar believed that Tombo's only reason for coming forward after Bailey's initial arrest for the murder of Shawn Moore was that he knew he would be found out anyway. If Dr. Tombo had been put on the stand during the murder trials, Cassar was sure that there was a chance the jury would have found Ron Bailey guilty but mentally ill. In that case, he still would have been sent to prison and he would still be serving a life sentence, but it would have been a prison with a psychiatric unit.

Redemption for the now experienced magistrate was testifying against Dr. Tombo in the arbitration hearing. Aside from his initial nervousness when he began his testimony, he let Dr. Tombo have it. There wasn't any doubt in his mind. He believed the only way Tombo got away with it for so long was by telling his patients, "Who are they going to believe? You or me?" In 1989, the former Dr. Tombo crossed the border into Canada and has never been heard from since.

When Ray Cassar looked back, he felt that even though the jurors who served on the Moore case said they could be impartial, he believed they couldn't be and were just saying they could because they wanted to be part of the trial.

As Cassar recalled the bench trial in the Kenny Myers murder case, he felt Tim Kenny did a phenomenal job in destroying the credibility of Dr. Joel Dreyer on the stand. In Cassar's own words, "He tore him to pieces."[250] At the end of his testimony, Dreyer had no credibility left.

Ray Cassar couldn't help but wonder about the cause and effect of Tombo's abuse. If Tombo hadn't abused Ron Bailey, would Kenny Myers and Shawn Moore still have been murdered? Tombo was a defining moment in Bailey's life, and Cassar believed Bailey wanted to get away from him. He was tired of being abused.

—

After divorcing his wife of twenty-nine years, Dr. Joel Dreyer remarried and moved to Murrieta, California in

250. Cassar, Raymond, Interview with author, February 27, 2024

1988. He was named the medical director at the Oak Grove Institute, a treatment center for children with psychological, emotional, and behavioral problems. Dreyer wasn't making the kind of money he had been in Michigan but still lived a lavish lifestyle.

He and his new wife seemed happy, but after seventeen years of marriage, she noticed bizarre behavioral changes in her husband. He had become reckless and embarrassing in public. He would often steal small things he could easily afford, and he began watching a lot of internet pornography. It was as if his entire persona had changed.

On Christmas Day in 2005, when a thirty-five-year-old woman was found dead from an overdose in Newport Beach, police discovered twenty prescription medications near her body. Two of those, OxyContin and Ambien, had been issued by Dr. Dreyer twenty-three days earlier.

As police began their investigation, they discovered that Dreyer was handing out prescriptions to just about anyone. He would often hand them out in places like parking lots, restaurants, and even his own home without ever doing any formal medical exam. The police were very familiar with him because some of the pharmacists in the area had reported their suspicions about Dreyer.

In 2007, the Drug Enforcement Administration began an investigation using undercover agents to get prescriptions from Dreyer. When his home was raided, they discovered that between 2004 and 2007, he had written prescriptions for 800 doses of Actiq, which contains Fentanyl, 37,000 doses of Xanax, 7,000 doses of Concerta, 18,000 doses of Ritalin, 12,000 Adderall pills, 68,000 Norco pills, over 17,000 oxycodone, and almost 79,000 hydrocodone pills.[251]

On July 24, 2007, Dr. Joel Dreyer was arrested at his home in Murrieta. The DEA, California Medical Board,

251. Hayasaki, Erika, "A Criminal Mind," *The California Sunday Magazine*, October 4, 2015

and the prosecutor considered Dreyer one of the biggest prescription drug dealers in Riverside County, California. He also had dealings in Mexico, where he traveled on a regular basis and wrote illegal prescriptions out of a pain clinic.

The California Medical Board revoked Dreyer's medical license immediately.

Two and a half years after his arrest, Joel Dreyer pleaded guilty in federal court to conspiracy to possess with the intent to distribute controlled substances.

Medical tests initiated by his family after they noticed the changes in Dreyer's personality confirmed he was suffering from frontotemporal dementia. Dreyer's defense attorney, William Ginsburg, said Dreyer had been suffering for years with a degenerative brain disorder that robbed him of his moral compass. He maintained that sentencing a mentally ill main to federal prison wouldn't serve justice. "He's gone mad," Ginsburg said.

The judge in his case refused to hold an evidentiary hearing to determine his competency. On December 13, 2010, Joel Dreyer, at the age of seventy-three, was sentenced to ten years in prison by US District Judge Virginia Phillips. "[He] prescribed some of the most addictive and dangerous opiates without even a pretense of a physical exam," she said. "I think he shows an astounding lack of self-awareness of the seriousness of his conduct."[252]

———

It was dogged police work that law enforcement attributed to Bailey's arrest and conviction. There were still unanswered

———

252. Burge, Sarah, "Psychiatric Crime Database and Disciplinary Actions: Psychiatrist Joel S. Dreyer Goes to Prison for 10 Years on Federal Drug-Prescribing Charges," CCHR International, December 15, 2010, accessed October 7, 2024, www.psychcrime.org/news

questions afterward in the Moore murder. If there was, in even the smallest way, an attempt at redemption for what he had done, Bailey consented to an interview about the Moore case, and Ray Cassar agreed to it.

Det/Sgt. Beaupre knew there weren't many legitimate stranger abductions, and when there was an arrest and conviction in a case, an interview with the killer could provide critical information on how a pedophile operates.

Looking back on the case, Beaupre recalled sixteen-hour days for those who came in at the start of the case. Every one of the 1,600 tips that had come in had to be investigated. "You don't have the luxury to throw any of them away," he said.[253] It was a once-in-a-career type of case, and it was a joint effort by several law enforcement agencies that solved it. He knew the case had come down to a battle between Stock, Blunt, and Dreyer.

Det/Sgt. Al Moffatt, who had tailed Bailey to Florida, wanted the outcome to be different. Like everyone else, he was hoping for Shawn's safe return, but as a cop, he was realistic. "What people have to realize is that there's evil in this world and bad people. No matter what you do, you've got to live with it."[254]

—

Like Frank Del Vero, Judge Stanley Latreille's life during the trial was much the same. Mentally, he took it home with him every night. He agreed that the Moore kidnapping and murder was a "sad coming of age" for Livingston County.

Livingston County was seen as a "backwater" community. Many suspected that law enforcement in and

253. Robertson, Nicole, "Dogged Police Work Was Key to Bailey Conviction," *The Brighton Argus*, October 8, 1986

254. Robertson, Nicole, "Dogged Police Work Was Key to Bailey Conviction," *The Brighton Argus*, October 8, 1986

around mid-Michigan and the courts in Livingston County weren't up to an investigative effort and trial that was getting so much attention, both locally and nationally. Judge Latreille admitted afterward that even he was doubtful of a first-degree murder conviction.

By the end of the trial, Frank Del Vero and David Morse had proven him wrong.

The trier-of-fact had to maintain an unconditional appearance of fairness. He couldn't reveal his own thoughts or biases in the case, and given the fact that it involved the brutal murder of a child made it that much more difficult. "It was hard for me because there was some horrible testimony," he said. "The case is part of the background of my life, but I would not want to do it again."[255]

—

Ten years after Shawn's murder, the Brighton community still hadn't forgotten about the teenager who had been kidnapped and murdered at the hands of a serial sadistic pedophile in 1985.

With Shawn's bike—the one he had been riding on that fateful August day—hanging in the garage at their home in Horizon Hills, the Moores truly believed their son's spirit was with them.

Even ten years later, they were still dealing with the abduction and murder of their son. Sharon Moore spoke with the media near the anniversary of the abduction. "Just a little while ago, I was cleaning out a cedar chest because we were getting ready to re-carpet. I was going through this chest, and I came across a scrapbook that belonged to Shawn. I wasn't ready for that." She said she broke down crying.

255. Stuart, Maria, "Trial Was 'a Sad Coming of Age,'" *The Brighton Argus*, August 30, 1995

All throughout the community they were still recognized, and they still received much love and support.

The community was so affected by Shawn's murder that at his grave, there were often small tokens and gifts left for the teen. Many times, those cards, flowers, and coins were left by strangers who never knew him.

Sharon Moore still taught second grade at Farley Hill Elementary School in Pinckney. Bruce had retired and worked out of the family home in Brighton. He had become a world traveler after his retirement from the *Ann Arbor News* and started a business called Leisure Communications. He traveled from Europe to South America and several places in between as part of his new job.

Ten years after that day, Bruce spoke of how important it was for people to realize that, although a stranger abduction was a rare occurrence, it could happen to anyone's child.

Shawn's mom added, "Never take your children for granted."[256]

---

256. Moorehouse, Buddy, "Never Take Your Children for Granted," *The Brighton Argus,* August 30, 1995

22
Questions Remain

When Det/Sgt. Cory Williams read that a pedophile by the name of Richard Lawson had firsthand information about the Michigan "Snow Killings," he knew exactly what that meant. The police report Williams was reading was from Pennsylvania, and no one there had any idea what Lawson was referring to. At the Livonia Police Department in Michigan, Cory Williams did. Lawson was referring to the Oakland County Child Killings.

—

Cory Williams grew up in Berkley, a Detroit suburb, and graduated from Berkley High School in 1979. His father had worked for the Berkley Police Department, and he had retired as a detective just two years before Cory's high school graduation.

After his graduation from high school, Cory joined the Livonia Police Department as a cadet. That lasted nineteen months, until the department was forced to lay off their cadets. He had loved his venture into law enforcement but faced the reality and began painting houses before he joined the army.

In his military career, he became a paratrooper with the 82nd Airborne, flourished as a sniper, and eventually as an instructor before being discharged in 1986.

After his discharge, Williams phoned the chief at the Livonia Police Department and asked if there were any openings. He wanted to come back, the chief hired him, and he graduated from the police academy in 1987. Williams worked five years in uniform, six years in narcotics, and was promoted to Detective Sergeant, where he ended up doing investigations for the rest of his career. While he worked there, eight of those years were spent working with his own brother, while his other brother, like his dad, worked for the Berkley Police Department.

—

Before Cory Williams's career in the military and law enforcement ever began, the phone rang at the Williams home on January 2, 1977. At the other end of the line was his dad's lifelong friend, Bob Bell. Bell was in a panic. His granddaughter, Kristine, was missing. The former detective's high school-aged son, Cory, listened to the subdued conversation his dad was having over the phone and later learned from his mom that Kristine had walked to the nearby 7-Eleven store just down the street from his own house, the same store where he and his brothers often visited, and she hadn't been seen since.

Retired from the Berkley Police Department, Lee Williams had just started working for L. Brooks Patterson as an investigator for the Oakland County Prosecutor's Office. The elder Williams worked the case of his best friend's granddaughter's disappearance both at work and on his own time. Nineteen days after that panicked phone call, Kristine Mihelich's body was found.

Cory and his dad never talked about Kristine's disappearance and murder.

—

In 2004, Cory Williams was assigned to a Livonia cold case from 1989 involving the shotgun murder of a father of five who owned the Detroit Cab Company. The man who committed the murder, a former cabbie named Richard Lawson, and his accomplice, a juvenile named Richard Mudica, fled Michigan after the murder and ended up in Atlantic City, New Jersey, where they ditched the guns used in the Detroit homicide.

Richard Lawson had picked up his accomplice, a homeless fifteen-year-old runaway, in California. Mudica was selling newspapers on the street when Lawson, a known pedophile who, by the time he was a teen, had been charged with numerous sex crimes involving the molestation of juveniles, befriended him. In exchange for sex, Mudica got free booze and a place to stay. The two had come to Michigan to rob Lawson's former boss. Lawson knew he took large amounts of cash to his home in Livonia every night.

After leaving Atlantic City, the two traveled the east coast, committing armed robberies in several states including Maine, Vermont, and Pennsylvania before being caught. Lawson was sent to prison in Maine for nine years while Mudica was returned to California because he was a juvenile. After Lawson's release from prison, he returned to California.

Cory Williams was reading the arrest report from Dormont, Pennsylvania when he read about Lawson's statement about the Michigan "Snow Killings." The unsolved murders of four children in Oakland County in the mid-'70s were well known across the state and nationwide.

Williams's plan was to prove Lawson and Mudica were involved in the Detroit cold case from five years earlier; then, if Wayne County Prosecutor Kim Worthy would allow it, he would offer Lawson a deal of some sort for whatever information he might have in the Oakland County Child Killings.

Kim Worthy gave the okay to offer Mudica immunity in exchange for his testimony about Lawson's involvement in the Detroit murder. The following day, Lawson, who was now living in San Diego and trafficking Latino boys from Mexico, walked into the lobby of the San Diego Police Department to report to his probation officer. Cory Williams was in the lobby waiting for him and arrested him for the 1989 murder in Detroit.

In the early seventies, Richard Lawson had been an informant for the Detroit Police. He prowled the Cass Corridor and gave his information to the head of the Detroit Police Sex Crimes Unit, who at that time was Isaiah McKinnon. According to McKinnon, "Lawson had an uncanny knowledge of the underworld of pedophiles. He had a knowledge none of us could get because it's a secret society."[257]

In his own way, Lawson would pick up juvenile boys up and down Woodward Avenue, have sex with them, then try to get information regarding the Oakland County Child Killings. Some of the information he provided about his associates was valuable, and it included the names of other pedophiles in the Detroit area who became prime suspects in the Oakland County unsolved murders. They included Ted Lamborgine, Bob Moore, Chris Busch, and Gregory Greene.

Cory Williams was getting ready for Lawson's murder trial in Livonia when Det/Sgt. Garry Gray from the

257. Keenan, Marney Rich, *The Snow Killings*, Exposit, Jefferson, NC, 2020

Michigan State Police called him. MSP was reopening the investigation into the Oakland County Child Killings after thirty years, and Gray was asking Williams to be a part of it. Gray didn't realize that Cory Williams had a promising lead on the thirty-year-old unsolved killings. Williams told the MSP detective that he was working on the lead he developed from Richard Lawson, and Gray was anxious to hear about it.

—

In 1976, immediately after Mark Stebbins's abduction and murder, police had interviewed thirty-five-year-old pedophile Arch Edward Sloan. Sloan was an auto mechanic and tow truck driver. He was living with his parents in Southfield in 1976. Mark Stebbins's body had been found in Southfield. When the news of Stebbins's murder hit the media, Sloan's parole officer saw the news reports and immediately thought of Sloan as a suspect.

Arch Sloan was interviewed soon after, and he gave permission for the Southfield Police to search his 1966 Pontiac Bonneville. An evidence technician dusted the car for fingerprints, but none of those matched Mark Stebbins's. The evidence technician also collected hairs, fibers, and other debris from the floor of the Bonneville. None of the debris from the teen's clothing matched the debris lifted from Sloan's car either.

Twenty years after the Oakland County Child Killings, evidence from the killings was submitted to the FBI Laboratory in Quantico, Virginia. The evidence had been held by MSP, and DNA analysis was a new investigative tool on the horizon. An item labeled "Pontiac debris," taken from Arch Sloan's car, was included.

Cory Williams knew that some of the other evidence in the OCCK cases was missing, including a slide that contained a hair from victim Timothy King's groin that was retrieved during his autopsy. That slide was eventually found in 2008 at Detroit's FBI laboratory.

In 2009, Cory Williams retired from the Livonia Police Department. Wayne County Prosecuting Attorney Kim Worthy asked him to come to work in her office as an investigator, and while he was working other cases for the prosecutor's office, he was also still working on the Oakland County Child Killings. Williams found another package of slides related to the OCCK case at the MSP Northville lab that was labelled "dirt, fur, fiber." An MSP lab scientist examined those slides and discovered human hairs. When those were analyzed, a total of five hairs were isolated from the slides, and three of those hairs had been found on Timothy King. The fourth was a hair found on Mark Stebbins's clothing. They were sent to the FBI Laboratory in Quantico.

Of the hairs submitted to the FBI for DNA analysis, three of them had the same mitochondrial DNA sequence. They were all left by the same person but didn't belong to Arch Sloan. The first was found on Mark Stebbins's clothing on February 19, 1976. The second was left behind in Arch Sloan's 1966 Pontiac Bonneville and was found on February 23, 1976. The third was found on Tim King's groin area thirteen months later at his autopsy.

Det/Sgt. Cory Williams believed that Sloan knew who the Oakland County Child Killer was, but Sloan refused to talk. Four years of investigation, several hundred interviews, and more than two dozen DNA swabs still hadn't identified whose hair had been found in Arch Sloan's car and on two of the Oakland County children.

—

By 2015, Cory Williams's relentless pursuit of justice for Mark Stebbins, Jill Robinson, Kristine Mihelich, and Timothy King, along with other devoted law enforcement professionals from MSP, Denise Powell and Becky MacArthur, was still moving along, even though it had been almost forty years since the first murder. In 2011, Det/ Lt. Denise Powell was named as director of the task force investigating the re-opened cases.

When Williams graduated from the police academy in 1987 and started working full-time for the Livonia Police Department, everyone there was already familiar with the names Ronald Bailey and Jose Tombo because Northville bordered Livonia, and their names had dominated the news for the previous two years. As many of the leads developed when the case was reopened in 2006 had faded, much like other cold case investigators who have looked at the murders, Williams said, "We should take a look at Bailey."[258] Williams recalled that when he started working at Livonia, he had seen pictures of Bailey after his arrest and recognized him from the Ward Presbyterian basketball team that he used to play against as a youth.

Det/Sgt. Garry Gray from MSP was doing the follow-up investigation into Ron Bailey when the Oakland County case was initially reopened. As part of that, Gray got Bailey's hospital records from Northville. At briefings and meetings, Gray emphasized that they could "check Bailey off the list," adding he was locked down at the hospital and couldn't leave.[259] Everyone assumed he was correct.

In 2015, when the task force began looking at Bailey again, Cory Williams said he wasn't comfortable with the old records. The Wayne County prosecutor he was working with suggested interviewing Bailey and running a ploy

258. Williams, Cory, Interview with author, September 4, 2024
259. Williams, Cory, Interview with author, September 4, 2024

on him to see if he would talk. The guise would be an investigation into Jose Tombo.

—

Cory Williams and Becky MacArthur sat in the conference room at the Michigan Department of Corrections waiting for Ron Bailey. Williams and MacArthur shook his hand before Bailey, wearing the standard prison garb, sat down across from the two investigators.

Williams had already decided not to read Bailey his Miranda warnings because they wanted him to open up and build a rapport as one of Jose Tombo's victims. They told Bailey the statute of limitations had changed in Michigan, Tombo could still be charged, and they planned on tracking down all of the victims to complete the investigation. It was all a ruse.

When Ron Bailey heard the two investigators were there as part of an investigation into Jose Tombo, he started talking openly about his time at Northville Psychiatric Hospital. There was no hesitation in the discussion because he truly believed he was a victim of the former doctor and legitimately felt as if he had been abused. Bailey described Tombo as a creep who carried around a syringe to get what he wanted from patients. Tombo would shoot up patients who didn't give him what he wanted with Thorazine. If a patient wanted a privilege pass, they had to have sex with Tombo. Bailey told Williams and MacArthur he wasn't the only one having sex with the doctor. There were other male patients whom Tombo liked too.

The interview with Ron Bailey wasn't centered solely on Tombo. Bailey spoke of his family life, too, and the trouble he had been in in Livonia when he lived there. As the interview progressed, Williams asked about Tombo's lifestyle and whether or not he liked kids. Cory Williams was curious if Tombo had an apartment and if Bailey had been there.

As Bailey described his abuse by Tombo, he also made it sound as if he were special to Tombo too. While Ron Bailey described his life with Jose Tombo to Cory Williams and Becky MacArthur, Williams noticed there was no expression in his face, either one way or the other. Normally during an interview, there was at least a small point of commonality in some way, maybe even a smile at some point, but Ron Bailey spoke with no emotion. Williams thought it was almost as if Bailey had no soul.

When Williams and MacArthur left the prison after their first interview with Bailey, they had learned more than they ever thought they could. Ron Bailey was often taken out of the hospital by Tombo, and the two of them would go to bars. Bailey was free to come and go and was allowed to have his car on the hospital campus. He would leave on Friday and come back on Sunday evening. There was a patient board with his name on it, and he would simply move a small magnet to show his in or out status. When he was checked out of the hospital, he was allowed to work at Sears at the Livonia Mall, and he would stay with friends in some of the areas where the Oakland County Child Killings had occurred. In fact, Ron Bailey was discharged from the Hawthorn Center on January 5, 1976, and Mark Stebbins was reported missing on February 15.

Cory Williams and Becky MacArthur knew they had to either exclude him as a suspect or, if he was involved in some way, get him to talk.

The second meeting with Ron Bailey was much different than the first. Williams waited for a month or so before the two investigators headed back to the prison with a buccal swab in hand. If Bailey refused to give a DNA sample, Williams was all set to get a search warrant from the Honorable Timothy Kenny, who had, since prosecuting

Bailey for the murder of Kenny Myers, become the chief judge in Wayne County Circuit Court.

Cory Williams cut to the chase. They were there investigating the murders of four children in Oakland County from 1976 and 1977. The gig was up, and they were zeroing in on Ron Bailey as a suspect. They told Bailey they would be talking to his old friend Jack Zaccardo and several of his other old cronies, and they wanted Bailey's DNA.

Ron Bailey's physical demeanor immediately changed. Williams and MacArthur had struck a nerve. Bailey began trembling, clearly uneasy about their second visit. They began asking the convicted killer questions about his knowledge of the Oakland County Child Killings. They asked if he was involved in any way. They assured him that it would work in his favor if he told them up front rather than making them dig any further for answers. When they asked for a buccal swab for his DNA, he asked why they wanted it.

Williams was up front with him and said they were going to compare it with the DNA profile in the Oakland County cases, then forward his DNA profile to every state between Michigan and Florida. Bailey nervously agreed to give them the sample, but there was no doubt he was visibly shaken as he signed a consent form.

Williams could see that Bailey, who normally had beautiful penmanship, could barely write his own name.

Ronald Bailey was one of the last suspects considered in the Oakland County Child Killings. When the Oakland County Child Killings began, some of the investigators felt he would have been too young at the time of the killings in the seventies. In reality, he would have been just shy of turning seventeen when Mark Stebbins went missing.

Cory Williams had uncovered a child pornography ring operating in the Detroit area at the same time of the Oakland County murders. The production of films and magazines took place behind closed doors, and kids were lured by pedophiles who stalked parks, skating rinks, and arcades. Those involved would use other teens to lure their victims away. "It was an ugly, hidden world that nobody wanted to touch at the time," Williams said.[260]

After Tim King's murder, *People Magazine* ran an article in December 1977, stating:

As one police detective points out, Timmy King's body was dumped on Gill Road just a few miles from Northville State Hospital. The killer had to travel down a badly torn-up section of Eight Mile Road to reach the Gill dump site, a route someone unfamiliar with the area would tend to avoid because of the construction. The detective speculates that the killer knew the area well and might even be an outpatient at the hospital.[261]

In early 1977, just as Dr. Tombo was increasing Ron Bailey's grounds privileges to leave the hospital, Timothy King was reported missing.

The buccal swab containing the DNA sample from Ronald Bailey was compared with the DNA profile in the Oakland County Child Killings. It wasn't a match.

Williams and MacArthur had long talks after interviewing Bailey. There was no doubt in either of their minds that even though Bailey's DNA didn't match the profile of the hairs taken from Arch Sloan's car, Mark Stebbins's clothing, and Timothy King's body, he still could have been working with Sloan, Busch, Greene, or Lamborgine and have some role in the murders. Cory Williams, along with others, firmly

260. Kennan, Marney Rich, *The Snow Killings,* Exposit, Jefferson, NC, 2020

261. McCall, Cheryl, "A Shadowy Child Killer Claims Four Victims and Holds Detroit's Suburbs in a Grip of Fear," *People Magazine*, December 5, 1977, quoted in Kennan, Marney Rich, *The Snow Killings,* Exposit, Jefferson, North Carolina, 2020

believes there are still other murder victims of Ron Bailey spread between Michigan and Florida.

Ronald Lloyd Bailey, now back in the Michigan prison system, is serving a life sentence without the possibility of parole.

For More News About Rod Sadler,
Signup For Our Newsletter:

http://wbp.bz/newsletter

Word-of-mouth is critical to an author's long-term success. If you appreciated this book please leave a review on the Amazon sales page:

https://wbp.bz/doreviews

ALSO AVAILABLE FROM WILDBLUE PRESS

https://wbp.bz/CrackCityStrangler

THE CRACK CITY STRANGLER: The Homicides of Serial Killer Benjamin Atkins offers a chilling, in-depth account of the horrifying crimes committed by one of America's most notorious serial killers.

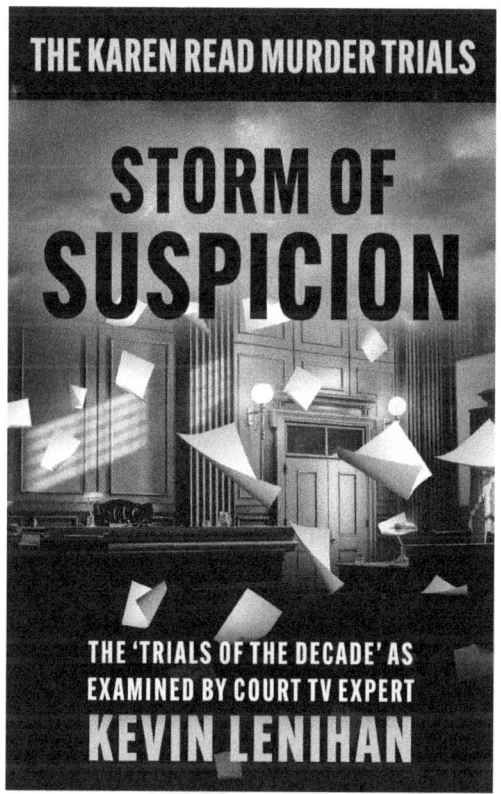